PRAISE FOR MODERN ACHIEVEMENT

"*Modern Achievement* is breaking the mold! To be an effective leader for the future, outdated paradigms must be replaced with the kind of innovative approach you'll find in this book. Asheesh and Marshall have dug deeply into this sea change in work and life, drawing from the collected wisdom of top management thinkers as well as young strivers from around the world to create a revolutionary guidebook to success and leadership for the next generation."

—**MEL ROBBINS**, *New York Times* bestselling author
and host of the award-winning *Mel Robbins Podcast*

"Marshall and Asheesh are the right people at the right time to tackle the important work of modernizing the definition of achievement. They approach the task with humility and ambition in equal measure. This book is a must-read and destined to be a modern classic."

—**DR. JIM YONG KIM**, twelfth president, World Bank

"Fixed-Flexible-Freestyle provides a profoundly useful framework for thriving in turbulent times. By embracing the inevitable messiness of achievement, this wise book teaches young leaders how to iterate their way to fuller, more meaningful lives."

—**DANIEL H. PINK**, #1 *New York Times* bestselling
author of *Drive*, *When*, and *The Power of Regret*

"Asheesh Advani has a global perspective on success and achievement that is rare. This book is forward-looking and practical. Every young person should read it!"

—**AHMAD ALHENDAWI**, secretary general, World
Organization of the Scout Movement

"Who better than the CEO of JA Worldwide and the legendary Marshall Goldsmith to meld the wisdom of the past with the fresh thinking of the new generation to redefine success for a changing world? Both timeless and timely, *Modern Achievement* is a necessary book for today's aspiring leaders."

—**HUBERT JOLY**, former CEO, Best Buy, and
author of *The Heart of Business*

"I wholeheartedly endorse *Modern Achievement*. It's a source of inspiration and a guide for readers to embrace their unique paths, adapt to the ever-changing world, and lead with authenticity and purpose. Get ready to be inspired, to grow, and to lead with this transformative book."

—**DAVIDO**, Grammy-nominated pop star;
founder, Davido Music Worldwide

"A thoughtful, wise, practical guide for students and young adults."

—**AMY C. EDMONDSON**, Harvard Business School professor
and author of *Right Kind of Wrong* and *The Fearless Organization*

"*Modern Achievement* is a terrific book, especially for younger people. It combines the wisdom of past leaders, such as Dale Carnegie, and adds valuable and powerful insights for today's generation. Kudos to Asheesh Advani and Marshall Goldsmith on a new manual for success!"

—**JOE HART**, president and CEO, Dale Carnegie
& Associates, and co-author of *Take Command*

"This wonderful book is like a private mentor and guide whispering wisdom to you during pivotal moments in your life."

—**CAROL KAUFFMAN**, founder, Institute of Coaching; assistant professor, Harvard Medical School

"Asheesh received the Tony Hsieh Award for his innovative leadership of Junior Achievement Worldwide. Marshall is one of the world's top leadership experts. The fixed-flexible-freestyle approach to leadership is brilliant and can help individuals, teams, and organizations. Every aspiring leader should read this book."

—**KEITH FERRAZZI**, author of *Never Eat Alone* and #1 *New York Times* bestseller *Who's Got Your Back*

"*Modern Achievement* is an important modern-day manual that redefines the journey of persistence, hard work, and success for today's fast-paced world. I would recommend this book to anyone about to embark on the journey."

—**MR EAZI**, African pop star and pioneer of Banku music

"*Modern Achievement* is brilliant. In a world where careers are increasingly non-linear, unfolding like spirals rather than along predictable lines, traditional career advice focused on long-term goal-setting feels obsolete. Asheesh and Marshall have succeeded spectacularly in remedying this by laying down the principles and practices essential for navigating portfolio careers. This book is essential reading for anyone under forty—or better yet, anyone under ninety, since we all need to keep learning, growing, and redefining our purpose throughout our lives."

—**SALLY HELGESEN**, coauthor of the international bestseller *How Women Rise* and author of *Rising Together*

"We are long overdue for a reexamination of the concept of achievement, and I can't think of two better people to tackle that task than Asheesh Advani and Marshall Goldsmith. The two have shared powerful stories from their own lives and experiences to create a book that will help redefine achievement in today's rapidly changing world."

—**ROBERT GLAZER**, #1 *Wall Street Journal* and *USA Today* bestselling author of *Elevate*; *Elevate Your Team*; and *Friday Forward*

"Be original. That is the advice that I share with young people. I love the framework in *Modern Achievement*, as it allows each individual to find lessons for life based on their unique strengths and goals. Young people everywhere will enjoy this book."

—**ANUPAM KHER**, award-winning actor, director, and international bestselling author of *The Best Thing about You Is You*

"*Modern Achievement* is drawn from the fascinating personal journey of the authors, including overcoming a chronic stutter, as well as the truly global experiences of Junior Achievement that transcend geography and time and embrace the wonderful differences that make us all individuals. If you want to understand some highly practical lessons and a process that can increase your level of achievement—and more importantly, fulfillment—along the way, this is the book for you!"

—**ADAM WARBY**, chairman, Heidrick and Struggles; chairman, Software One; CEO emeritus, Avanade

"This book presents a transformative guide for the new generation of leaders to carve their path to success. *Modern Achievement* is an indispensable companion for those seeking to make an indelible mark in the modern era."

—**HORTENSE LE GENTIL**, author of *The Unlocked Leader* and *Aligned*

"My own achievement journey has not been linear, so this book resonates deeply on a personal level. Every young adult, educator, and parent will benefit greatly from reading it. More broadly, this book points the way for the US education system to embrace a more flexible, purposeful, and inspiring definition of achievement."

—**JEFF WETZLER**, co-CEO, Transcend, and author of *Ask*

"Written for young achievers, *Modern Achievement* is full of practical insight for any leader looking to adapt to an ever-faster-changing world. Having had the opportunity to work closely with Junior Achievement Worldwide and Asheesh Advani, and being intimately familiar with Marshall Goldsmith's leadership vision, I am delighted that the world now gets to learn and benefit from their combined wisdom and experience."

—**RENS VAN DEN BROEK**, partner, McKinsey & Company

"In the evolving landscape of success, this book represents a major shift from the linear path of doing X to get Y to a whole new paradigm. While paying homage to the wisdom of icons like Dale Carnegie and Stephen Covey, the innovative Fixed-Flexible-Freestyle framework offers thirty actionable lessons that update the idea of achievement (something we all thought we knew). A must-read for anyone who wants to grow, learn, and lead!"

—**URS KOENIG**, founder, Radical Humility Leadership Institute; former UN peacekeeper; and author of *Radical Humility*

1OO COACHES
—PUBLISHING—
AN IMPRINT OF AMPLIFY PUBLISHING GROUP

amplifypublishinggroup.com
publishing.100coaches.com

Modern Achievement: A New Approach to Timeless Lessons for Aspiring Leaders

For more information, please contact:
100 Coaches Publishing, an imprint of Amplify Publishing Group
620 Herndon Parkway, Suite 220
Herndon, VA 20170
info@amplifypublishing.com

Library of Congress Control Number: 2024906291

CPSIA Code: PRV0424A

ISBN-13: 978-1-63755-825-6

Printed in the United States

From Asheesh:

For my children, Alexander and Eliot, as they start their achievement journeys

From Marshall:

For my children, Kelly and Bryan

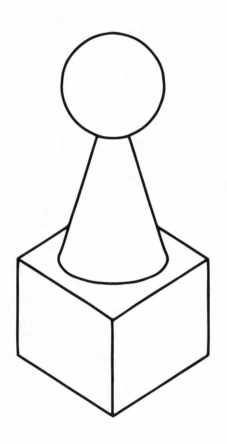

MODERN
ACHIEVEMENT

A NEW APPROACH
TO TIMELESS LESSONS
FOR ASPIRING LEADERS

ASHEESH ADVANI AND MARSHALL GOLDSMITH

illustrated by ayse birsel

100 COACHES
—PUBLISHING—
AN IMPRINT OF AMPLIFY PUBLISHING GROUP

CONTENTS

My Modern Achievement Story—and Yours   xii

Embrace a Fixed-Flexible-Freestyle Approach to Achievement   10

PART I: FIXED

SELF

1. Meritocracy Is Not Dead   28
2. You Can't Complain Your Way to a Happy Life   38
3. Write It Down   48
4. Go Meta   60
5. Connect beyond the Screen   72

CAREER

6. Present Your Story   84
7. Keep Your Personal Burn Rate Low   94
8. Look beyond Your Parents for Advice   102
9. Be a Good Mentee   112
10. Find People Who Push You   124

PART II: FLEXIBLE

SELF

11. Reframe—Know the Power of "Yet"   138
12. Pay Attention to the Weighting, Not Just the Score   150
13. See Education as an Investment Return, Not Just an Investment   162
14. Perform Sequential Tasking, Not Multitasking   174
15. Embrace the Mess   188

CAREER

16. Think "And," Not "Or"   206

17. Don't Let Feedback Get in the Way of Your Success   218

18. Learn to Balance Simplicity and Complexity   230

19. Leave Them Wanting More   242

20. Make Other People's Goals Your Own   252

PART III: FREESTYLE

SELF

21. Embrace Your Inexperience and Cluelessness   270

22. Create Protected Time   288

23. Do It Now   302

24. Experience Different   316

25. Freestyle Your "Self"   330

CAREER

26. Design Your Passion   334

27. Go Plural   348

28. Make Friends Five to Ten Years Older—
    and Younger—Than You   364

29. Share Your Story to Inspire Others   378

30. Freestyle Your Career   394

Be Fixed, Flexible, *and* Freestyle   396

Acknowledgments   402

About the Authors and Illustrator   406

Index of Contributors   408

MY MODERN ACHIEVEMENT STORY — AND YOURS

As the chief executive officer of Junior Achievement (JA) Worldwide, I have the opportunity to meet many of the most achievement-oriented young people around the world. JA reaches over fifteen million young people per year in over one hundred countries, delivering educational programs in entrepreneurship, financial literacy, and work readiness. My work is as gratifying as, and more rewarding than, anything I have ever done, and it became only more gratifying and rewarding when we were nominated for a Nobel Peace Prize—a huge honor for the organization that has brought attention to the important connection between education, economic empowerment, and peace.

ASHEESH ADVANI

When I was fourteen years old, I was one of those JA students. But I didn't think, *One day, in my forties, I will become CEO of Junior Achievement. What do I need to do to get there?* In fact, if you met me as a child, you would be forgiven for thinking I would struggle to lead anyone anywhere.

I was born in Mumbai, India, but immigrated to Toronto, Canada, with my family just before my sixth birthday. My brother, Aneel, who is three years older, helped me understand what was going on and navigate the move. Not that I was unhappy. I just didn't have a lot of self-confidence, partly owing to a severe stutter I developed after we arrived in Toronto. That stutter deeply influenced what I believed I could do. I didn't run for student council or participate in school performances that I would have loved to be a part of because I dreaded auditioning and avoided anything that would require me to get on stage. One time I was asked to recite a brief poem during an assembly in front of all my classmates, teachers, and many parents in attendance. I could not get the words out of my mouth. *Iiiiii wwhhhaaaa* . . . . After what felt like an hour but was probably ten long minutes, I finished reciting the poem that should have taken a minute or so. When I left the stage, I avoided eye contact with everyone and was convinced my social life was over and I would never have any friends.

My parents signed me up for weekly speech therapy sessions at the world-leading Hospital for Sick Children in Toronto, and by the time I was thirteen, my stutter was sporadic rather than continuous. But sporadic in the context of my teenage years and hopes of attracting girls meant my self-confidence hardly made me feel date-worthy. The only thing I had confidence in was my athletic abilities, which did not align fully with what my parents wanted for Aneel and me. They tried to instill in us a value set for working hard and doing well in school. Aneel embraced these values from an early age. He excelled in school, won national math contests, went to debating championships, got into Harvard, and went to medical school. Meanwhile, I was the kid who skimmed the first and last pages in a book that was assigned for homework, considered my work done, and headed out to play street hockey, basketball, or anything else that would help me make friends.

It wasn't that I didn't want to achieve—I was in Junior *Achievement* after all. I just didn't have much ambition. If you asked my thirteen-year-old self where I wanted to work when I grew up, I probably would have answered, "In a stable government job." That's because my family lived through the upheaval of the partition of the British Indian territories into Pakistan and India in 1947, forcing millions of people to move and turning many of them into refugees and migrants, including my parents and grandparents, who emigrated from the province of Sindh, where our roots had extended for generations. For many Indian families displaced from their homes, stability was appealing. And in India, the stable jobs that offered social mobility and success for the working classes were largely in government sectors, like in foreign service, administrative service, and the military.

It was my brother who convinced my parents to send me to the University of Toronto Schools (UTS) to change my educational—and life—trajectory. UTS was a unique high school that operated within one of Canada's leading universities, the University of Toronto. I needed to commute ninety minutes each way via public bus, rapid transit, and subway to get there, but it was worth every minute. UTS was a magnet for some of the hardest-working students that I had ever met and provided a doorway to a whole new set of opportunities. I started to excel at academics, not just athletics. When Aneel got into Harvard, I strove to match what he accomplished and eventually applied to the Wharton School at the University of Pennsylvania. I figured I'd get an undergraduate business degree, then go to law school and have the option of that "stable government job" practicing law, or perhaps I'd take a risk with a career in politics. One of those would be my path to achievement—a linear progression to success.

That's not how my story turned out.

From the moment I got to college, I knew I wanted to explore and experience different work environments and industries. I took summer internships in banking and publishing. I became, among other things, a door-to-door salesman, a research assistant for a book, an associate for a strategy consulting firm, a banker, and a consultant for the World Bank. I helped start an investment firm in India, got a graduate degree, taught at a major university, and created a pioneering company in person-to-person loans called CircleLending. All before I turned thirty.

My initial career steps may look like a hodgepodge to those who think achievement should or must be linear, but each was intentional in the moment. What I had no way of articulating at the time was that my nonlinear achievement journey, which continued in my thirties and forties, followed a definition of achievement different from the one I grew up with.

Classic books on achievement define it based on linear progression to accomplish a goal. They feature compelling stories of adversity and triumph over tragedy and contain many timeless lessons that remain immensely valuable. But authors like Napoleon Hill (*Think and Grow Rich*) and Brian Tracy (*Maximum Achievement*) focus their work on singular goal setting and attainment. In 1963, Hill could call his book *The Science of Personal Achievement* because his *entire* approach to achievement was singularly focused: set a goal, write it down, put the focus and effort into achieving it, and you will.

Hill and the classic achievement writers of the past wrote for a world that was more centralized, static, and hierarchical and less global, dynamic, and diverse by every measure. I saw how I struggled with sustaining long-term goal setting under the conditions of uncertainty, complexity, and rapid change. Thus, defining personal achievement and success based purely on long-term goal attainment felt outdated, not just to me in understanding my achievement story but to whom this book is for—people like my sons who have just started to write their own achievement stories and the millions of JA students and alums around the world who have inspired me every day for nearly a decade. According to the World Economic Forum's *The Future of Jobs Report*, most young people starting their achievement journeys will change jobs potentially twenty times and their career direction seven times on average. Moreover, more than 60 percent of jobs for the future have not been invented yet. That means no matter how you write your achievement story during your twenties and thirties, in your forties and fifties you will need to learn new things, reskill yourself, and pivot to new opportunities either within your field or outside your area of initial expertise.

In modern achievement, *all* steps and lessons, not just goals—no matter how nonlinear or seemingly unrelated—should be seen as part of a larger achievement process. Each one furthers your understanding of who you are, where you want to go, and how you want to challenge and change yourself, your career direction, and indeed the world. This approach is essential in an unpredictable world that requires constant change, adaptation, and resetting as new technology, information, and data constantly become available.

Thus, a modern definition of achievement needs to support nonlinear approaches to success and rewards and celebrate the tasks and processes associated with goals, not just the goals themselves. And here is the definition I have come up with:

Modern achievement is a new way of thinking about the journey to success and fulfillment that values the process of reaching your goals and objectives as much as their attainment.

To be clear, this definition of achievement doesn't dismiss goals and goalsetting as essential to your success; we all naturally want

MODERN ACHIEVEMENT IS A NEW WAY OF THINKING ABOUT THE JOURNEY TO SUCCESS AND FULFILLMENT THAT VALUES THE PROCESS OF REACHING YOUR GOALS AND OBJECTIVES AS MUCH AS THEIR ATTAINMENT.

and need goal attainment. It just acknowledges that multiple and changing goals are and will be a natural part of life and, in turn, values the process more. But you need to train yourself to live this kind of achievement journey. While from the outside it may appear as though I moved from success to success, my journey has been messy and fraught with rejection, obstacles, and moments of self-doubt. Yet I learned to see it all as part of the process of achieving. I have come to view my setbacks, mistakes, and failures as positives and to see pivoting and resetting as opportunities to build self-efficacy. Once you start to see all these things as part of your growth process, you immediately start to perceive and respect them differently. That's what this definition of modern achievement and the lessons in this book help you do.

My modern definition of achievement and the lessons I created around it are also much broader when it comes to notions of individual empowerment. I have learned from my journey and meeting aspiring leaders from around the world in leading JA Worldwide that young achievers like many of you are all about personal, professional, and social empowerment. Your entrepreneurial spirit is fierce. You want to create your future on your own terms but also value flexibility, collaboration, and diversity. You embrace the notion of a "portfolio career" that comprises multiple roles. You expect kindness and empathy from your leaders. You crave creative control and the ability to solve some of the world's biggest challenges. You understand the importance of prosocial motivation and self-care to your happiness, your professional success, and your intellectual, emotional, spiritual, and physical well-being.

This book honors all those things, but it also respects the needs and approaches of others *and* the timeless lessons from the classic books on achievement that remain relevant and influential to young people's success. That's why I call this book a new approach to timeless lessons: it honors your desires and directions and allows you to thrive while still aligning your way of achieving with both the best lessons of the past and the goals of the people you will work with and for. Because the process modern achievement values is not just about you. It is also about the people you surround yourself and collaborate with—the relationships you make—which is why you won't just find lessons and stories from me in this book. In all the numbered lessons, you will find insights on achievement from leading thinkers who have influenced me, comments from some of the best career coaches I know, and stories from young achievers from around the world, who, like you, are writing the proverbial first chapters in their achievement stories.

But only one person appears in every lesson with me: Marshall Goldsmith. This book exists only because Marshall changed my life. He has served as a coach, mentor, and friend who has pushed me to think differently about myself and my impact on others.

Marshall is one of the world's most influential leadership thinkers and a bestselling author and editor of dozens of books, including *Triggers*, *What Got You Here Won't Get You There*, and *The Earned Life*. But I am not collaborating on this book with him because of the millions of books he has sold or any of his other many accomplishments. I think of him as a modern sage because he shares wisdom and enhances the self-efficacy of everyone he meets, including me.

Our friendship started with an awkward phone call. I was driving down a narrow street in Boston, navigating traffic from all directions, and had Marshall on speaker phone. I had not even Googled him before this introductory call, so I did not know who he was and what he had accomplished. He asked me about my background, and I asked him about his. We both resisted the temptation to mention anything about our past accomplishments. I spent most of the time talking about what I wanted to do in the future—helping young people reach their full potential—rather than what I had done in the past. I think that's what convinced Marshall to accept me into his cohort of coaches, a community of leadership thinkers that includes some of the world's leading executive coaches, speakers, authors, entrepreneurs, and leaders.

This book is the next step in our collaboration. It is guided by Marshall's mission to help you achieve positive, lasting change for yourself and others. He wants to help you make your life a little better and overcome limiting beliefs and behaviors to achieve greater success, which is what he has done for me. But while we are collaborating, Marshall and I are not taking the traditional coauthor roles. He and I share a passion for helping people, but our stories and experiences are vastly different. Thus, our stories and thoughts will remain separate in each lesson—two "I's" rather than one "we." After I have laid out my story and the lesson and have presented a classic connection, coaching comment, or young achiever story, Marshall will offer stories and insights from his life.

All of this is designed to make the lessons bigger, more useful, and more actionable for you. That's our singular goal of this book: to help you use the start of your modern achievement journey so you can embrace the process of exploration to pursue opportunities, learn about unknown paths and other possibilities, and understand yourself and how to work for and collaborate with others. The more prepared you are to do this, the more prepared you will be to achieve and lead in the face of future challenges and changes.

Modern Achievement is for you: the leaders of tomorrow. You have helped me understand myself and my journey through your lens. This is my attempt to pay it forward. Enjoy the process!

INTRODUCTORY LESSON:

EMBRACE A FIXED-FLEXIBLE-FREESTYLE APPROACH TO ACHIEVEMENT

The summer after my first year in university, I interned for a bank in Canada but arranged to leave early to take another internship at Fairchild Media in New York City. I wanted to learn about the publishing industry and received an offer to work for their men's lifestyle magazine, but it shut down the week before I started. Instead, Fairchild offered me an opportunity to move my internship to their flagship publication: *Women's Wear Daily*, the "Bible of fashion." I knew nothing about women's fashion. Yet there I was, going to fashion photo shoots, talking to women on the street about where they'd shopped for the accessories they were wearing, and writing it all up for a magazine that needed daily content.

One Saturday, when no one else wanted a summer weekend assignment, I was asked to do a restaurant review. I said "yes" without a second thought. How many college students get to do restaurant reviews for a New York magazine?! I was sent with a photographer to take pictures of the chef while he bought tomatoes at the nearby greenmarket and then made his famous gazpacho, which I was supposed to write about in the review. The chef proudly served me the soup and waited for my reaction. I had never tasted gazpacho before.

My first comment? "The soup is cold."

The chef rolled his eyes and walked away. With just four words, I had eviscerated my credibility and ruined a delightful morning with the chef. That's how clueless I was. And in hindsight, that was OK. I had just experienced one of my first lessons in my approach to modern achievement: embrace your inexperience and cluelessness. What I was doing that day in New York was what I call *freestyling* today. That's a word you won't find in classic books on achievement, but it is one of the three words that define my framework for these lessons on modern achievement.

I call this framework Fixed-Flexible-Freestyle.

Fixed-Flexible-Freestyle is a human-centered framework for thinking differently about achievement in a rapidly changing world. It helps us to interpret rules and lessons about how we learn, how we collaborate with others, and how we claim our individual power to grow, succeed, and lead.

I first embraced a Fixed-Flexible-Freestyle approach when I became CEO of JA Worldwide in 2015, but I wasn't thinking about individual achievement then. JA Worldwide was the first truly global organization I led. I had always thought of myself as "global"—born in India, raised in Canada, educated at universities in the United States and England, married an American with Danish roots, led teams in five countries—so I started with some level of confidence. But leading JA Worldwide and its three-hundred-plus legal entities and staff working on the ground in more than one hundred countries, I immediately learned the limitations of my experience when it came to global diversity. At JA, my ability to understand the direct communication style of a colleague from the Netherlands versus the indirect communication style of a colleague from mainland China could be the difference between success and failure. Following traditional top-down approaches to leadership didn't always work either. For example, the staff on the ground working in Indonesia knew much more about supporting achievement-oriented young people in Jakarta than most "educational experts" living in the United States or United Kingdom.

Moreover, JA is not just globally diverse; it is also huge. As I said at the start of the book, JA delivers educational programs in entrepreneurship, financial literacy, and work readiness to more than fifteen million young people *each year*. In some countries, we reach more than 10 percent of all school-aged children, teaching them about business, economics, and the future of work through experiential learning and programs such as job shadowing. All of this is free for students and schools.

To make that possible, the JA Worldwide network of local, national, regional, and global teams raises substantial funding every year from donors. Those donations allowed us, during the COVID-19 pandemic, to transform the organization to add a direct-to-student channel, allowing some of our programs to be accessible outside of school systems for the first time. For an organization that was founded in 1919, that level of disruption and change was not easy. For all this and more, *Fast Company* recognized JA Worldwide for having one of the top 100 Best Workplaces for Innovators, the only nonprofit to make the list alongside companies such as Google, Microsoft, and Genentech. That honor celebrated JA's ability to work across boundaries without conflict and recognized the way our decentralized teams work together to grow the organization.

And all that work was supported by the Fixed-Flexible-Freestyle framework.

The catchy name comes from Jonas Prising, the chairman and CEO of ManpowerGroup, a global staffing firm that employs more than five hundred thousand people across the world. When I started at JA Worldwide in 2015, Jonas was the vice-chair of the board and chair of the strategy committee. Together, with the visionary chair of the board, Francesco Vanni d'Archirafi, we worked with our colleagues across the world to develop a new plan for JA's global strategy that we

FIXED-FLEXIBLE-
FREESTYLE IS A HUMAN-
CENTERED FRAMEWORK
FOR THINKING DIFFERENTLY
ABOUT ACHIEVEMENT IN A
RAPIDLY CHANGING WORLD.
IT HELPS US TO INTERPRET
RULES AND LESSONS
ABOUT HOW WE LEARN,
HOW WE COLLABORATE
WITH OTHERS, AND HOW
WE CLAIM OUR INDIVIDUAL
POWER TO GROW, SUCCEED,
AND LEAD.

called "Raising Aspirations." The idea was simple: since JA focuses on raising aspirations of the youth that we serve, we should raise our own aspirations and leverage our global network to magnify our impact. JA has one of the largest distribution networks in the world for reaching young people and now has partnerships with more Fortune 500 companies than any other nongovernmental organization (NGO). Because we thought of ourselves as one global organization rather than three-hundred-plus separate legal entities, we asked ourselves this question: How could we collaborate to use these assets to do more for the world?

In pondering this question, I shadowed Jonas at ManpowerGroup just like a JA student would as part of our job shadow programs. For a day, I immersed myself in the life of a Fortune 500 CEO, attending meetings with him and his direct reports, joining conference calls, and discussing the challenges of working across geographies and empowering teams. When Jonas told me about the Fixed-Flexible-Freestyle framework he was trying to develop at ManpowerGroup, primarily to clarify decision rights in different countries, I loved it immediately.

A Fixed-Flexible-Freestyle framework was exactly what JA needed, not just to clarify decision rights but also to move faster at creating change by empowering teams at all levels of our networked organization. I asked Jonas if I could borrow it for JA, and he not only told me I could borrow it but encouraged me to amplify it, transform it, and make it our own. And that's exactly what we did to empower individuals and local teams within a regional and global framework.

At first, Fixed-Flexible-Freestyle had a very clear definition at JA Worldwide: fixed meant global (guidelines, practices, and rules that apply to all national offices across JA), flexible meant regional (enabling regional leaders and teams in places like Europe and Africa to create their own guidelines, practices, and rules customized for their regions), and freestyle meant local (empowering the teams on the ground in every region to make decisions about how to serve students and build sustainability). The clarity and simplicity of the framework helped me explain to the six-thousand-plus local, regional, national, and global JA board members how a cohesive global strategy could be customized based on regional differences and local needs. The benefit was not just at the organizational level but at the individual level, where staff members could make their own decisions about the best way to implement marketing, program design, revenue generation, people development, and many of the other elements of JA's work, using a common framework with common language, without needing to consult and renegotiate operating agreements between JA's many entities.

As the Fixed-Flexible-Freestyle framework took hold, we realized the framework also allowed for customization based on place and time—the very thing most hierarchies, franchises, networks, and rulebooks do not allow for: more autonomy and opportunities for customization of . . . everything. That's when I started to wonder whether Fixed-Flexible-Freestyle could be adapted into lessons for individuals, especially aspiring leaders and JA students who are preparing for their own careers.

The three dimensions of fixed, flexible, and freestyle lend themselves to adaptability, which is essential for today's rapidly changing, globally diverse world. Allowing for more autonomy and opportunities for individual customization of life and career lessons certainly sounded like what I needed for myself and wanted to share with others, especially my twin boys, Alexander and Eliot, who were about to graduate and start university.

So I reimagined the Fixed-Flexible-Freestyle framework as an individual approach to learning lessons on modern achievement.

Fixed

Fixed lessons don't change at their core, even as the world around us does. They connect to and honor classic research and writings on achievement and ground you while you explore more flexible and free-style lessons. Think of them as the basic rules for any game: they apply no matter the time or place the game is played or who is playing it.

Flexible

Flexible lessons compel you to think broadly and differently (i.e., more flexibly) about what you are doing as time progresses and where you live and work changes. They help you revise or reconsider your thinking and account for new understandings as you grow. Context matters! Think of them as the strategies that teams and individuals use when playing games: they follow the rules but adapt the approach according to who, where, and when they are playing.

Freestyle

Freestyle lessons are about designing and innovating *you*. They compel you to think creatively about your unique strengths. They encourage you to build your passions, understand your values, embrace differences, and connect your strengths and stories to others. Think of freestyling as if you were an athlete on a team: How can you individually *and* collaboratively maximize your potential as you grow to lift yourself and the team (i.e., others) to success at the same time?

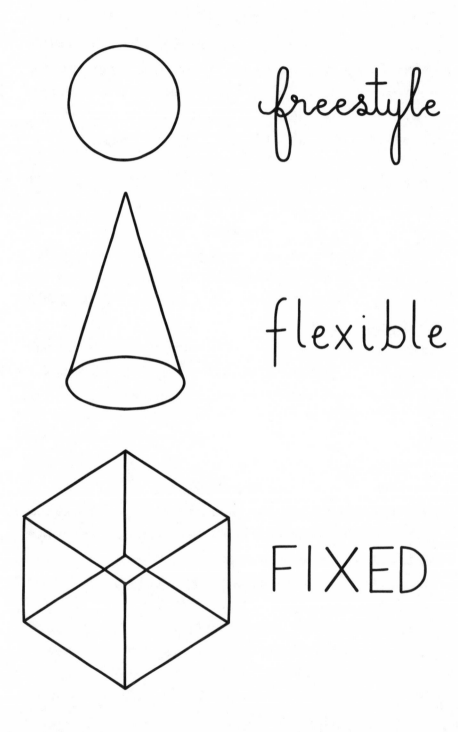

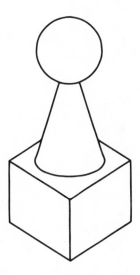

Think of fixed, flexible, and freestyle as the dimensions of a structure. Each has its own length, width, and height that come together to define that structure. The lessons fill the space of each dimension: fixed lessons hold you up, no matter what changes around you; flexible lessons keep you steady as you grow; and freestyle lessons point you out to the world. How you balance the lessons within those dimensions gives your pyramid of achievement its shape. Learn to balance all three dimensions, and you will not only achieve but grow as a person and as a leader the workforce and workplace of tomorrow needs. Overweight one or two of them, and you become unsteady.

For example, the freestyle lesson I learned that day in New York with the chef—*embrace your own inexperience and cluelessness*—was about exploring the unknown and being willing to play different roles that I was uncomfortable with to innovate myself, learn new skills, and create the life I wanted. Simply put, I was clueless that morning in New York because I *chose* to take that internship and that assignment. Choosing to put yourself in environments that allow you to learn new things, even though they do not form a linear path to success, exposes you to multiple opportunities for designing and creating your future.

But like every lesson in this book, this lesson has its limitations. While the experience of trying new things and taking risks with new jobs and assignments is part of the journey to achievement, you can't navigate a path to achievement, let alone change existing structures, without understanding your values and why you are making your choices—and you can't use cluelessness as an excuse for ignorance. I had not done my research about gazpacho before taking the assignment, and that left me too inflexible to consider that soup could be cold. When the chef walked away after my review of the soup, he showed me I was a little too clueless. Since then, I have learned to do the work and balance empowering my freestyle approach with my fixed and flexible approaches, which has helped me succeed within existing organizational structures.

That balance propelled me forward and helped me to develop the self-efficacy (belief in your own ability to succeed) modern achievement requires. As Marshall Goldsmith says, self-efficacy is born from personal responsibility. You need to take responsibility for each dimension of the framework. The process of learning them shows you have more agency than you may realize. From building relationships and developing new skills to exploring side hustles, modulating the energy you bring to work, reframing your reactions to situations positively or negatively, and learning to ask to do and be more . . . there is so much you can choose to control and influence if you embrace a Fixed-Flexible-Freestyle approach in order to not just achieve more but achieve *better*.

Using this framework can allow you to succeed in different organizational structures, learn to collaborate and compromise, put yourself in environments that open you up to explore, test your assumptions, and find your values, purposes, and passions. I say "can" because the framework is designed to let you live your story as you want to write it.

FROM MARSHALL
ASHEESH'S CHALLENGE TO ME — AND YOU

This book gives me a special opportunity to try to help you—the young achievers and aspiring leaders, who are essential to our future but who I have spent very little time with—at the start of your achievement jour-

MARSHALL GOLDSMITH

neys. Most of my professional life has been spent working with people at the highest level of business, coaching the coaches and executives at the top or those well on their way to getting there. When I wrote a book called *What Got You Here Won't Get You There*, I was writing for successful people to make them more successful. Their hard work had paid off, but something was holding them back from reaching the next level. That something was themselves—their behaviors and habits and often a desire to win at all costs. They needed to learn to get out of their own way.

I learned a lot working with those people, and I have become quite good at helping them. Asheesh offered me a new challenge. Not just in coaching him, which I have enjoyed doing, but in thinking about how what I have learned and done and continue to do can help high-potential achievers and aspiring leaders in a positive way. That is very different from what I have done in the past, and it inspired me in a way no other person has.

Asheesh has a life perspective and experience that no one I have met or read about has. The combination of his entrepreneurial story, education journey, innovative style of leadership, and now the magnitude of his job as the leader of Junior Achievement Worldwide (which connects him to millions upon millions of young people around the world and gives him access to their insights and ideas) adds up to something unique.

A few years ago, Asheesh was selected for a leadership award named after Tony Hsieh, the founder of Zappos and author of the book *Delivering Happiness*. The award was for leading people through empowerment rather than control, through influence rather than authority. That is, I believe, what Asheesh has done with his advice for aspiring leaders in this book, and I have encouraged him to root it in his personal experiences and journey, which I have tried to complement with my own experiences and advice. Asheesh has learned what I did decades earlier, as I was starting my own achievement journey, and what we both want for you to understand: the better you are at making positive change at the start of your career to try to overcome bad habits and behaviors before they affect you as a leader, the more you will achieve for yourself and others as a leader.

HOW TO TREAT THE LESSONS IN THIS BOOK

The things you can control and influence also extend to how you treat the lessons in this book. You can jump in anywhere you want. Let your curiosity guide you. Modern achievement is about life and work, so the lessons are divided not only into fixed, flexible, and freestyle but also into self (life) and career (work). But there is no linear progression within any of these divisions. I have tried to order them in a way that makes them easiest to read together, but the lessons within each part and division are not sequential; they are observational based on how I and others behave. They are also by no means comprehensive or finite. The lessons included here have been revised after being vetted by achievers of all ages, but you might rephrase them and add to them too. There are many more lessons out there that may be meaningful for understanding yourself and your place in the world. Regardless of how you approach them, seeing them through the dimensions of a Fixed-Flexible-Freestyle framework will help you understand their value to your achievement journey—and your happiness.

Fixed lessons don't change at their core, even as the world around us does. Think of them like the basic rules for any game: they apply no matter the time or place the game is played or who is playing it. These fixed lessons also connect to and honor research and books on achievement that are considered classics in the field and have had an influence on me, Marshall, and countless other leaders. You may or may not be aware of some of them. Perhaps you've encountered Napoleon Hill's *Think and Grow Rich* or Dale Carnegie's *How to Win Friends and Influence People*, which remain top-selling books today. But other names like Zig Ziglar, Frances Hesselbein, Roosevelt Thomas, Stephen Covey, Jim Rohn, Peter Drucker, and Brian Tracy may be less familiar to you. Yet many of their lessons are just as salient and influential today to the fixed lessons on modern achievement as they were in the past, which is why every fixed lesson that follows features a "classic connection" to books and other work on achievement.

That said, when I use the term "classic," I am also referring to some more recent books that I consider to be modern classics such as Angela Duckworth's *Grit*, Carol Dweck's *Mindset: The New Psychology of Success*, Keith Ferrazzi's *Never Eat Alone*, Linda Hill's *Becoming a Manager*, and Robert Waldinger's *The Good Life: Lessons from the World's Longest Scientific Study of Happiness*. Those authors and more are also featured in the classic connections that follow to help these fixed lessons ground you while you explore more flexible and freestyle lessons, embrace the process of modern achievement, and rise into leadership.

The first set of lessons focus on your life (self), and the second set of lessons focus on your work (career).

PART 1
FIXED

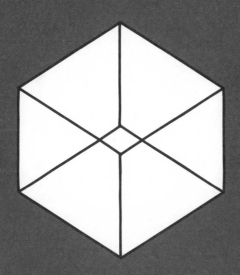

1. MERITOCRACY IS NOT DEAD

2. YOU CAN'T COMPLAIN YOUR WAY TO A HAPPY LIFE

3. WRITE IT DOWN

4. GO META

5. CONNECT BEYOND THE SCREEN

SELF

1.

MERITOCRACY IS NOT DEAD

As you know from the first pages of this book, my parents' message to me and my brother, Aneel, as we grew up was clear: education matters and hard work pays off. Even though they didn't earn a lot of money—my father was an engineer at IBM studying computer science at night to get ahead, and my mother was a secretary—their hard work allowed us to move from a small apartment in an immigrant neighborhood to houses in the suburbs, moving every few years as our economic prospects improved. You also know it took me longer than it took Aneel to effectively grasp my parents' message, but it eventually stuck and remains a big reason why I can't accept the current zeitgeist that claims meritocracy is dead.

Do not get me wrong: I do not think we live in a world where meritocracy thrives for everyone. A meritocracy is defined as a system in which everyone gets what they earn—where abilities, achievements, and merit matter most and determine how people are chosen for positions and how we find success, power, and influence. When class, race, ethnicity, sex, or any other personal traits have outsized impacts on how we move through life, how others perceive us, and how we get access to certain institutions, the meritocratic ideal is clearly compromised.

Access to institutions of higher learning is one example of flawed meritocracy. As Adam Grant, an organizational psychologist at Wharton and bestselling author, notes, "Harvard, Princeton, Stanford, and

Yale have more students in the top 1% of family income than in the bottom 60%." Several important books have done deep dives on this inequality and explore the apparent fallacy of and absolute problems with meritocracy. The titles of two of them are enough to give you pause: *The Meritocracy Trap: How America's Foundational Myth Feeds Inequality, Dismantles the Middle Class, and Devours the Elite,* by Daniel Markovits, and *The Tyranny of Merit: What's Become of the Common Good?* by Michael Joseph Sandel.

In fact, the concept of meritocracy—and by extension the word merit—is such a lightning rod that some people I consulted called for a less "provocative" title for this lesson, like "Hard Work Pays Off" or "Effort Matters." However, this sidesteps the relationship between effort and merit: *exceptional achievement requires exceptional effort in all you do, from your education and your job to your relationships and the kindness and empathy you show others.* But here's the rest of that sentence: you must believe that effort will pay off. For me, that has meant challenging the terms of meritocracy, not abandoning the idea altogether.

Whether you are born into privilege or poverty, some portion of your success still comes down to how you earn it, and, yes, that is founded on hard work and effort. Even innate talent and unlimited opportunity get you only so far if you don't put in the time and effort to hone that talent and seize those opportunities. Nothing is absolute in life. Even if 90 percent of achievement is bound by circumstance, identity, and many "-isms," the 10 percent based on individual effort is essential. But if achievement is just about effort, where is the joy of improvement, knowledge, and growth? Merit is not only how you are rewarded or compensated for your work and effort but how you feel about those things. You can try as hard as you can, but you need to have an internal compass that informs your idea of what constitutes merit in order to achieve. Put another way, merit requires achievement—and vice versa.

This belief in meritocracy has been a key for me in building self-efficacy—the belief in yourself and your abilities to achieve your goals. I first learned this by overcoming my stutter and gaining confidence to excel in school. I also developed my self-efficacy from extracurricular activities such as Junior Achievement. Whether an afterschool club like mine or something much larger, JA has dozens of programs in and outside of school to enable you to learn about the business world with job shadows and immersive experiences, develop financial literacy skills by roleplaying, and build confidence by becoming an entrepreneur. At JA, you learn by doing. For example, the JA Company Program teaches teenagers to build businesses with a real product or service, as part of a team of other teenagers holding roles and titles such as CEO, CFO, and other executive roles. As a kid with a chronic speech impediment, there was nothing that built my confidence more than becoming CEO of a student business and speaking to a room full of friends who came to respect me and follow my lead despite my stutter. I loved the experience so much that it prompted me to launch a multischool investment competition for students and take on additional leadership roles as I entered high school.

To build the self-efficacy you need to pivot, adjust, adapt, and deal with or create change, you must produce this same resourcefulness in yourself. You also need to make the effort to find role models and surround yourself with people who can propel you forward. How do you find those people?

Start by doing a little research. Look around you: Who can you emulate and say, *If they can do it, I can too*? As an Indian kid who moved to Canada, I did volunteer work for the political campaign of one of the first-elected politicians with South Asian ancestry, Murad Velshi. Working on his campaign helped me to see that I could indeed aspire to more than just a stable government job, which my parents wanted for me. When I had my college admissions interview in my final year of high school, I found another role model in my college interviewer. He was a partner in one of the largest law firms in the world. The interview was in his law office, overlooking the Toronto skyline. While he looked and dressed nothing like me, he was such a good communicator—warm, impressive, gracious, and thoughtful—that he made me want to be like him, not just as a lawyer but as a human.

Take a moment now and make a list of five people who come from backgrounds like yours. Knowing what you know about their success—how they did it and why—reflect on why you picked them.

Identifying and studying those role models allows you to form your own mental models for achievement and break through the barriers that make you think you can't accomplish things. They will also help you visualize what success looks like for you—from material things to love and happiness, to where you want to live, to what you want to study, to where and how you want to work, to the impact you want to have in the world. Being able to visualize all that focuses your effort to achieve them and builds self-efficacy.

Visualizing your success also draws successful people to you, and you will need those people to achieve your goals. In life and leadership, you will need the aid of others. You will need their fiscal, physical, emotional, and mental assistance. You will need to get them to support your point of view. I firmly believe cooperation and competition with others are not oppositional forces and are often the best parts of achievement; they can lead to great relationships. And the lessons of

I FIRMLY BELIEVE
COOPERATION AND
COMPETITION WITH
OTHERS ARE NOT
OPPOSITIONAL FORCES
AND ARE OFTEN
THE BEST PARTS OF
ACHIEVEMENT; THEY
CAN LEAD TO GREAT
RELATIONSHIPS.

achievement throughout this book are all about relationships, which bring you greater fulfillment and happiness and can help you think more positively—another key factor in self-efficacy. But here again, effort is not enough to build those relationships, especially when aspiring to leadership. People need to believe in you, and you need to believe in them. But why would anyone believe in you as a leader if you don't believe you will succeed? Your self-efficacy could be the difference between getting people to support you or your idea, navigating the inevitable obstacles you will face, dealing with and creating the change you seek, and more.

CLASSIC CONNECTIONS

Two authors of classic texts on achievement we are considering in this book, Napoleon Hill and Brian Tracy, did not come from privilege and thus place a high value on hard work and effort.

For Napoleon Hill, hard work and effort are the cornerstones of his fifth principle in *The Science of Personal Achievement*: "Go the Extra Mile, Always." He lists several reasons that effort gives you an advantage, including "the law of increasing returns" (increased compensation), "favorable attention" (going out of your way to do for others attracts them to you), "a positive, pleasing mental attitude" (which in turn attracts positivity back), and "taking personal initiative" (creating opportunities for yourself).

Brian Tracy, on the other hand, prioritizes self-efficacy through effort. The opening chapter of *Maximum Achievement* is called "Make Your Life a Masterpiece" and is all about putting effort into visualizing your success—painting "a masterpiece on the canvas of your life." While circumstance can affect how you paint, most of our limitations are self-imposed. "You perform as well as you believe yourself capable of performing," Tracy writes. For Tracy, great achievement begins with the choice to visualize success: we choose what will make us happy in what we are doing and then choose to dedicate ourselves to the pursuit of those things.

I also want you to consider this lesson's connection to the leadership work of Linda Hill, a professor at Harvard Business School. Since Hill's original research for her book *Becoming a Manager*, she has continued to study the personal transformation involved when someone becomes a boss. According to her research, that transition gets harder all the time. The overarching reason? "In [the managers'] prior jobs, success depended primarily on their personal expertise and actions," Hill writes. "As managers, they are responsible for setting and implementing an agenda for a whole group, something for which their careers as individual performers haven't prepared them." No framework can fully prepare you for something you haven't been asked to do, but this lesson and the other lessons in this book are intended to help you build awareness and self-efficacy. You will also need the effort required for this lesson to meet the challenge Hill wrote about in the *Harvard Business Review*: "Create the conditions for your success." As Hill says, "New managers often discover, belatedly, that they are expected to do more than just make sure their groups function smoothly today. They must also recommend and initiate changes that will help their groups do even better in the future."

FROM MARSHALL
EARNING YOUR PATH
TO ACHIEVEMENT

I grew up poor in Valley Station, Kentucky—as in my-school-had-an-outhouse poor. My high school came in next to last in academic achievement in the state. The academic standards were low. Yet only 20 percent of the people I went to elementary school with managed to graduate that high school. Fortunately, I still had some great teachers, including an in-house advantage my classmates did not: my mother had been a first-grade teacher. I say "had been" because my father thought women shouldn't work (which is how we ended up so poor). So, as part of "tending to the house," she spent her time teaching me. By the time I started school, while the other kids tried to grasp the concept of one plus one, I knew how to add and subtract, multiply, and divide. I told my mom after the first day in school that I was the smartest person who ever lived!

I went on to beat the graduation odds and get my bachelor's degree in mathematical economics from Rose-Hulman Institute of Technology in Indiana (where I received an honorary PhD in engineering in 2023!) followed by an MBA at Indiana University's Kelley School of Business and a PhD at UCLA's Anderson School of Management. I eventually landed a job at Dartmouth College in New Hampshire. Near the end of my time at UCLA, I met Paul Hersey, a pioneering organizational behavioral scientist who taught and trained top business leaders. Paul let me follow him around, and I absorbed his methods. One day, he asked me if I thought I could do what he did, *and he let me.* When I won over the extremely conservative executives at MetLife (basically because I wasn't boring), I started working with Paul officially. That set me on the path to forming my own management education business and earning a life I never imagined as a child sitting in that outhouse at my school.

Earning: that's an important word when considering your goals. Even if I had been born into privilege, my success would not be merited unless I had earned it. Something truly earned requires maximum effort to push as far as you can. But living an earned life means something more. We are living an earned life when the choices, risks, and effort we make in each moment align with an overarching purpose in our lives, regardless of the eventual outcome. I realize the idea of an "eventual outcome" goes against classic definitions of goal achievement: set a target, work hard, earn your monetary reward. But what you earn must be about more than personal ambition. Goals and rewards are important, but the effort that goes into achievement must be connected to a higher purpose. It's the earning, not (just) the destination.

What is your higher purpose today? Ask yourself that and keep reexamining your answer as you grow to keep your efforts aligned with it. Commit yourself to "earning" every step toward that purpose and making it a habit. Like the circumstances you are born into, the outcomes or rewards will not always be fair and just, but the feeling you get from what you earn beyond those rewards will drive your self-efficacy on your achievement journey.

2.

YOU CAN'T COMPLAIN YOUR WAY TO A HAPPY LIFE

When I was young, my mother told me a story from Hindu mythology about two brothers who had the same teacher. One of their assignments was to go out in search of someone who could teach them new skills. The first brother returned and said to his teacher, "Everyone I met has certain skills that I do not have, so I can learn from everyone." The second brother returned and said, "I have certain skills that each person does not have, so I cannot learn from any of them."

I try to see the world like the first brother: filled with opportunities to learn from others. As I advanced in my career, I became more confident as I learned new things—and most of that learning occurred through interacting with others and looking for the positive in all my interactions. Today, when I look to the future, I still feel there is so much more to learn, so much more to do.

While the story my mother told me influenced my worldview, it doesn't fully explain why I look at the world in this way. My friends once tried to figure it out. I'm part of a "forum" of eight friends who meet monthly, organized as part of the Young Presidents' Organization (YPO). During one of our forum retreats, we hired a professional moderator who asked us to dig deeper to understand one another. In my case, we explored my relentless optimism and learn-from-everyone outlook. The conclusion was that, as a young immigrant from India, I had tried hard to fit into my adopted homeland of Canada, learning from everything and everyone I could so that I could fit into my new surroundings. I must have turned each negative experience into a positive experience as a coping mechanism to avoid unhappiness. This created a habit that became a lifelong, ingrained practice. I don't know if my forum's analysis was accurate or not. (Others with similar immigrant experiences have had different outcomes and exhibited different behaviors.) But it affirmed that optimism and a thirst for learning are inextricably linked in my personality.

Seeing the world in an optimistic way has made me a much happier and more successful person, and I continue to look for the good in everything and have worked hard to maintain and ensure that belief in everyone I connect to. But it is not just *my* belief. Study after study has shown that optimists do better in life, are more resilient, and live longer and healthier lives.

The first study most people point to was done by Dr. Martin Seligman. Known as the "father of positive psychology," Dr. Seligman was hired as a consultant by MetLife in 1982 to identify which sales-people would be more successful in order to reduce training costs. He developed a test that found that, of more than fifteen thousand people who took the company's employee screening test, optimists outsold pessimists by 56 percent. To this day, MetLife recruits opti-mistic professionals, saving the company tens of millions of dollars through employee retention and increasing its market share.

One of the big reasons optimistic people are more successful is that when they experience setbacks, they don't give them perma-nence. They think, "Next time I will fix that" or "It will get better." Pessimists, on the other hand, think the setback is permanent. They think, "Nothing is fixable" or "We're doomed." The less permanence you give things, the more you will move forward through failures and successes with energy and enthusiasm and will build self-efficacy—the belief you will succeed. And once you believe you will succeed, your chance of success goes up. In fact, the term "self-efficacy" comes from the pioneering work of the psychologist Albert Bandura. He found that turning negative thoughts into positive thoughts is one of the critical elements of developing self-efficacy. Optimistic thinking enhanced one's sense of self, while pessimistic thinking was more debilitating.

Seeing the world as an optimist doesn't always make me a popular person at dinner parties. I'm *too* optimistic and don't have much patience for gossip or complaints. I'm not saying complaints are never warranted, and speaking out against injustice is better than silence. I'm saying that doing that alone without believing change can happen and changing how you see the world is not the path to modern achievement. In the age of doom-scrolling and people living in echo chambers that affirm their points of view—usually by complaining about the other side—it is easy to go down a rabbit hole of negativity: to complain about how wrong, exclusionary, and insensitive "they" are. We then look for others to fuel our anger and pessimism. And that is too often the objective: to see things one way and drown out all compromise, understanding, and other ways forward—to flip things completely to your side and exclude those who think differently.

Yes, there have been a few studies that have shown that optimists aren't always the most successful. One study found that while optimistic employees earn more than pessimistic ones, optimistic entrepreneurs earn less than pessimistic ones. But I would argue that optimism is a core belief of an entrepreneurial mindset. Pessimists may earn more through business cycles, but optimists are more likely to start businesses in new industries and new product categories that drive innovation.

The good news is that optimism is learned over time, not something you're born with. It starts with a shift in your mindset from one of "I can't" to "I can," from "these are my limited skills" to "I'll keep learning and growing throughout my career." Stop giving things permanence. Don't think of setbacks and failures as condemnations of you or your abilities overall (that you are not good at anything). That's a pessimistic body blow to self-efficacy. Instead, see them as narrowly contained to a specific instance or skill you can work on—and an opportunity to learn.

That said, saying all this is easy. It takes effort to maintain optimism, and one of the best ways to do that is by practicing gratitude. Gratitude—being thankful for what you have—breeds optimism and self-efficacy. Natalie Miller-Snell, a leadership coach and host of the *Seize the Day* podcast, represents this idea beautifully in what she calls the "Gratitude Cycle."

GRATITUDE CYCLE

THE GOOD NEWS IS THAT OPTIMISM IS LEARNED OVER TIME, NOT SOMETHING YOU'RE BORN WITH. IT STARTS WITH A SHIFT IN YOUR MINDSET FROM ONE OF "I CAN'T" TO "I CAN," FROM "THESE ARE MY LIMITED SKILLS" TO "I'LL KEEP LEARNING AND GROWING THROUGHOUT MY CAREER."

In my family, we have developed a habit of saying three things that we are grateful for on a regular basis. We selected three, rather than one or two, for a specific reason. The first one or two things are usually easy to identify—a good grade on a test, a goal scored in a game, a great meal. It becomes harder to find a third thing and nudges the mind to turn neutral and otherwise negative experiences into positive ones (e.g., missing the school bus but still getting a ride to school, dealing with a health issue for a loved one but still being able to care for them). When one of my sons dropped his ice cream cone, his third example of that day was being grateful that he has a family that gives him ice cream. That turns a negative into a positive simply by using "even though": "Even though my ice cream cone fell today, I am grateful to have a family that goes out for ice cream." Try it yourself now and keep it going!

Doing this exercise daily, starting with "even though," makes gratitude a habit. The mind starts to look for the positive in everything. Ask yourself, *What am I grateful for?*

CLASSIC CONNECTIONS

There is no shortage of classic literature on optimism and achievement. Napoleon Hill advised readers to have a "positive mental attitude" and "pleasing personality." Dale Carnegie's approach in *How to Win Friends and Influence People* relied on helping people build stronger relationships by using a few thoughtful techniques, such as giving honest and sincere appreciation and talking in terms of the other person's interest. You then win people over by avoiding making enemies and using "a drop of honey" in dealing with them. I also love what Marshall wrote about Frances Hesselbein (the former executive director of Girl Scouts of the USA and CEO of the Frances Hesselbein Leadership Institute): "She never complained. She never whined, and it was always about us and not about her. In fact, the first of her 'battle cries' was what she proudly called her blood type: 'B+ (Be Positive)'!"

Marshall introduced me to Frances a few years before she passed away, and I am forever grateful for his introduction. She asked me to sit beside her, looked me right in the eyes with a piercing stare, thanked me for leading Junior Achievement to become more global and more diverse, and expressed her hope for our growing impact on young people worldwide. She exuded optimism and positivity even after she turned one hundred!

I also want you to focus on a single enduring line from Jim Rohn that may influence your optimism more than anything else—a line I have heard achievers of all shapes and sizes quote: "You are the average of the five people you spend the most time with."

Rohn started his career with Sears before becoming an entrepreneur and author of several books, but the line was one he used as a motivational speaker and has been repeated by many high achievers as being essential to their self-efficacy and success. Surrounding yourself with successful people who propel you forward, build you up, and have a positive spirit is critical to your optimism. I found that through my forum in YPO as an adult, but it started much earlier with my school friends, college friends, and the friends that I chose in my twenties. I believe if my brother had not believed in me and encouraged my parents to send me to a different school, my path to success would look very different. It changed my life by surrounding me with other kids who were academically motivated. They got me thinking I could be successful. Who is doing that for you? Identify them and spend more time with them!

FROM MARSHALL
PRAGMATIC OPTIMISM

My mission is to help others and the people around them have happier lives, but in today's competitive world, it's difficult to remain optimistic. It's easy to get caught in a "poor me" cycle if we dwell on the negative aspects of life and work, the fast pace of our lives, the constant barrage of emails, a 24/7 workplace, and so on. But without a positive attitude, we can't face those obstacles to happiness. A positive spirit is an unambiguous feeling of optimism and satisfaction that conveys both happiness and meaning. But what happens when we are faced with dire circumstances?

For those moments, I turn to the *Bhagavad Gita*. The *Gita* is a battlefield dialogue between Arjuna and Krishna. Arjuna is talking about his terrible situation and the two choices he has: bad and worse. While he is talking about a war, the real war is with himself and the choice he has. Krishna listens and says: "What is, is." That line—"What is, is"—is the foundation for pragmatic optimism.

The pragmatic part means facing reality. This is not a time for happy talk. No motivational speeches are going to make a bad situation go away, especially one like a natural disaster or a global pandemic that happened through no fault of your own. Don't sugarcoat things. Don't play games with yourself. *What is, is.* Accept and face that. Optimism means making the best of that reality and making peace with your decision and results, forgiving yourself for any mistakes, forgiving others for what they've done, and saying, "OK, here we are. The reality is the reality. Now, how can we make the very best of this that we possibly can?" You don't have to like the choice—Arjuna had only bad and worse choices—but whatever the result, don't complain and carry it around, letting it infect you and your optimism moving forward. If you have done what is right and done your best, take a deep breath and make peace.

3.

WRITE IT DOWN

About half of all Americans make New Year's resolutions, which means that at least half of the country starts the year with a belief that they can be better at something. That's optimism! Perhaps unsurprisingly, because of my optimistic nature, I have always been one of those annual resolution people. I can see them in my journals going back to the start of my career, marking what I wanted to achieve and how I wanted to do more to support and deepen relationships with my kids, my wife, my parents, my colleagues, my family and friends, and the other important people in my life. In my thirties, my resolutions evolved into lists of things I wanted to accomplish, experience, and learn, like becoming a hot air balloon pilot, writing a book, and traveling the world. Then, every December, I would read what I wrote and rate myself on how well I performed on the past year's resolutions before making new ones in January. On a scale of one to five, I gave myself mostly threes and fours.

But while I had made a habit of making and reviewing my annual resolutions, I had no plan for how to get better at keeping them and ensuring that I remembered what they were over the course of the year. Chances are you have a similar resolution story. Recent surveys show that people eighteen to thirty-four are the largest New Year's and annual resolution-making demographic, mostly focusing on physical and mental health. Yet you are no better at keeping them than any other demographic group: no survey reports more than 10 percent of

SUSTAINABLE LONG-TERM ACHIEVEMENT REQUIRES A PROCESS-ORIENTED APPROACH — SMALL, CONCRETE STEPS TO DEVELOP HABITS THAT CREATE THE BEHAVIOR CHANGE WE WANT, ACHIEVE (AND EVEN SURPASS) OUR GOALS, AND BUILD SELF-EFFICACY.

people keeping their annual resolutions—or any big resolution—for long. Most people don't even keep them beyond January. Many quit after just a week.

Some of our failure with resolutions comes from setting unrealistic goals and pursuing them without what Napoleon Hill calls "definiteness of purpose." Some comes from "planning fallacy," in which we underestimate how much time, money, and/or effort a project, action, or change will take—a miscalculation optimistic people tend to fall victim to. But the larger issue with resolutions is that most people follow a classic goal-oriented approach to achievement: set big goals, pursue them with purpose and singular focus, and by the law of attraction, your behavior will change. But that's exactly why resolutions for behavior change fail: this goal-oriented approach equates failed effort with failure.

Most goal-oriented approaches to resolutions prioritize results over effort—goals over process. We think we have failed by only partially reaching our goal, rather than celebrating the smaller successes of the process that moved us closer to achieving them. Sustainable long-term achievement requires a process-oriented approach—small, concrete steps to develop habits that create the behavior change we want, achieve (and even surpass) our goals, and build self-efficacy.

Two people helped me understand the importance of this process-oriented approach: Marshall Goldsmith and Angela Duckworth.

It was not until I met Marshall Goldsmith that I fully understood the power of daily routines to improve self-efficacy. Marshall's book *Triggers* is a prescription for taking personal responsibility for behavior change and recognizing environmental and psychological triggers that set you back. One of his recommendations is to use a daily routine of "active questions" to ask yourself daily (daily!) what you have personally done to address a given issue. In this process, the way you frame the question matters even more than what the question is because each question is designed to measure your effort, not your results.

This lesson is fixed because, while the questions will change in your achievement journey, the question-asking process never stops. I understood this all too well when Marshall included me in the "Life Plan Review" (LPR) group he assembled for his book *The Earned Life*. The group was like *Triggers* on steroids. Fifty high achievers, from CEOs to Olympic athletes, checked in all summer long to report on how we did with our wide-ranging questions: *Have I done my best to be a good partner? Have I done my best to be a good father? Have I done my best to get better at tennis?* We completed a spreadsheet by writing down self-evaluations for each question on a scale from one to ten. If I thought I was a hard grader about my annual resolutions in the past, I was no match for these amazingly successful people. No one in the group gave themselves more than sixes or sevens, because they saw they could have achieved more with more focus and effort on the process.

Angela Duckworth helped me better understand the strategy behind Marshall's question process and the value of taking small, concrete steps to behavior change. I met her in graduate school when she started dating my friend Jason. They eventually married and moved to Philadelphia, close to where they both grew up. Today, Angela is a well-known professor of psychology at the University of Pennsylvania, and her first book, *Grit: The Power of Passion and Perseverance*, has become a modern classic, which helped form my views of human behavior and character. In her book, she defines grit as "passion and perseverance for long-term goals." So how do you achieve the sustained interest those goals require? You break big things into small things. She cites the work of Albert Bandura (see lesson three), who found that when two equal groups of elementary school students had to learn math, the ones who learned to break down the work into smaller goals achieved more in the end than those who tried to learn all the math at once. In fact, Angela used this approach to write *Grit*: when she thought about writing the whole book, she was overwhelmed and got nowhere; when she broke the book down to its smallest piece—simply writing one sentence—she built on that success to write another and then another . . .

Marshall's daily questions and Angela's grit only work with what she calls "intentional and consistent observation of our behavior" or "self-monitoring," which facilitates learning when pursuing any goal. "Once I realize I'm not getting to the gym," she writes, "I can ask myself why. Perhaps I'll discover that my gym routine is sort of boring and I should try jogging or yoga instead. Or that I need to motivate myself by bundling the chore of going to the gym with something I absolutely love to do—like talk to my best friend on the phone or watch episodes of *Top Chef*." Again, how you achieve your behavior change is less important than taking a process-oriented approach.

In our family, we use a framework called "stop, start, and continue." I learned it from Andy Snider when he introduced it to my colleagues at a management retreat. I met Andy more than twenty years ago when his leadership advisory company had an office next to mine. We became friends, developed a mentoring relationship, and I have hired him to serve as a meeting facilitator to run management retreats at every organization that I have led. Andy knows most people take feedback personally. After all, that's how it's usually presented: it's about judgment—you point out what people did wrong, what they need to improve, and what their flaws are. Andy recommends saying something like, "Hey, in order for me to get my work done, could you stop doing this, start doing this, continue doing this?" This approach is great for self-monitoring and feels much less stressful for both the giver and receiver than long feedback sessions do.

We adapted this stop-start-continue framework to replace annual resolutions in our family. For example, my sons adapted it to succeed in difficult classes, get work done without procrastinating, or keep up with their daily affirmations by *stopping* wasting time on TikTok, *starting* each day with an affirmation, and *continuing* to seek help as problems arise in their difficult classes. The stop-start-continue, process-oriented approach places the emphasis on concrete changes in behavior that lead to sustainable results, not the results themselves.

That need for sustainable behavioral change is the reason this lesson is called "write it down." Both Marshall's question-asking process and Angela's breaking-big-things-into-small-things process require writing things down for them to work. Our family's stop-start-continue process started many years ago, when our twin boys were seven and my wife and I started a tradition of writing them letters after their birthday. The letters recounted our past year together, the things we were proud of having worked to improve, and all they achieved. At the end of my letters, I reflected on things they could improve through stop, start, and continue—and got their buy-in before writing them down in the letters (e.g., "I'd like you to continue to reflect on three things that you are grateful for every day," and "I'd like you to stop biting your nails"). The boys have saved them all in binders and keep adding each new letter every year as a milestone of progress.

Reflecting on these letters, I understand more than ever how writing down my annual resolutions was the one thing I did absolutely right. Most people do not do this. In fact, I find many people are terrified of it and thus never learn the benefits of doing so. Angela Duckworth notes that writing things down is essential to self-monitoring and directly counters the ostrich effect. The ostrich effect (or ostrich problem) is exactly what it sounds like: we would rather stick our heads in the sand and deliberately avoid, reject, and ignore negative information that would cause us pain rather than confront it. Without writing anything down (from goals to daily questions and our progress on them) you don't *become* an ostrich; you *start out* as one!

"Writing it down" opens you up to another benefit Angela notes: sharing your progress with others keeps "reality in full view." That's what I learned sharing my daily questions with the Life-Plan Review group of high achievers that Marshall recruited from his network: we made each other feel we could be better. When you surround yourself with people who are as or more successful than you or more self-critical and let them see what you have written down, it tends to drive you to raise your bar.

CLASSIC CONNECTIONS

While most classic books on achievement take a goal-oriented approach, this lesson's process-oriented approach echoes their focus on taking responsibility for the changes you want to make, notably seen as the first habit of Stephen Covey's *The 7 Habits of Highly Effective People*: be proactive or "response-able" in choosing your behavior. The processes in this lesson and indeed the entire Fixed-Flexible-Freestyle framework more closely align with the work of a modern classic: Carol Dweck's *Mindset: The New Psychology of Success*. A growth mindset is "based on the belief that your basic qualities are the things you can cultivate through your efforts, your strategies, and help from others" and that "your true potential is unknown." People with a fixed mindset believe that our qualities are permanent and working to improve through learning is futile.

Dweck's "fixed" is very different from the "fixed" lessons in the framework, which are timeless but require a growth mindset: You must believe that all learning and work—personally and professionally—is meaningful, rewarding, and worthwhile, even when you fail. There's no better evidence of this than the way this lesson helps you build a growth mindset Dweck describes by doing the following:

- Acknowledging and embracing your imperfections.
- Replacing the word "failing" with the word "learning."
- Valuing the process over the end results.
- Learning from other people's mistakes.
- Having a sense of purpose and keeping the big picture in mind.

FROM MARSHALL
THE DAILY QUESTIONS PROCESS

The LPR group Asheesh participated in started with this process: *Every day, challenge yourself to answer a series of questions related to specific behaviors that you know are important but are often easy to neglect. Write each question out in an Excel spreadsheet and answer them on a scale of one, for "not at all," to ten, for "the best I possibly could."*

My list is thirty-two questions long, but there is nothing magical about the number thirty-two. Use any number that works for you, no matter how big or small. The most important part is that your questions are "active."

I learned about active questions from my daughter, Dr. Kelly Goldsmith, E. Bronson Ingram chair and professor of marketing at Vanderbilt University's Owen Graduate School of Management. Kelly explained to me that the standard practice in almost all organizational surveys relies on what she calls "passive" questions—questions that describe a static condition like, "Do you have clear goals?" That question is passive because it often causes people to think of what is being done to them rather than what they are doing for themselves. "Active" questions are the alternative to passive questions. There is a huge difference between "Do you have clear goals?" and "Did you do your best to set clear goals for yourself?" The former is trying to determine your state of mind; the latter challenges you to describe or defend a course of action.

Thanks to Kelly I start with six "active questions" that I believe, based on my research with thousands of people, lead to higher satisfaction with life. Each question begins the same way, with "Did I do my best to . . ." Did I do my best to set clear goals? Make progress toward goal achievement? Be happy? Find meaning? Build positive relationships? Be fully engaged?

By beginning my questions with "Did I do my best to . . ." it is almost impossible to blame someone else for my efforts. No one can be responsible but me! For example, if I am not/ was not happy today, someone screwed up—and that someone would be me. After all, despite all my blessings in life—a wonderful wife and kids, good health, loving my job, not having a boss—I can still sometimes get caught up in day-to-day stress, forget how lucky I am, and act like an idiot. It helps to get a daily reminder of the importance of happiness and gratitude.

My remaining questions are about health, exercise, saying or doing something nice for my family, and following up with my teaching and coaching clients. The questions have evolved over time, but many remain the same, which is why they are in this fixed part of the framework: the questions you ask can be as flexible as you want, but the process is fixed and works well for any stage of life. It forces us to confront how we live our values every day. We either believe that something matters, or we don't. If we believe it, we can put a question about it on the list and do it! If we don't, we can face reality and stop asking ourselves about it.

The results speak for themselves: according to our research, of the people who do the daily questions process every day, 34 percent get better at everything they asked about, 67 percent got better at four things, 91 percent got better at something, and almost no one got worse.

So try it out.

Write down the questions that you should ask yourself every day. I find that it does a wonderful job of keeping what is most important to you in your head. Even the process of writing questions will help you better understand your own values and how you can live them daily. Feel free to use my questions or others you hear, but please remember my questions reflect my values and might not work for you.

If you're stuck, imagine a person was going to call you every day and listen to you answer questions about your life. What questions would you want to ask yourself every day? Now, if you really have courage, ask someone to listen to your answers every day just as Asheesh and those other high achievers did to push themselves to be better in the things that mattered to them.

4.

GO META

Learning continues even when school stops, and that goes beyond developing skills to be better at our jobs or understanding new technologies. It's a skill that's about self-improvement—understanding and bettering ourselves. *Who am I? What matters most to me? Where do I want to go? What do I want?* Answers to those questions require reflecting on what you have done and learned before. The more you comprehend and take responsibility for and control of this learning, the more perspective and control you will have about the decisions you make and actions you take. This awareness of how you learn, or "learning about learning," is called meta-learning.

Meta-learning or "going meta" means intentionally stepping out of your role as a learner to ask the following: What am I learning? What am I seeing or noticing? What connections can I make to other things? The wisdom that comes from this physical, emotional, mental, and spiritual perspective on yourself gives you a deeper appreciation throughout your career and life for what you have gone through. It adds another dimension to everything from behavior change to decision-making for yourself and others as a leader.

While your experiences and what you want and need will evolve, the reflective process of going meta remains constant. As you change, so will your answers, and as you use those answers to understand yourself, you will also learn to present and revise your story (see lesson seven), especially in key moments that trigger and inspire reflection.

META-LEARNING OR "GOING META" MEANS INTENTIONALLY STEPPING OUT OF YOUR ROLE AS A LEARNER TO ASK THE FOLLOWING: WHAT AM I LEARNING? WHAT AM I SEEING OR NOTICING? WHAT CONNECTIONS CAN I MAKE TO OTHER THINGS?

For example, two crazy, challenging years after CircleLending had been acquired by Virgin Money, I stepped down as CEO. I had been thinking, *What's next?* careerwise months after the Virgin acquisition. But it takes time to plan the next phase of your life, and I didn't have much time for reflection or anything else, really, when I was working for Richard Branson. When I left in 2009, my friends and family were telling me that I should take a little time to breathe and reflect before jumping into something new. My friends in the Young Presidents' Organization told me that I should take a year to travel and introduced me to Dick Simon, who used travel with his family to step back, reflect on what he had learned, and plan his next phase. It seemed the perfect opportunity to do something special. I had some financial security, my wife Helen's work situation had some flexibility, and our twins wouldn't be starting kindergarten until the following fall. So we started thinking about how to take advantage of the opportunity and ended up going to India for six months.

While not everyone has the chance to take an overseas trip or sabbatical between jobs, the ability to step back and reflect on what I had learned and what I wanted to do next was critical. Six years later, I found myself in a similar situation: after leading Covestor, I stepped down as CEO when the investment management company was sold to Interactive Brokers. Once again, I found myself in the process of reinvention and asking myself, *What's next?*

In 2015, as we started to negotiate the sale of Covestor, I attended the funeral of Arthur E. Chase. Arthur was eighty-five and had lived a full life as a businessman and politician. He founded the Chase Paper Company and then Checkerboard Ltd. (one of the largest stationery companies in the United States and one of the first to use recycled paper). He served in the Worcester, Massachusetts, city government and was subsequently elected state senator. And in 1991, while serving in the senate, he designed and sponsored the creation of the Massachusetts Academy of Math and Sciences at Worcester Polytechnic Institute—a residential magnet school for advanced students in math and science, which endures as one of the best public high schools in Massachusetts.

Funerals—like graduations, landmark birthdays, weddings—are singular moments that often compel us to (re)evaluate and reflect on our lives, especially when we are in moments of transition. Arthur's dedication to young people in the founding of the school surely influenced my thinking, hearing speeches from former students and tributes from friends and family about how passionate he was about education. When the Junior Achievement Worldwide opportunity presented itself a few months later, I connected the dots between what I had heard at Arthur Chase's funeral and what I felt would be the right next step for me. Rather than raising funds to build another start-up or tech company, I would raise funds for JA—using my skills to help young people around the world. JA felt like the right step.

In reflection, I was better prepared for these and all my calculated and uncalculated career jumps because I had regularly gone meta and reflected on what I wanted, where I was going, and who I wanted to be. By writing down my experiences, thoughts, and what I wanted to do in my journals since I was young, I had made achievement process-oriented for me and created a space to reflect on myself—what I had learned, what I had seen and noticed. That gave me perspective through self-reflection, which made me a better leader and, most importantly, a better person.

Certainly, COVID-19 forced many of us who weren't on the front lines to go meta—take a pause as the world shut down, ask what we wanted next, and stop what we were doing to pursue new directions or return with new understanding. But you don't need a global pandemic, a funeral, a major life event, or a career or job change to go meta—or to reflect on your experiences and memories.

Instead, you can begin this lesson in perspective through the entertainment you consume: reread your favorite books and stories, rewatch your favorite TV shows, videos, and movies, and relisten to your favorite podcasts.

Revisit these touchstones as key moments in your personal development. Do it multiple times as you grow older. It helps to select some learning objectives or self-reflection questions when you do so: *What have I learned since I last read, watched, or listened to this? What did I forget or miss the last time? What is it making me feel or motivating me to do—or not feel?*

The key to meta-learning is waiting at least a few years to understand where you were, are, and where you might go, rather than doing this every few months. I'll bet there are plenty of things you consumed three years ago that you haven't gone back to since.

I like to do this with my favorite authors in business and find new meaning in Marshall's success stories, David Schwartz's stories in *The Magic of Thinking Big*, and legendary salesman, author, and motivational speaker Zig Ziglar's successful selling stories. I love Jeffrey Archer's achievement stories, John Mortimer's Rumpole stories about character and justice, and *Yes, Minister*, a British sitcom and book series that is a satire about people, politics, and bureaucracy. I understand what I like about these stories, because I have gone back to them and reflected on what they mean to me and how I've changed between each reading. I get more out of them each time. Plus, I am entertained all over again, which makes the process fun.

Of course, not everything you go back to will be more impactful. I have gone back to some of the writing I edited for a college magazine and cringed. I have reread some Jeffrey Archer books and winced at how I could have liked the book and how the world has changed since I read them last. That's important too. Going meta is about learning more about the good and the bad. It helps you understand where you were and how far you've come—and opens you up to where you might go or what you need to change to get you to the next level in your achievement, by seeing opportunities in reflecting on your accumulated experience.

CLASSIC CONNECTIONS

The classic literature on achievement is filled with chapters on self-discipline and the mental mastery lessons in behavior that change requires—it is hard and uncomfortable. But few of them talk about this change in terms of empathy or appreciating the world from others' points of view. One of the few that does is Dale Carnegie's approach in *How to Win Friends and Influence People*. The third lesson in being a leader is "talk about your own mistakes before criticizing the other person." Carnegie forces leaders to turn the spotlight on their own shortcomings and mistakes and then use them to motivate others—even if you are still making the mistakes or trying to correct those shortcomings. That has a powerful effect on others and creates a shared experience (i.e., empathy!). "Any fool can criticize, condemn, and complain—and most fools do," Carnegie wrote. "But it takes character and self-control to be understanding and forgiving." Understanding and forgiveness are also extremely hard.

Carnegie's words have a very modern echo in Dr. Brené Brown's *The Power of Vulnerability: Teachings on Authenticity, Connection, and Courage*. Going meta requires vulnerability, which Brown defines as "the feeling we get during times of uncertainty, risk, or emotional exposure. This includes times when we're showing our feelings and we're not sure what people will think and times when we really care about something and people will know that we're sad or disappointed when it doesn't work out." Being this vulnerable requires one to be brave: "Being brave is feeling scared or awkward, accepting those feelings, and moving forward anyway."

FROM MARSHALL
THE SECRET TO BECOMING THE PERSON YOU WANT TO BE

Once you practice these fixed "self" lessons from Asheesh, you are likely going to figure out what you like and don't like about yourself and which behaviors and traits you want to change for the better. But as Asheesh laid out in the last lesson, change like this is often impossible because most of us are so optimistic (and delusional) that we try to change everything at once. We get so overwhelmed with becoming a "New Me" that when it doesn't happen as quickly or easily as we'd like—and people don't notice that we made changes—we give up. Discouraged and disheartened, we make excuses for our failure and harbor beliefs that trigger all manner of denial and resistance—and we end up changing nothing. We fail to become the person we want to be.

So, what do you do? When you see your frailties in the face of behavioral change and know what you want to change, you can use the previous lesson (write it down). If you need to decide what to change and where to put your efforts, you can go meta and use this version of a tool from my book *Triggers* that I've taken teams, organizations, friends, peers, and myself through called "The Wheel of Change."

The Wheel of Change has two axes. The more/positive-to-less/negative axis tracks the elements that either help us or hold us back. The change-to-keep axis tracks the elements that we determine to change or keep in the future. Thus, in pursuing any behavioral change, we have four options: change or keep the positive elements and change or keep the negative. Three of the options are more dynamic, glamorous, and fun, but they're all equal in importance.

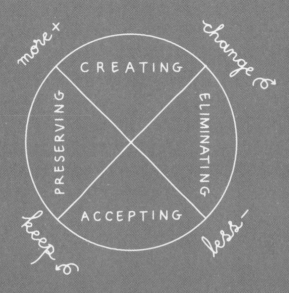

WHEEL OF CHANGE

1. **Creating** represents the positive elements that we want to create in our future. When we imagine ourselves behaving better, we think of it as an exciting process of self-invention. The challenge is to do it by choice, not as a bystander. Are we creating ourselves or wasting the opportunity and being created by external forces instead?

2. **Preserving** represents the positive elements that we want to keep in the future. It requires soul-searching to figure out what serves us well and discipline to refrain from abandoning it for something new and shiny and not necessarily better.

3. **Eliminating** represents the negative elements that we want to eliminate in the future. Eliminating is our most liberating, therapeutic action, but we take it reluctantly. Maybe we'll need it in the future. Maybe it's the secret of our success. Maybe we like it too much.

4. **Accepting** represents the negative elements that we need to accept in the future. Our ineffectuality is precisely the condition that we are most loath to accept. It triggers our finest moments of counterproductive behavior. It may feel like admitting defeat, but it is incredibly valuable when we're powerless to make a difference.

When you choose to use creating, preserving, eliminating, and accepting to challenge yourself to figure out what you can change and what you can't, what to lose and what to keep, you can surprise yourself with the bold simplicity of your answers and can thus take significant, real steps toward becoming the person you really want to be.

5.

CONNECT BEYOND THE SCREEN

had just started working on this book and working on the ideas that would become this lesson when I sat down to lunch with one of my twin sons, Alexander.

"In terms of the jobs and internships I've had," Alexander said, "the ones that were online-only I didn't feel connected to at all. With the one job I had in person, I did feel connected. It wasn't even that it was a better job or opportunity. I just got to be with the people all day. It was more of an experience."

But while Alexander agreed with what I intended to say about the relationships that scaffold our success, he dismissed my suggested lesson titles about relationship management.

"I would just say, 'Connect beyond the screen,'" he said.

When I was my sons' age, I had two ways of connecting when I wasn't with someone: mail and phone calls. I'm not sure my kids know how to mail a letter, and a phone call is like kryptonite to them. But they can see the world and each other through their screens and have myriad ways to connect without picking up a pen or dialing a number—text, Snapchat, WeChat, WhatsApp, Instagram, TikTok, FaceTime, Zoom, Discord, Slack . . . When the global pandemic shut the world down, those screens became the main way most of us could connect. In the years that followed, some things stayed and remain online, some are in person, some are hybrid. Alexander prefers the latter: "You can't start a connection or connect super well over a Zoom call," he said.

And he is not alone. Connecting through the screen may seem like social behavior, but study after study shows excessive use of social media leads to feelings of social isolation, not connection. According to many studies, these feelings of loneliness were on the rise for many young people long before most of us had heard of the coronavirus. For example, the BBC's Loneliness Project found the rates of loneliness among fifty thousand people ages sixteen to twenty-four—those who grew up with social media—were the same as they were among senior citizens. But the pandemic did exacerbate this loneliness among young people with virtual school and jobs, leaving many frequently or always feeling lonely.

But loneliness is not inevitable, the challenges of connection are not new, and social media can be good and useful in moderation in helping us make those connections. What I want to emphasize here is that saying relationships matter and making them work beyond the screen requires, well, *work*.

My wife, Helen, and I met during our first year of college and dated all four years of college. After graduation, she accepted a job at CARE, the international humanitarian organization, and then headed to India for a year of development work. I ended up in Amsterdam with Monitor and then studied in England. And that was just the beginning of years of international distance between us. But we made seeing each other in person a priority. We created the "two-month rule," in which we arranged to meet every two months somewhere—no matter where or how busy we were. We built shared memories in India, France, Belgium, Morocco, Spain, and Scotland. We had no money and were barely able to afford meals, let alone flights. But we used our time together to question what we would do next. And we did it openly and honestly.

Openness and honesty are what all great relationships require to propel them and you forward. That's what brought me so close with the members of my Young Presidents' Organization (YPO) group. With the sole exception of the months following the shutdown for COVID-19, our group meets in person monthly. They have given me so much more than I could ever give back. After every career transition, the group helped me stay centered and supported me through my identity shift to the nonprofit sector. But our work together has gone way beyond our professional challenges. We open up about our health issues, aging parents, and family tragedies—all in a confidential setting. When we were forced to move online during the pandemic, we were grateful for Zoom, Microsoft Teams, and other platforms that made it possible to connect through the screen. It was hard to go as deep as we had before, but because we had that in-person foundation, we sustained our connection until we could meet in person again. That is true of most relationships: connections that start beyond the screen— at school, work, jobs, or other in-person activities—can be sustained through the screen as long as you work to keep connecting in person.

That's why this lesson is the last fixed lesson in self and not career. You might take steps later in your achievement and leadership journey, like joining a YPO forum or MasterMind group, but they will fail without understanding what it feels like to have and the importance of open, honest, and deep in-person relationships. Personal connections can teach us skills for professional connections and vice versa (and in the age of work-life integration, there is less of a distinction between them), and both start with you, not the work you do.

In the age of hybrid offices and remote work, establishing these relationships is something you need to work on harder than previous generations had to—but they remain as important as ever. I couldn't raise investment funding for CircleLending without in-person meetings and calls and couldn't raise philanthropic funding for JA without traveling the world. And I couldn't do either unless I had worked on every area in my life at connecting beyond the screen and *kept* working at it.

In-person relationships made in the schools we attend, places we work, fields we play on, events we go to, parties we attend, meals we share, clubs we join, and out in the world are the ones we need to sustain us throughout our achievement journeys. The feeling you get from these connections beyond the screen influences you and gives you influence. Look for anything that gives you those opportunities to see those faces in person.

CLASSIC CONNECTIONS

Robert Waldinger's second book came out in 2023, but its origins are long and deep. Waldinger, a clinical professor of psychiatry at Harvard Medical School, is the author (with Marc Schulz, PhD) of *The Good Life: Lessons from the World's Longest Scientific Study of Happiness*. The study is the Harvard Study of Adult Development, which started in 1938. Waldinger directs the study, and in 2015 he delivered one of the most watched TED talks ever on it (forty-four million views and counting). The title was a question we all ask a version of at some point in our lives: "What makes a good life?" The answer according to the study's data? Relationships. "Good relationships keep us happier and healthier," says Waldinger. "Period."

Simply put, loneliness kills. Our social connections can predict our mental and physical health throughout our lives. The stronger our relationships are, the more socially connected you are, the happier, longer, and healthier your life

IN-PERSON
RELATIONSHIPS MADE
IN THE SCHOOLS WE
ATTEND, PLACES WE
WORK, FIELDS WE PLAY
ON, EVENTS WE GO TO,
PARTIES WE ATTEND,
MEALS WE SHARE,
CLUBS WE JOIN, AND
OUT IN THE WORLD
ARE THE ONES WE
NEED TO SUSTAIN US
THROUGHOUT OUR
ACHIEVEMENT JOURNEYS.

is. Waldinger notes that young people, since the start of the study through to today, have said they wanted to be rich. In the study, those who leaned into relationships with family, friends, and community achieved that goal more than others. Saying relationships matter isn't just a platitude—it's science. The best ones, Waldinger notes, are messy, complicated, and hard work. But the "payoff" in your achievement journey—the success Marshall talks about—is big in every way.

FROM MARSHALL
FOUR THINGS SUCCESSFUL PEOPLE DO TO HAVE GREAT RELATIONSHIPS

Some relationships are sources of power and provide guidance and help; others need to be avoided, ended, or minimized because they represent unwanted detours, excess weight, or distraction. Some relationships are permanent, such as our families, or become that way, such as life partners, close friends, mentors, and professional colleagues; others are transient—they come and go as circumstances dictate. But the strongest endure, not necessarily because of frequency of contact but because of the nature of the relationship. In my book with Alan Weiss, *Lifestorming: Creating Meaning and Achievement in Your Career and Life*, we noted how relationships fuel our journeys—in achieving more in all we do. Some of those relationships are virtual. Alan and I noted this years before COVID-19 forced so many of our relationships online. The nature of those relationships remade and maintained on Zoom might be different from the connections we talked about then—called "followers" or "friends" or, literally, "connections." Many permanent and transient relationships are enhanced by social media and then Zoom. However, there is a difference between using social media as a communications tool for face-to-face relationships *and using it as a source for developing new relationships.*

With these distinctions in mind, let's now focus on sustaining your journey through relationships, whether permanent or temporary or virtual, with these four goals in mind:

1. *Give to get.* Relationships are two-way streets. For them to be fulfilling, we must invest in them; we can't simply be takers. That is, don't hog the road! What we offer needn't be tangible (although it can be); it can be listening, support, feedback, or empathy.

2. *Build them on trust.* Trust is the belief that others have your best interests in mind and that you have their best interests in mind. Honest feedback and advice, even when painful, are part of caring for the other person.

3. *Don't make them a zero-sum game.* I am not diminished by someone else's victories. For me to win, you don't have to lose. For you to win, I don't have to lose. We rejoice in success and bemoan loss for either party.

4. *Make them appropriate.* At some point in your achievement journey, your promotion to leadership will turn peers into subordinates and former superiors into peers. You can reach a level of familiarity and ease in personal

relationships that may not be right for a professional relationship. Similarly, social relationships have their own unspoken rules. You probably wouldn't act the same way with your college friends as you would with your prospective mother-in-law.

Above all, as you pursue these goals, remember what Asheesh said and the words of Robert Waldinger: what makes most successful people so successful is that they have great relationships. Practice living these four goals, and you will have them too!

6. PRESENT YOUR STORY

7. KEEP YOUR PERSONAL BURN
    RATE LOW

8. LOOK BEYOND YOUR
    PARENTS FOR ADVICE

9. BE A GOOD MENTEE

10. FIND PEOPLE WHO PUSH YOU.

CAREER

6.

PRESENT
YOUR STORY

met Michael Wenban the summer of my junior year of college when I worked in the Toronto office of Monitor Group, a multinational consulting firm that is part of Monitor Deloitte today. Michael was a senior partner, and we stayed in touch after I returned to school for my senior year. When I found out he was coming to the University of Pennsylvania for a recruiting trip in the fall, I arranged for us to meet for dinner at Bookbinder's, a legendary seafood restaurant in Philadelphia's Center City. But I didn't choose Bookbinder's just because of the food. I chose it for its history and its potential to create a lasting memory. US presidents dating back to Teddy Roosevelt dined there alongside local politicians, gangsters, athletes, movie stars, and other performers. Pictures of Babe Ruth, Tennessee Williams, Elizabeth Taylor, Frank Sinatra, and hundreds of other local and national celebrities filled the restaurant's walls along with . . . mine. The day before the dinner meeting, I had arranged to have my picture replace another on the wall behind me at our table before our dinner! (I was editor of a school magazine in college, so I used this pretext with the restaurant manager so he would hang a photo of me with others on the leadership team.)

As Michael and I started catching up during our first course, I gestured at the walls. "You know, a place like Bookbinder's recognizes not just great achievement, but also great potential." That's when I motioned toward the wall behind me. A smile of recognition crossed Michael's face.

"You're kidding," he said as he rolled his eyes. "You are good."

I thanked Michael for all he had done for me. Not only had he hired me for the summer and served as a mentor, but he had offered to write a letter of recommendation for a scholarship to study at Oxford (Michael is British). Because of him, I felt I had the credibility to earn a spot on the wall someday. That said, I told Michael I wasn't sure I wanted to go to graduate school right away. I might want to return to Monitor after graduation instead and plan on graduate studies after a few years. I sought his advice.

As I presented my story, Michael knew what I was doing: I was sharing my ambitions candidly (asking for his help) and visually (with the photo on the wall). And that's what he wanted to hire: someone who would and could do that. That's what the people who mentor you will look for in your stories as well: how you present a story about what you've done or are doing, explain how that story connects to your hopes and ambitions, and invite them to be part of the journey.

But that evening I was doing something more than just presenting my story to Michael. I was connecting my value to him through my story, and that opened him up to what I had to say.

An essential part of achieving is becoming more persuasive, but you're not going to persuade people if you don't connect with them. And you're not going to connect with them on a deeper level and build relationships if they don't think you have empathy. Empathy means showing that you understand and even share the feelings of others. That you have compassion for how they think and feel. That you have tried to imagine yourself in their shoes. Becoming a more empathetic person is the same thing as becoming a more persuasive salesperson.

Thus, to be a great, persuasive salesperson, your superpower needs to be empathy, and presenting your story is a never-ending masterclass in empathy. That's why I focus on presenting my stories openly and

AN ESSENTIAL PART OF ACHIEVING IS BECOMING MORE PERSUASIVE, BUT YOU'RE NOT GOING TO PERSUADE PEOPLE IF YOU DON'T CONNECT WITH THEM. AND YOU'RE NOT GOING TO CONNECT WITH THEM ON A DEEPER LEVEL AND BUILD RELATIONSHIPS IF THEY DON'T THINK YOU HAVE EMPATHY.

authentically. Stories open me up to you and you up to me and hopefully also to what I am persuading you to do—a few points of information that make you want to know more.

Note, I am not saying *tell* your story but *present* it. That is a skill that requires intent, focus, and direction. It requires effort—thought, planning, and research to know your audience so it lands where you want it to land and opens them up to sharing their stories. For example, after I decided to apply to Oxford, I met with a professor who wrote one of the seminal books in the area of economics I wanted to study and would decide if I got to work with him as a graduate student, much like a job interview. I prepared for that meeting by reading not only what that professor had written but whose research he cited and referenced in his articles. I followed the breadcrumbs back to articles that others had written that cited him too. When he heard me reference the same things he'd read and the other researchers who had referenced him, his whole demeanor changed to *this American college kid really knows his stuff*.

With Michael, our story together played out in rather unexpected and powerful ways. I knew he went to Cambridge, and when I chose to go to Oxford for my graduate degree rather than accept a position at Monitor, our whole relationship changed. It was now no longer about *please hire me* but about *tell me about your experience*. He regaled me with stories from his time in England and advised me about places to go, people to meet, and experiences to have. And of course, he would defer my position at Monitor until after I finished.

I ended up working for Monitor in Amsterdam the summer before I moved to England, but by the following summer, I decided to stay in Oxford to pursue a PhD and went to work not at Monitor but at the World Bank, which was the place to pursue my interest in development economics. But as luck would have it, Monitor was building a practice area to collaborate with the World Bank and other international institutions. That allowed me to keep Michael and Monitor as part of my story: I wasn't turning down their offer; I was merely delaying it *again* and becoming more experienced by virtue of working at the World Bank. Our stories eventually came together when I returned to Monitor a few years later and worked at their headquarters in Cambridge, Massachusetts. It was there that I created CircleLending.

My point is that even though the skill of presenting your story is a fixed lesson, your story is not. So don't get stuck in it. Keep updating it, retelling it, pivoting it for how your interests change as you get older. Remember this: presenting your stories isn't just about reliving your experience but about demonstrating your value.

When I interviewed for the CEO role at Junior Achievement Worldwide, I learned that the chair of the CEO search committee had written several books about leadership. So, I read them. When I presented my story during the interview, I cited one of those books because it connected the dots between something I did and what he said. He smiled and knew what I was doing, and so did everyone else. I was so transparent about how I had researched my audience and was connecting my story with theirs that I called attention to the strategy in answering a question from another interviewer. It allowed the CEO search committee to understand me better, appreciating the transparency and skill of connecting with people. I made sure they knew that was the point, and a strength as opposed to a manipulative tool.

That's the foundation for bringing others along with you, whether you are selling yourself, an idea, a product or service, your team, or your organization: make them see it as their idea, too, and own it as part of what they want to achieve. When someone is as invested in a project as you are, they have ownership, even if it wasn't their idea to begin with. By seeing themselves in your story, they know your way can meet the organization's goals—and your own goals too. By making the ideation process collaborative, you gain immediate buy-in. That leads to greater connection and collaboration up and down and across an organization.

So, how to get started?

Find an anecdote that brings out your best and worst characteristics in a way that is also interesting and memorable. These stories can highlight your strengths that demonstrate your skills in moments of triumph or shine light on your weaknesses, showing people you are vulnerable enough to admit failure and learn from it. After all, if you are interviewing for something that attracts other high achievers, then everyone has a resume and references. Everyone has skills and experience. Everyone is already a person of interest. What makes you, you?

But buyer beware: stories can be powerful tools in the other direction as well. They can build us up or hold us back. They can be tools for blame and excuses or encouragement and motivation. They can unite us or drive us apart. Not being familiar with or opening ourselves up to each other's stories, fully and genuinely, leads to what some people have called an "empathy deficit" in our society. This is especially prevalent in politics but in business as well, where disconnects thrive when we don't hear the stories of people we disagree with—when we've assumed the other side is always the enemy or the source of our problems, holding us back from achieving more.

Look around you: Whose stories are you listening to the most? Do they open you up to possibility and opportunity and new relationships and drive your self-efficacy, or do they shut you down?

Listening to the stories from people who are not like you is also one of the best ways to confront your biases and privilege. You can't and shouldn't hide your privilege. I am fully aware that I have had more opportunities than many people in this world by virtue of my parents' values and my educational pathway—but that makes me work even harder to seek out and listen to the stories from others about what life is like for them and ask how they feel. Changing the community of people you surround yourself with can have a dramatic effect on your capacity for empathy and put you in the right or better environment to succeed.

CLASSIC CONNECTIONS

Many classic books on achievement present their personal stories before laying out their processes. The authors understand that you won't care as much about what they have to say unless you have some empathy for them.

In *The Science of Personal Achievement*, Napoleon Hill sets up his "Seven Factors of Definite Purpose" with a story about his growing up in Kentucky, about his mother dying when he was ten and his father remarrying. He draws us in by showing how he leaned on his reputation as a bad kid to overtly hate his stepmom, but she reframed his hate by saying Hill wasn't the meanest boy but the smartest, who just didn't know what to do with his smartness. This created a sense of admiration for her and his father and their resourcefulness to build a life for their family.

In *Maximum Achievement*, Brian Tracy shows us how he learned to ask the question "Why are some people more successful than others?" after working in sawmills, as an itinerant farm laborer, and then a salesman working on commission. He asked questions of the successful people around him and became a voracious reader to learn everything he could about how people in the jobs he was doing got results and built a multimillion-dollar global sales organization.

In *The 7 Habits of Highly Effective People*, before Stephen R. Covey gets to detailing any of those habits, he shares short stories from people struggling with personal issues. He then demonstrates empathy for them by sharing a story about when his son was struggling in school. Covey writes, "[My wife and I] began to realize that if we wanted to change the situation, we first had to change ourselves. And to change ourselves effectively, we first had to change our perceptions."

No better way to help someone else understand that than to present your story first.

FROM MARSHALL
WHAT'S YOUR BIG REVEAL?

The first thing I do when I start new relationships is share my story, and then I want to hear theirs—that's what bonded me to Asheesh. It wasn't his resume. Lots of people have great resumes. It was his story and how he told it. Yet too many people struggle to present their stories. They even hold back on sharing their most interesting and special skills.

You see this all the time in movies, especially comedies and thrillers. It's the "Big Reveal" when we discover tangentially that a heretofore unimpressive character has abilities we never suspected. I suspect a lot of you feel that way about yourselves: You yearn for your specialness to be known to all but struggle to present it, partly because you struggle to identify your special skills and personality traits. But talking about them pragmatically is an essential part of presenting your story.

Here is an exercise that can help you get started.

Ask yourself: *What about you, when finally out in the open, would surprise people and leave them thinking, "Who knew?"* Maybe it's something you collect, volunteer work you do, or writing you had published. Maybe you know how to write code, won a prize in your age group at some tournament, can dance, or do stand-up comedy. My point is that once revealed, your quality of "Who Knew?" is an eye-opening experience for other people who thought they knew you, leaving them to infer that you have hidden depths of passion, commitment, and resourcefulness, that you're more capable than they thought. It elevates your credibility in their eyes. It's the ideal net result: you are earning credibility.

Now, extend this exercise to the workplace by asking: *What is the Big Reveal—your Who Knew? quality—that will raise your credibility among your peers and bosses? If everyone knew, what positive difference would it make in your life? Why are you hiding it?*

7.

KEEP YOUR PERSONAL BURN RATE LOW

W hen I was a sophomore at the Wharton School of the University of Pennsylvania, I decided to get fully engaged in one student club: the college magazine, *The Wharton Account*. The idea of running a physical magazine feels so outdated now that the internet, smartphones, generative AI, and other technology have consumed print media, but in the early 1990s, it was thrilling to work at a magazine, even more so when I was selected as editor-in-chief.

At that time, Wharton was the only undergraduate business school in the Ivy League, and I recognized this created an opportunity for the magazine. All the Ivies had students studying history, politics, and economics, who wanted to learn about business and signal to employers that they were interested in finance and management consulting. So I proposed we expand our magazine's reach by creating clubs at each of the Ivy League campuses and including articles from them in every issue. We contacted our friends on the other campuses, recruited them and the people they recommended as editors, and repositioned *The Wharton Account* with a new tagline: the "undergraduate business magazine of the Ivy League." It was ambitious and audacious. The rebranding expanded our reach and drew major corporate advertisers, expanding our ad revenue budget by 300 percent and allowing us to print the cover in color—a first in the magazine's history. In the winter 1993 issue, we published our most popular cover story, "The Life of an Analyst."

The lure of being a financial analyst after graduation was strong—
for many there was no better job to challenge you and put you on a
fast track to wealth—but few liberal arts majors knew what being an
analyst meant and what it took to be a successful one. In our story we
interviewed grads from Brown, Cornell, Dartmouth, Harvard, and Penn
who worked as analysts on Wall Street and at major companies, and we
detailed how they spent their days at work. Next to their pictures, we
put sidebars with typical biographical information (grad year, major,
where and in what city they worked, etc.). But what captured our
readers' attention was what came next: each analyst's personal burn
rate. We listed their annual and monthly salary and bonus followed
by how much they were paying in taxes, rent, college or car loans,
transportation (tolls, taxis, public transportation, etc.), food, clothing,
phone, and entertainment. We then listed each analyst's monthly
savings, which came to $1,255 . . . *combined*. An average of $251. The
high was $585 per month. The low $45—just about breaking even in
one of the most lucrative and sought-after positions for Ivy grads.

Few of the undergraduates we spoke to had any clue about this
information. Even the people I went to Wharton with were incredu-
lous. They knew business and economics. But this was an eye-opening
course in personal finance, revealing one of the biggest reasons people
get stuck in jobs and in life: like most of those analysts, they take on
expenses—housing, education, material goods, entertainment—that
they think they should have but may not be able to afford.

For example, in the early days of leading Covestor, a social networking and investing marketplace, I interviewed an excellent can-
didate for a senior executive position who was eager to work with
us. When we got to negotiating the terms of the offer, he sheepishly
explained he needed a higher salary because he had built his personal
burn rate to the point that he could not accept any job for less than

$350,000! While his heart was committed to working in a fast-paced start-up, his cost structure required him to pursue corporate roles for large enterprises. His country club membership in Connecticut, jumbo mortgage, and private school tuition for his kids made it untenable to work for less. It was too risky for us as a start-up to hire executives with such a high and inflexible personal burn rate. We did not make him an offer.

There is so little personal financial education in our schools, and too many families fail to talk about money and finances. Ask yourself: Do you know what your family's burn rate is or was when you were growing up? What kind of expenses and debt did they have? How much did they save? The lack of transparency and knowledge around that limits our understanding as we grow up, shrouds subjects like burn rate in mystery, and potentially takes away choices that could have been considered, if not solved with more knowledge.

A Fixed-Flexible-Freestyle approach to achievement requires an entrepreneurial mindset—for you to have the ability to pivot, adjust, and adapt to take advantage of and pursue those opportunities and to recover when things do not go as intended. You might change jobs twenty times in your career, not always by choice. Your flexibility in those situations, bad and good, depends on your burn rate. Keeping it low increases your freedom and opens you up to things like taking time off between jobs and pivoting to entrepreneurship and experiences that are better than moving from job to

YOU MIGHT CHANGE
JOBS TWENTY TIMES
IN YOUR CAREER, NOT
ALWAYS BY CHOICE.
YOUR FLEXIBILITY IN
THOSE SITUATIONS, BAD
AND GOOD, DEPENDS
ON YOUR BURN RATE.

job. Optionality may be where it's at for you. A low burn rate allows you to take a job that isn't necessarily the highest paying one but one that builds your passion, gains you required experience and new skills, or allows you to pursue a side hustle. But if your side hustle has major potential but cannot pay you for a year, the only way you are going to be able to continue pursuing it without a partner or investors who can fund the expenses is if your burn rate is low and your savings allow you to fund it.

Too many people ignore, dismiss, or refuse to understand and confront their burn rate and its implications for their professional goals and aspirations. Without keeping it low, it is going to be much harder to execute the flexible and freestyle lessons to come.

Use what you learned in lesson four and write down everything about your personal finances, ask questions about what you see, and find things to stop, start, and continue spending money on. Talk to your parents, family, and friends about their burn rate. Heed the next lesson and look beyond your parents for advice. Ask them what they think they did right and wrong—what they regret and would do over, what they wish they knew when they were your age. Read and listen to some of the countless personal finance experts out there. Use this knowledge to think about not only what you can give up but what you could do and where you could go to achieve more and burn less.

CLASSIC CONNECTIONS

"Successful people must know themselves, not as they think they are but as their habits have made them. Therefore, you are requested to take inventory of yourself so that you may discover where and how you are using your time." So wrote Napoleon Hill more than a half century ago in "Budgeting Time and Money"—his twelfth principle in *The Science of Personal Achievement*. Hill wanted readers to stop drifting through life, have a major purpose, and plan for its attainment. He understood that without a budget of time and money (i.e., a low burn rate), that would be impossible. In fact, Hill combines points of both Marshall's story and mine when it comes to your burn rate: keeping time *and* money burning low—slowly, carefully, and consciously—is an essential step to becoming what Hill calls a "non-drifter." His suggestions for analyzing and budgeting income and expenses are dated, but he laid out a plan for attacking it that still applies today. As he notes, much like this lesson about achievement, "The material may not make dramatic reading, but it does hold the secret of your destiny for the rest of your life."

FROM MARSHALL
PAYING THE PRICE FOR
AN EARNED LIFE

Some years ago, I was one of the speakers at a Women in Business conference. The speaker before me was a pioneering woman in the tech industry, a founder and CEO of her own company and something of a celebrity. She said she didn't conduct mentoring sessions too often because running a company was a demanding job and she'd be spending all her time mentoring women if she accepted every invitation that came her way. Instead, she stuck to the three things in life that mattered to her: spending time with her family, taking care of her health and fitness, and trying to be great at her job. She didn't cook, do housework, or run errands.

Having grabbed the full attention of every woman in the room, she doubled down on her message: "If you don't like cooking, don't cook. If you don't like gardening, don't garden. If you don't like cleaning up, hire someone to clean up. Do only what is core to you. Everything else, get rid of it."

A woman in the audience raised her hand, declaring, "That's easy for you to say. You're rich."

The CEO wasn't buying that excuse: "I happen to know that the lowest salary in this room is a quarter of a million dollars. None of you would be invited here if you weren't doing well. Are you telling me that you can't afford to hire someone to do the stuff you don't want to do?"

This CEO was delivering a hard truth that's tough to accept: to pursue any kind of fulfilling life, especially an earned life, you must pay a price. She wasn't talking about money. She was talking about making the maximum effort on the important things, accepting the necessary sacrifices, being aware of the risks and the specter of failure, but being able to block them out. Some of us are willing to pay that price. Others are not for reasons that are compelling but also, when all is said and done, regrettable.

What we focus on or give up today does not yield a reward we can enjoy today. The benefit from our self-control is far down the road, given to a future version of us whom we do not know. It's why we'd rather spend our spare cash on ourselves now than save it and let the wonders of compound interest turn it into a useful sum thirty years later.

8.

LOOK BEYOND YOUR PARENTS FOR ADVICE

After I joined Junior Achievement (JA) Worldwide as the CEO, I had the honor of being invited to judge a business-plan competition for students from the Middle East/North African (MENA) region. Operating under the brand INJAZ (which translates to "achievement" in Arabic), JA Worldwide is one of the few global NGOs that works with schools and universities in Saudi Arabia, and a team of girls from the country was competing in the MENA regional competition. The chief financial officer of their student company (JA companies are real student-led enterprises, not hypothetical or simulations) caught my attention as she answered our questions about the company's margins, growth plan, and how it succeeded in selling its products. She was great at responding to the judges' questions about financial topics, and I could see her eyes light up (visible despite her facial covering) as she spoke about their results. I sought her out after to tell her how impressed I was. "I think you have a knack for finance," I said. "I think if you wanted to, you could have a career in financial services." A week later she sent an email saying how impactful it was for her to be encouraged to have a career as a businessperson and financial professional. She said that my comment encouraged her to pursue further study in finance! I have kept in touch with her over the years since that first meeting and watched as she found a job with one of the Big Four accounting firms, gained certifications in financial modeling from the Corporate Finance Institute, and completed an MBA.

Now consider another story: After a speech at a JA conference in Calgary, a young woman from a small town in Saskatchewan, Canada approached me. She said when she heard me talk about how my brother and I went to Ivy League schools in the United States, she was stunned. "As a Canadian, can you even go to Ivy League schools?" she asked. No one had mentioned this as a possibility to her before, and it seemed so out of reach. "Absolutely it is possible," I said. "Be sure to take some time to prepare for the SAT and do some work to understand the entry requirements." Years later, she sent me a beautiful message on LinkedIn about how she went home after the JA conference, researched what she needed to do to take the SAT, took the test, and applied and got in to Harvard. "You put the idea in my mind," she wrote. "I didn't even know it was possible."

Finally, consider this moment following a talk about self-efficacy I gave at Endicott College in Massachusetts. I opened the floor to questions from the students, and a young woman stepped forward and bravely asked, *How do you overcome self-doubt?* I told her that earlier in the day, I had ninety minutes of self-doubt at work while dealing with a complex matter. But I have learned over the course of my career to recognize that self-doubt is temporary and that I'm not unique in having it. In other words, everyone has it. I explained how optimistic people realize that negative events are neither permanent nor unique to them. I cited the work of Martin Seligman, who spent several years interviewing hundreds of thousands of executives and discovered that the top 10 percent are all optimists (see lesson three). "With practice and an optimistic approach," I said, "you will be able to move past your self-doubt and even see it as an advantage."

What these three stories have in common is that they each illustrate the power of having people who are not your parents or guardians give you advice. That advice can influence your career direction, your sense of possibility, and even your mindset in profound ways— in ways that even the same words from your parents often don't or can't. That advice not only leads to self-knowledge but lays the foundation for mentorship in your achievement journey. This is a lesson in the power of identifying coaches and mentors who help you build self-efficacy—taking responsibility for building the confidence you need to achieve.

Simply put, we all need mentors or coaches beyond our parents or family. Parents can be helpful in your career, of course, but relationships with those who guide you professionally and personally are quite different. Don't get me wrong: I love my parents; I would do anything for them and am grateful for all that they do for me. But parents can be blinded by the need to protect their kids and keep them safe. They too often rely on what they think they know about their kids and push them in one direction without seeing others. Remember, it was my brother who pushed my parents and me to go to the school that changed my career trajectory by introducing me to people who challenged me in ways I never had been before. When you find your own coaches and mentors, it builds your awareness and confidence without feeling beholden to your parents or obliged to loop them in. Finding them is its own accomplishment, showing that you can be as much as you want to be.

As you aspire to achieve more and lead, you need this belief. Recall the second lesson of this book: there are no self-made people. Teachers, employers, friends, and coaches . . . the best of them want you to get better and expand your value, starting when you're a student and continuing into your first jobs as you encounter things you never have before. How do you ask for a promotion or a raise? What can you do better? How do you make your goals the same as your boss's or company's? These are not things learned in classrooms, and every organization is different. Multiple perspectives are needed. Seize every opportunity to get them.

In some small but meaningful way, that's what I represented to the people in those three stories: an opportunity to learn, grow, and maybe even build a relationship for the future.

There's that word again: relationships—they are key to achieving success *and* happiness in your career and life. Every success I have had is built on the advice, help, and support of others. Some of those relationships are new, some ongoing for years, both constantly or on and off as circumstances changed. But the best of them came through my own efforts.

And here's a secret: most people like me want to help. Working with JA Worldwide, I may have had the opportunity to meet and give advice to more young people than most. But JA has thousands of high-achieving volunteers in more than one hundred countries who give their time to JA students and young alumni and often go above and beyond in developing relationships with them. Many of them see it as their responsibility and understand the importance of giving their time and advice. They want you to get better and expand your value.

Too many times, I hear people say, "I don't want to bother them" as an excuse for not approaching someone for advice and mentorship. But you must. Don't be afraid to ask. Many people would be happy to be bothered in the right way, especially if you phrase the text message, email, or request in a concrete and thoughtful way that respects their time. Say, "If you're too busy, it can wait." That gives them an out. What's the worst thing that could happen? They don't respond, they are too busy, or they say no. That's OK too. Any response can be the start of a relationship. I know when I have to say no, I have that little feeling of guilt, so the next time or the time after I might say yes.

Again, I am not suggesting that you disregard or disrespect your family. In some families and cultures, asking for advice beyond the family or community is disrespectful and gives the impression you're ignoring your parents or elders. I am saying that success requires risk-taking. Open yourself up to people and perspectives that put you outside your comfort zone—not just those who are doing what you want to do but those who have achieved in ways you never considered. They all have stories they want to share. Listen to what they have to say. Ask them questions. And then listen *again* to the answers. Do what all three of the people in these stories did: open yourself up to their advice.

CLASSIC CONNECTIONS

The four parts of Dale Carnegie's *How to Win Friends and Influence People*—principles for handling people, making people like you, winning people over to your way of thinking, and being a leader whom people want to follow—are a timeless master class in forming lasting relationships. At their core, they are about having a positive approach when starting those relationships. Consider "Don't criticize, condemn, or complain." We would all be wise to heed that in our polarizing times, which seem to value disrespect and judgment over questions and connection. That diminishes a person in your and their eyes, violating two of Carnegie's principles at once: be charming and make people feel important.

The key to that, according to Frances Hesselbein, is to listen. Hesselbein was a former CEO of Girl Scouts of the

USA, CEO of The Frances Hesselbein Leadership Institute, and, according to Marshall, one of the greatest leaders he ever met. In her book *My Life in Leadership*, she wrote one of the best descriptions of listening and leadership Marshall says he ever read: "Listening is an art. When people are speaking, they require our undivided attention. We focus on them; we listen very carefully. We listen to the spoken words and the unspoken messages. This means looking directly at the person, eyes connected; we forget we have a watch, just focusing for that moment on that person. It's called respect, it's called appreciation—and it's called leadership."

Skills like those that Carnegie and Hesselbein taught us are the secret for reaching out to other people and spinning what Keith Ferrazzi calls a "web of relationships." In his modern classic *Never Eat Alone and Other Secrets to Success, One Relationship at a Time*, Keith calls isolation from people who could help you make more of yourself a kind of poverty that goes beyond financial resources. He writes about the people he met when he caddied at a golf course that he could never afford to be a member of: "The web of friends and associates was the most potent club the people he caddied for had in their bag." As an adult, he realizes "the very successful people I know are, as a group, not especially talented, educated, or charming. But they all have a circle of trustworthy, talented, and inspirational people they can call upon." Do the work to be a connector. Make your circle bigger!

TOO MANY TIMES, I HEAR PEOPLE SAY, "I DON'T WANT TO BOTHER THEM" AS AN EXCUSE FOR NOT APPROACHING SOMEONE FOR ADVICE AND MENTORSHIP. BUT YOU MUST. DON'T BE AFRAID TO ASK.

FROM MARSHALL
ASK FOR HELP

As Asheesh laid out in the second lesson of this book, the myth of the self-made individual is one of the more sacred fictions of modern life and deserves our skepticism. It endures because it promises us a just and happy reward that is equal to our persistence, resourcefulness, and hard work. It's not impossible to achieve success on your own, but the more salient question is this: Why would you want to when you could surely achieve a better result by enlisting help along the way? An earned life is not more "earned" or glorious or gratifying—or even more likely—just because you tried to achieve it all by yourself.

Too many of us try to go it alone. Our near-clinical reluctance to ask for help is not a genetic defect, like color blindness or tone deafness. It is an acquired defect, a behavioral failing we are conditioned to accept from an early age. Don't buy into the conditioning. The probability of your creating an earned life increases dramatically by asking for help, and you need it more than you know in your life and career. In fact, "Did I do my best to ask for help?" was on my list of daily questions only recently, when I asked myself what task or challenge in my life could be more profitably and efficiently dealt with alone rather than with solicited help from other people—and couldn't come up with an answer. You should too.

Consider all the times someone—friend, neighbor, colleague, stranger, even foe—has asked you for help. Was your first impulse to refuse them? Resent them? Judge them? Question their competence? Deride them behind their back for needing help? If you're like most good people I know, your first impulse was to help. You'd demur only if you lacked the capacity to help—and you'd probably apologize, regarding your inability as somehow your failure. So before you reject the idea of asking others to help you, consider this: If you are willing to help anyone who asks for your help without thinking ill of them, why would you worry that other people won't be as generous or forgiving when you're the one seeking help?

The Golden Rule—treating others as you wish to be treated—works both ways, never more so than when help is on the table. I think we can agree that some of the greatest feelings in life come when we help others, right? Why would you deprive others of the same feeling?

9.

BE A GOOD MENTEE

M entorship is a two-way street. Finding mentors is just the first step. Now you need to become a good mentee: opening yourself up to those mentors' advice, making them want to keep investing in you and your success, and building a connection to you. This is where many mentorships fall apart. What and how are you giving back to your mentors?

One of my first significant mentor-mentee relationships was with Howard Schwartz. I met him through Monitor, and he became the first non-family investor in CircleLending, the pioneering online person-to-person lender I founded. Our relationship might sound like an odd pairing on paper. CircleLending wanted to disrupt the way people borrowed money with peer-to-peer loans, enabling mortgages, business loans, and personal loans with lower costs and more flexibility than banks could provide. Howard was the head of financial services for Capgemini, a top consulting firm to banks, evaluating them and assessing trends in banking to make mergers and transactions successful. Howard was *the* bank guy. But he loved CircleLending, recognized that peer-to-peer financial services was just beginning, and wanted to use his knowledge and contacts to help us grow. And since I had it in my head at that time that a bank might eventually acquire us, I knew Howard could ensure what we built would be attractive to financial institutions one day.

Howard helped me create CircleLending's first advisory board. He hosted dinner parties for our staff and investors at his home in

Brookline. The invitation to this annual event became coveted within the fintech community in Boston (long before "fintech" became an everyday term). He was our go-to person for credibility with potential investors: if the goal of the first meeting with those investors was to get a second meeting, the goal of the second meeting was to get them to have a call with Howard. We rarely needed another call to close the deal.

Howard also introduced me to his former client Jim Tozer, who became an investor and my next CircleLending mentor. Jim was a founding director and investor in LendingTree, the online lending marketplace, which had a successful IPO in 2000. He turned our advisory board into a real board of directors and gave me an education I didn't know I needed. He challenged me to run CircleLending like a public company, setting quarterly goals and then resetting them if we didn't achieve them. Jim knew we wouldn't achieve them at first because we were still learning and working with a lean budget. (The running joke was that our budget for marketing was about the same as his budget for lunch). But he knew that missing and resetting those forecasts would make us better and better at forecasting.

Until I met Jim, I didn't fully appreciate what it meant to have a board. Because of my relationship with Howard, I thought boards were avuncular advisors to CEOs rather than hold-you-accountable-and-point-out-when-you-don't-hit-your-numbers-and-fail-to-deliver-on-your-promise-so-you-become-better-at-managing-expectations entities. Things got real in those board meetings, and they taught me discipline when running CircleLending, which in turn earned the respect of serious institutional investors.

At this point in the story, you can clearly see what Howard and Jim contributed to my achievement story. So what did I give, and they get, from mentoring me? How was I a good mentee to Howard and Jim? First and foremost, I opened myself up to their advice. I asked questions and sought their help for many activities ranging from recruiting new employees and investors to evaluating whether a partnership was a good fit for our company. As importantly, my gratitude for Howard and Jim never went unspoken. I was a first-time CEO in my late twenties, and I never let them forget how thankful I was for making me a better leader and CircleLending a stronger company.

But for me to truly be a good mentee, I had to understand Howard's and Jim's motivations for what they were doing for me. This is the essential question you need to ask to be a good mentee: *What do your mentors want—what are their motivations—for what they do for you?*

To answer that question, you need to listen to your mentors' stories, not just include them in yours. When I did that with Howard and Jim, I found a big part of their motivation was that they enjoyed mentoring and investing in me way beyond the checks they wrote. They took great satisfaction in assisting in my personal development and professional success, and my words of gratitude were often all they needed in return. But for Howard and Jim, there was also something more.

Howard didn't know much about the internet or digital marketing when he first invested in CircleLending, so he got an education in those things and met the leading tech industry analysts who were studying peer-to-peer lending. He met investors and other interesting people in the start-up world—the hot new kids on the fintech block so to speak—who didn't connect with his banking world. That helped him build his network in tech. He enjoyed social gatherings, so hosting that big annual gathering at his house was special for him too. Howard also got great happiness from serving as a validator and expert with tech investors who were learning about the future of banking.

Jim had served on the board of LendingTree, so his interest in my ecosystem and need for education about it was low. What he wanted from our board development was to make CircleLending appealing to a potential acquirer and to educate me on how to do this. I genuinely enjoyed spending time with and learning from Jim, and he could see that. He took pride in being the teacher, and so I made sure I was a great student he could take pride in.

What I was doing for Howard was what we call "reverse mentoring" today. Reverse mentoring happens when a younger person mentors an older person on anything from new technologies and software to how to better communicate with their generation. Today, given the speed of change, all mentoring has an element of reverse mentoring, which is exactly what you can offer a mentor in return, at any stage of your career.

But don't ignore the other things: notes of gratitude, regular updates, showing interest in what your mentors do, making time, asking the right questions . . . all this and more will ensure people don't just have your back; they want to push you forward when asked. Simply put, being a good mentee is all about relationship management.

The need for that relationship management starts the moment you make that first connection. For example, I sat next to Harsh Shah at a Junior Achievement awards event in Canada. Harsh was one of the award recipients, and he asked if he could stay in touch—and then he did. He started by thanking me for allowing us to connect. Then, he asked for advice respectfully and only where he thought I could be of real help, for example with summer jobs or introducing him to people in financial services where he started his career. He always let me know how the advice or connection panned out and how grateful he was. When Harsh didn't need anything from me, he kept me posted on what he was doing. He made me feel our connection in a genuine way. All it took was just one short email—"Just wanted you to know I got this job" or "Hey, the person you introduced me to gave me a great

THIS IS THE ESSENTIAL QUESTION YOU NEED TO ASK TO BE A GOOD MENTEE: *WHAT DO YOUR MENTORS WANT — WHAT ARE THEIR MOTIVATIONS — FOR WHAT THEY DO FOR YOU?*

piece of advice, and I'm so glad you introduced us. Thank you!"—to keep building and sustaining our relationship. And when I asked for Harsh to be a part of this book, he understood my motivation and immediately made himself available for an interview.

Could I have said no to Harsh when he asked for help? Of course. Rejection is always a possibility, and you have to be OK with that as you strive to achieve more. But remember: most people often have a little guilt when we have to say no and might say yes down the road if you keep asking. So heed Marshall's advice in the previous lesson and don't be afraid to ask—and keep asking when the next opportunity comes. No, you are not bothering us. Most people are like me: they are interested in others and want to share what they know. We just want to be bothered in the right way: be respectful of our time and give us an out if we can't respond right away. But when we do respond, that's when the clock starts on our relationship.

CLASSIC CONNECTIONS

Dale Carnegie's *How to Win Friends and Influence People* is an enduring master class for relationship management, particularly this lesson: "Become genuinely interested in other people." Carnegie understood that for someone to want to act on your behalf and contribute to your success, you need to make that person feel important—even if that person already has earned their credibility. In Carnegie's telling, even George Eastman, founder of Kodak and one of the wealthiest people in the world, was moved when someone took sincere interest in a part of his story that Eastman himself had almost forgotten.

This ability to "arouse enthusiasm" with others is a big part of what the Carnegie Foundation calls "human engineering," and according to their research, being good at this accounts for 85 percent of your financial success—far more than any technical knowledge.

Today, too many people dismiss or fail to show interest in and appreciate the wisdom in others' stories, especially when those people do not look, worship, and live like them.

This, however, is not a new idea when it comes to achievement. Marshall speaks often about the late Dr. Roosevelt Thomas Jr., who reshaped corporate America's attitudes about workplace diversity in the 1970s with his insights on the unappreciated influence of what he called "referent groups." As Marshall notes, Thomas contended that each of us feels emotionally and intellectually connected to a specific cohort of the population. We think of this concept as "tribalism" today, but in the early 1970s, the idea of referent groups to explain social upheaval and the differences among people was a breakthrough concept. His point is as important to your achievement today as it was to people's achievements then: if you know a person's referent group (who they feel connected to, want to impress, and crave respect from), then you can understand why they talk and think and behave the way they do.

Problem is that most of us also have a counter-referent group. We base our allegiance and choices on what we oppose rather than what we support, which is what these classic connections in these fixed lessons try to remedy.

That has led to what I call a "wisdom deficit." One way to escape this deficit is to apply a good mentee mindset to the classic connections offered in these fixed lessons. I am acutely aware of the lack of diversity in the lists of classic books. But I appreciate Carnegie's and others' contributions to my achievement story and what they can mean to yours. Please don't let who the authors were, when they lived, or the outdated parts of their stories serve as reasons to dismiss their timeless advice. I hope you receive these classic connections in that spirit—as an opportunity to open yourself up to their advice and add what you know to the mix.

As Marshall writes, "You don't have to agree with people in other referent groups, but if you appreciate the influence exerted by such group, you are less likely to be stupefied by their adherents' choices or dismiss them as 'idiots.'"

FROM MARSHALL
THE CREDIBILITY MATRIX

In following Asheesh's advice about being a good mentee, you are taking important steps in earning credibility. In my book *The Earned Life*, I note that credibility is not bestowed on you; you *earn* it—and you must earn it twice: first with great work and then by being recognized for that great work.

So how do you earn credibility? Peter Drucker, a visionary and influential thinker on business and management, says that in life, it doesn't matter if you're smart or you're right; what matters is that you made a positive difference in people's lives. Making that difference is one of two dimensions when it comes to earning credibility. The other is proving ourselves. From our earliest days, we seek approval from people who can influence our future: parents, teachers, coaches, bosses, customers . . . each becomes a decision maker who holds sway over us. Eventually, proving ourselves to these people becomes second nature, but that's when we start making mistakes that damage our credibility rather than enhance it.

To help you determine when proving yourself to others is a worthwhile activity and when it is a waste of time or does more harm than good, I developed a "credibility matrix" that illustrates the connections between the two dimensions.

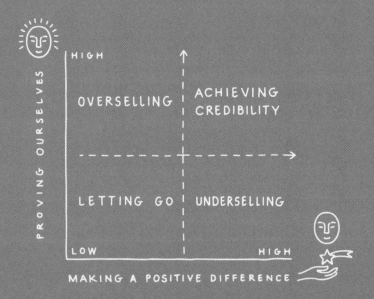

CREDIBILITY MATRIX

In engaging the matrix, you ask yourself two questions: *Am I striving to prove myself?* and *Will proving myself help me make a positive difference?* In some situations, your answers to those questions can be high or low.

You're in the most beneficial place when both are high and land you in the upper-right quadrant—"Achieving Credibility." You are proactively seeking approval that makes a positive difference in your own life or the lives of others, learning what you can, sharing what you know, and offering gratitude always.

In "Achieving Credibility" you are selling yourself with no fear and doubt that the outcome will make a positive difference, as opposed to "Underselling" (the quadrant below), in which your competency is not in doubt, but whether it will make a positive difference is.

The least beneficial quadrant is the lower right: "Letting Go." This is the "It's Not Worth It" quadrant, where straining to prove yourself will not make a positive difference, and you don't feel any need for approval. As Drucker advises, "We should focus our energy where we can actually make a positive difference in the world. Sell what we can sell and change what we can change. Let go of what we cannot sell or change."

The trickiest quadrant Is in the upper left: "Overselling Yourself." This is the "I Shouldn't Have . . ." quadrant, where earning approval would improve your credibility, but you get in your own way.

My most egregious example of falling into this quadrant was in the early 1990s. I had just returned from an International Red Cross family relief program in Africa. My experience was reported on the front page of the local newspaper, and Dr. Sam Popkin, a revered political science professor at the University of California San Diego, hosted a party in my honor. It was a perfect occasion for underselling myself, and yet that didn't stop me from pointlessly overselling my time in Africa to a small group of people at the party. I was giddy and full of myself, behaving like an overzealous "salesperson."

As the group dissipated, one older gentleman remained. Finally, I took a breath and said to him, "I'm sorry, I didn't get your name."

He put out his hand to shake mine and said, "I'm Jonas Salk. It's nice to meet you."

I didn't have to ask the man who invented the polio vaccine "And what do you do?" His name was his credibility, and his credibility was his name. He had earned that. I had not. It was one of the most embarrassing moments of my life.

10.

FIND PEOPLE
WHO PUSH YOU

On the day I graduated from college, I gave my parents a check for $8,000—money I received from the school as a refund. I presented the check to my incredulous father as we sat down for dinner after the commencement ceremony. The story of that $8,000 starts the fall of my sophomore year, when my classmate, Nobel Gulati, and I tried to take as many courses in a semester as we could. We took eight. The maximum allowed was six, which is what the dean said when she called me into her office—*two weeks before final exams*—and told me I needed to drop two courses. I explained that Nobel and I had received permission and signed consents to add the extra courses from our college advisors, had done all the work for the professors in the classes, and should be allowed to stay registered and finish our exams to receive the credit. She said she didn't care. The university couldn't survive if people broke the rules and took more courses than the permitted maximum. So I went to the two professors of the classes I needed to drop and told them what happened. They agreed it was unfair at this late date but couldn't help me. They also agreed that if I reregistered for the classes again in a future semester, I could just take the exams and they would give me the credit for the work I had done, which is what I did my senior year. When those professors indicated to the registrar that I had already taken the classes two years earlier, Wharton reimbursed me $8,000.

Not a single bit of that story happens without Nobel. (His name is Nobel because his parents—both scientists from Geneva—aspired for him to win the Nobel prize.) He pushed me to test every limit to maximize our learning and push the boundaries of what was possible when we were in college. We competed for the highest grades, cooperated to expand the reach of the school magazine where he was publisher while I was editor-in-chief, and encouraged me to try new things. When Nobel became convinced that we needed to learn to eat caviar—because "that's what successful people do"—he convinced me to go to the temple of caviar, Petrossian in New York City. (We took local commuter trains there and back to Philadelphia the same day and through the night, because we could barely afford the transportation, let alone a place to stay in New York City, in addition to the meal.)

Nobel and I even took our second semester of our junior year off—not abroad, *off*—to go to India to work on a feasibility study for an Indian joint venture for a US investment bank. He ended up working for that joint venture and moving to India after graduation. I decided to work for Monitor but learned so much from the experience of working in India, meeting Indian industrialists, and negotiating a joint venture. Nobel never stopped pushing me when we were together. When I was the best man at his wedding in Mumbai, he dared me to jump into the harbor, one of the most polluted bodies of water in the world. Because that's what Nobel does. He pushes me to do things that are outside my comfort zone.

We all need Nobels in our lives—from peers and mentors to coaches and leaders—to know just how far we can go. Who pushes you to achieve? Who gets you out of your comfort zone? Who helps you push through the proverbial pain and the aversion to risk? Who makes you ask, *What's the worst thing that could happen?* when opportunities happen and realize (most of the time) the answer is not so bad.

Can this dynamic create tension between people? Of course! But it is a necessary tension.

Who your Nobels are and what they do for you may change, so there is some flexibility in this lesson. But the need for those people remains fixed in your career. I also have Helen for the most important push I need in life: to be kinder to people no matter the situation and to care for others more often. She wants me to be as kind in my personal life as I have learned to be professionally by always thinking of others first. If we are on time for a dinner party, it's because Helen made me get out the door and not answer a few more emails. She's taught me not to fold pages in library books (because that's vandalism), to write thank-you notes (because appreciation makes the world better), and to wipe the toilet seat after using it, even if it is not dirty (because it's what you would want others to do for you). Getting pushed this way sometimes drives me nuts, but I've learned to see the positive in it.

But buyer beware: having people who push you can send you over the edge without some counterbalance. Nobel literally did this to me—he had me hanging off a cliff on a double black diamond ski trail because I believed him when he said we would just figure it out as he introduced me to skiing. That's another reason I'm grateful for Helen. That day in the polluted Mumbai Harbor, Helen was beside me, digging her nails into my arm to stop me from jumping in because she could sense I had not thought through the consequences of my actions. She was my guardrail when I almost jumped over one.

You need those guardrail people to balance the people who push you—to realize when enough is enough and the worst thing might be as bad as toxic pollutants in my lungs before the wedding and the return flight home. "Pushers" are often never satisfied. They refuse to accept defeat, limits, and sometimes rules. It's in their nature. Having someone as a check against that—pulling you back to safety if just to consider the risks and consequences—is essential.

When you have someone who pushes you, you also learn to push back and push it forward with others. With Nobel, I learned that competition and cooperation are not always in opposition and that you can cheer people on even if they are going after the same things you are—and getting them. You appreciate that others have skills and opportunities that you don't, and you want them to utilize them to achieve at the highest levels. And the stories you make together are magnificent.

For example, when I started CircleLending, I had my classmate and friend Peter Kuperman to push me to make it bigger. Peter is someone who goes for whatever he wants, and what he wanted was for me to add a zero to every number I asked for when raising money, to hire better employees, and to push harder to build a better product with more features and benefits. Simply put, I was aiming for the mountains; Peter told me to shoot for the stars. That terrified me at times, but it helped me channel confidence and belief in myself and the company to investors. Today, Peter even pushes my kids. He sends them text messages encouraging them to think bigger. As my son Alexander said, "Uncle Peter pushes us to do more on every front."

Alexander told me having someone like Uncle Peter inspired him to push himself and other students in his class who were struggling with the confidence they needed to succeed. That's building self-efficacy at every point in your achievement journey and leveling up to leadership.

WHO PUSHES YOU TO ACHIEVE? WHO GETS YOU OUT OF YOUR COMFORT ZONE? WHO HELPS YOU PUSH THROUGH THE PROVERBIAL PAIN AND THE AVERSION TO RISK? WHO MAKES YOU ASK, *WHAT'S THE WORST THING THAT COULD HAPPEN?* WHEN OPPORTUNITIES HAPPEN AND REALIZE (MOST OF THE TIME) THE ANSWER IS NOT SO BAD.

CLASSIC CONNECTIONS

Working together with people who push you in a more formal way to solve problems and achieve more connects directly to what Napoleon Hill called MasterMind groups (peer-to-peer mentoring groups). He first talked about them in his 1925 book, *The Law of Success*, but most people know them from *Think and Grow Rich* (1937) in which he described them as "Coordination of knowledge and effort, in a spirit of harmony, between two or more people, for the attainment of a definite purpose." A MasterMind group can focus on your success alone (like a personal board of directors) or the success of the group. Either way, they are a collective experience that Hill calls a "powerful force," offering wisdom and demanding your accountability. Today, MasterMind groups are available to people young and old through organizations and networks that create them for you. Or you can organize them by yourself by meeting regularly (biweekly, monthly, or quarterly) with a group of peers who are willing to support each other.

But Sharon Lechter makes an important point about these groups. In 2008, Lechter was asked by the Napoleon Hill Foundation to help re-energize his teachings and released several bestselling books in cooperation with the foundation, including *Outwitting the Devil* and *Think and Grow Rich for Women*. She notes that while these groups, like all the mentors in your life, will push you, guide you, present options you might not see, and teach you ways to navigate obstacles, they are "not people who make the decisions for you." Echoing Marshall's point about aspiration, Lechter writes, "Allowing someone else to make choices for you will lead you down a path that you are not necessarily meant to travel, pulling you away from your purpose and your vision. Instead, working with someone who will help you evaluate the information in front of you, so you can make a decision that is right for you, will accelerate your growth in all areas of your life. Always remember, you are the CEO of your life."

FROM MARSHALL
ASPIRATION PUSHES YOU FORWARD

Having someone who pushes you helps you overcome fears of uncertainty and risk. Far too many people settle for lives that they don't find fulfilling because they hesitate to take a risk that might not pay off. But while the people who push you can fuel your ambition, it is your choice to drive your aspirations forward.

Your aspirations are private matters, involving your pursuit of hidden capabilities and values. You alone know what you're up to. You judge the outcome. You perceive the slow but steady creation of a new you. You alone earn the sense of fulfillment that comes with working to care about something new. And you have the power to call it off. Like ambition, aspiration isn't about certainty but about growth—incremental growth.

It's only by aspiring to something—by enjoying, enduring, or resisting the process—that you know which outcome you prefer. You must engage the aspirational process (not imagine it) to understand the fulfillment. In the best case, you love what the process yields and keep pushing to become better at what you're doing. In the worst case, you find something else to devote yourself to. But at least you learned something, and you'll never regret not making the effort.

Regret-avoidance is not the point of aspiration, just one of its bonuses as you get closer to knowing whether your efforts will be satisfying or futile and you decide to reverse course. Regret is the price you pay when you don't pay the price. Nothing is stopping you from ending what you aspire to long before you regret the wasted time and energy you put into it. Consider that the best field generals are masters of retreat as well as attack.

I appreciate the irony that while I'm extolling aspiration as an essential motivating function that lifts us to perfect our noblest instincts, I'm also saying that it has a valuable braking function, like an early warning system telling us to stop and rethink what we're doing. Don't let this double role confuse you. Aspiration is your best friend, whether it motivates you or tells you to stop wasting your time.

It's certainly an improvement on achieving a long-held ambition, only to end up asking yourself, "Is that all there is?"

F lexible lessons compel you to think broadly and differently (i.e., more flexibly) about your achievement journey as time progresses, there are changes to where you live and work, new opportunities and career options present themselves, and you move into more senior positions and leadership. Think of them like the strategies that teams and individuals use when playing games: they follow the rules but adapt the approach according to whom, where, and when they are playing.

Each flexible lesson features a "Coach's Corner" with a comment from one of Marshall's network of coaches. We did not choose them because of their name on the door. You may not have heard of them or read their books, but they advise some of the most influential people in the world, and their insights are inspiring leaders and shaping the way they lead today. That said, I have asked all these coaches to present their comments through the lens of the start of their achievement journeys. Maybe they overcame obstacles, failures, or charted a different path than others and found success. Maybe something changed or evolved as they achieved more as aspiring leaders. Maybe they thought of something they learned or wished they had understood about modern achievement, which they have put into new perspective today. Taken together with my lessons and Marshall's comments, these coaches will make these lessons even more actionable for you.

As in the fixed section, the first set of flexible lessons focuses on your life (self) and the second set of lessons focuses on your work (career).

PART 2
FLEXIBLE

11. REFRAME — KNOW THE POWER OF "YET"

12. PAY ATTENTION TO THE WEIGHTING, NOT JUST THE SCORE

13. SEE EDUCATION AS AN INVESTMENT RETURN, NOT JUST AN INVESTMENT

14. PERFORM SEQUENTIAL TASKING, NOT MULTITASKING

15. EMBRACE THE MESS

SELF

11.

REFRAME — KNOW THE POWER OF "YET"

Whenever I talk about how I stuttered as a kid, I start with the speech therapy sessions I had once a week at the world-leading Hospital for Sick Children in Toronto that taught me to be a better public speaker. For example, one of the fluency exercises that I did at the hospital's speech therapy clinic was repetitive extemporary speaking with flash cards. The therapist would show me a flash card with a random word like "buttons" or "hockey," and I would try to speak for two minutes about that word without stuttering, starting each sentence fragment with a breath and speaking slowly. After a few months of doing this exercise, I became talented at extemporaneous speaking on virtually any topic. After a few years of doing this exercise, unrehearsed public speaking became my superpower. I learned to swap words and phrases on the fly for synonyms, anticipating what sounds would cause me to stutter.

Reframing the embarrassment and painful memories of stuttering as a skill-building opportunity to become an effective extemporaneous speaker who can think rapidly on my feet has been empowering for me. I could easily remember my stuttering entirely in the negative and how it stopped me from achieving things: the clubs that I did not join, the people I was scared to approach, and the leadership roles that I was not selected for. I just choose to remember the positives and reframe my journey around what I have achieved, notably the public speaking practice I had as a benefit of that weekly speech therapy.

My positivity and relentless optimism (see lesson two) apparently put me in the minority of most adults. Research shows that optimism peaks for most people when they are teenagers and diminishes for the rest of their lives. According to UNICEF's "Changing Childhood Project," younger people express greater optimism than older people in every country but India, Morocco, and Nigeria. But optimism doesn't have to decline with age. You can halt the decline and build your optimism muscles—and the self-efficacy you need—by mastering the ability to reframe and knowing the power of "yet."

Reframing focuses on skill-building instead of self-worth, as I did with my stutter. It builds on the optimism you develop in lesson two. Remember this: pessimists think setbacks are permanent—and they can feel that way as they hurt most in the moment. Pivoting to positivity through reframing requires you not only to believe that setbacks are not permanent but also to see their potential for learning and growth.

Think of reframing the same way you might learn to play a musical instrument. You need plenty of practice (and a good teacher), but you cannot expect to be good at it right away. That doesn't mean you're inept at it—unless you believe that. And too many of us are conditioned to believe that.

In the 1960s, Martin Seligman coined the terms "learned helplessness" and "learned optimism." People who see their adversity or failure as temporary and fleeting ("I made a mistake, but this problem won't last forever") or specific ("I made a mistake in this project, but that doesn't mean I'm too incompetent to manage projects of this scale") are far less likely to develop learned helplessness in relationship to their abilities and prospects. They don't narrate their achievement stories from the negative—all the grades they didn't get, schools they didn't get in to, goals they didn't reach, jobs they never got, investors who said no. They reframe them as part of what helped them achieve.

PIVOTING TO POSITIVITY THROUGH REFRAMING REQUIRES YOU NOT ONLY TO BELIEVE THAT SETBACKS ARE NOT PERMANENT BUT ALSO TO SEE THEIR POTENTIAL FOR LEARNING AND GROWTH.

I've seen more of the legacy of learned helplessness in many adults—even the high-achieving people I have worked with. They see someone who is better at something or more successful than they are and instead of saying, "How can I learn from them?" or, "If they can do it so can I," they say some version of, "They have an advantage over me" or, "They must have something I don't." In other words, they diminish their self-worth. They get stuck in negative stories about themselves. This also leads to "imposter syndrome"—even as they achieve and grow, high-achieving people doubt their abilities and feel like frauds, leaving them anxious no matter how well they perform (or others say they are performing).

Learned helplessness is related to what Sanyin Siang calls "comparison trapping"—something she sees causing anxiety in her students at Duke University, the high-achieving executives whom she coaches, *and* herself. Sanyin's solution? Reframe. "The problems we are helping others solve are the ones we're trying to solve ourselves," she says. "We are taught that we have to constantly prove ourselves. What if we flip it to say, *I have something to contribute. I have value. Let's talk about what that may be.* How do we have that conversation with ourselves?"

Reframing your achievement this way helps you understand how you see your value and the value of what you're doing. You accept there are always going to be people better than you at some things. There are always going to be people not as good as you at some things. All those people may achieve things that you don't. You can make yourself unhappy about it or use it as a call to action to keep working to be better at that skill. For those high achievers who struggle to say "I can do it" and suffer from imposter syndrome, this reframe forces you to acknowledge your contributions and how you might contribute differently than others, rather than what they have and you lack.

Reframing is foundational to moving away from learned helplessness and toward learned optimism. For example, "I'm terrible at asking for money, so I'll never get financing for my startup" becomes "I haven't prioritized asking for money so far in my life, but now that it's something I want to master for my growing business, I can learn this new skill in the same way I've learned so many others."

And you only need one word to start working the reframing process: "yet."

"Yet" is one the most optimistic and flexible words we have, and you need only perform this simple exercise to deploy its power: Instead of thinking *I can't do this,* think *I can't do this YET.* For example, don't say "I'm not good at math." Say "I'm not good at math yet." Meaning, "Maybe I haven't found how I can apply its value in 'the real world.'" Don't say "I'm not in the right job." Say "I haven't found the right job yet."

Try it with something you're working to achieve right now. Feel how it shifts your mindset to a positive story of what could be. That feeling is you empowering a growth mindset.

Of course, if you overdo reframing and say "yet" all the time, you can get stuck in the story of reframing, which is why it is not a free-style lesson. You can't "yet" your way out of asking for help to go it alone, to dismiss the impact of bad news, or to ignore a truth about yourself or a situation. Sorry, I am never going to like mayonnaise no matter how many times I say "yet." That's delusional. But building the muscle of learned optimism can be achieved without lapsing into the trap of breeding toxic positivity.

We all suffer from self-doubt and have pessimistic moments in our achievement journeys. I had them all the time when I created CircleLending and tried to reframe the conversation around social finance and peer-to-peer lending. Just like I wanted the people I pitched to let go of their perceptions of online finance, I had to reframe every failure, rejection, and obstacle as temporary and then learn from them and let go to push forward.

Learning to reframe a situation without deluding yourself is a powerful career driver when you need to pivot, negotiate, pitch your idea, and get others to follow your lead. If you work in an organization, even in a large company or multinational, having the tenacity and the ability to get people to support your point of view and get resources beyond what has been allocated requires resourcefulness and perseverance. Reframe conversations as you try to win people over and agree with your point of view. You won't always succeed, but you can see failure as a way forward you just haven't found—yet.

COACH'S CORNER
SANYIN SIANG
"PLAN FOR SERENDIPITY"

I was the student who had everything planned. I knew what I wanted to be (a doctor), where I needed to go (a top college), and what I needed to do to get there (excel at my classes and activities). I had what Asheesh might call a traditional fixed approach when it came to achievement: everything I did checked a box for my plan, and it worked. I got into Duke on a full academic scholarship. But college challenged my I'm-supposed-to-be-smart-as-defined-by-my-grades narrative. Classes were *hard*, and instead of getting help, I slid and then hid. When I stopped going to one class, I got a D, which cost me my scholarship. My world fell apart.

SANYIN SIANG

Putting my world back together turned out to be the best thing that ever happened to me. That's when I started planning for serendipity: planning for luck instead of planning for being a doctor.

By luck I don't mean lucky. I mean being prepared to see and seize opportunities that come from exploration of *ways* to achieve. Planning for serendipity led me to the portfolio career that I love today: a career with a range of engagements from leading a leadership center at a major university to advising top leaders and investing in tech startups and sports—jobs that I never knew existed let alone would have ever been interested in on my journey to be a doctor. My "failure" gave me an opportunity to sit down and rethink my plan for who I was and wanted to be. My predetermined path was gone, so I asked myself, *What's possible?* New types of learning and possibilities presented themselves to me. For example, maybe I wouldn't be a doctor, but what about medical ethics? I never considered that because of how fixed my approach had been. In high school, I worked through a checklist, and everything I needed to do to succeed was represented by a box to check. Now I was in pursuit of knowledge, learning, and growth rather than another checkmark.

The power of planning for serendipity is the power of "yet." It empowers you to embrace the different—to reframe where you are going and balance your fixed and freestyle approaches to achievement. "Experiencing different" [see lesson twenty-four] instead of just your major, your job, or the things you are good at can make you better at all those things. It pushes you to make your boxes bigger, go outside them, or, at the very least, understand and explore more of what is in them. It also prepares you to embrace what hasn't come yet. I tell my students that the types of jobs they'll be in three to five years from now don't even exist yet. Planning for serendipity prepares you for and opens you up to the possibilities.

All this makes planning for serendipity a perfect complement to this lesson and flexibility overall when it comes to achievement. If you stay fixed, you will always tend to focus on your deficiencies, not proficiencies. This happens to the highest achievers I know and is what often leads to imposter syndrome. I am not immune to it. I play my mistakes over and over in my head. But I know now I am not shackled by my past mistakes nor am I defined by my wins. I must have discipline and make it a habit to face my failures, learn from them, and channel that energy into my work—to make continual successes and find fulfillment as I continue to write my achievement story.

Plan for serendipity and know that whatever failures and successes you have had in the past can be powerful drivers for you to move forward. Choose where your story will go; that's your "yet." There is "yet" another chapter, another path to explore even within what you're doing or while you're doing something else. You always have a choice to change the meaning of what was and what you will become.

Sanyin Siang (teamsanyin.com) is a CEO coach, author, and the executive director of the Fuqua/Coach K Center on Leadership & Ethics (COLE) at Duke University. Sanyin helps leaders become even more successful and create value by focusing on mindset and behavioral change. Her award-winning book, The Launch Book: Motivational Stories for Launching Your Idea, Business, or Next Career, *helps readers build a leadership mindset for addressing the changes in their careers, businesses, and lives. In 2023, she was named a Coaching Legend by Thinkers50 and inducted into its Coaching Hall of Fame.*

FROM MARSHALL
WHAT HAPPENS WHEN WE OVERFOCUS ON ACHIEVEMENT

The people I work with are focused on achievement. That's a good thing. It's when you overfocus on achievement or one kind of achievement that trouble finds you. That's what happened to Sanyin. Her ego was attached to her results (e.g., grades), and when she didn't get them, her "world fell apart." But even when she achieved the results she expected, they didn't leave her fulfilled or happy. Each result left her needing more. She'd be happy when she reached her goal of being a doctor. That's the wrong kind of "yet," and one all too familiar to me.

By overfocusing on achieving results and the goals they set, the high achievers I work with need more and more to feel fulfilled. The problem high achievers have is they keep saying *I'll be happy when I* . . . (fill in the blank: earn this much, drive that car, buy that house, etc.). The reality is that just doesn't work. Because we never get there. We keep moving the finish line.

Half the people I coach are billionaires. I have learned from them that there's no amount of money you're going to make that's going to make you find peace in life or happiness. Nothing's wrong with making money to make money. Nothing's wrong with achievement for achievement's sake. As long as you don't believe either of those things defines your value as a human being. As long as you don't believe they are going to make you happy. Happiness and achievement are independent variables. You can achieve a lot and be happy or miserable. You can achieve nothing and be happy or miserable.

Achievement won't lead to fulfillment either. In fact, it often leads to the opposite: regret. Regrets happen when we imagine what might have happened had we done something else. That's the power of this lesson from Asheesh and the comment from Sanyin. Reframe: You don't have to carry regret around. You can change—restart—as you go through life. There is always a new you. There is no real you or fixed you. No one is making you be who you are but you. You just haven't explored who that person might become . . . yet.

12.

PAY ATTENTION TO THE WEIGHTING, NOT JUST THE SCORE

One of the most stressful choices many of us make is where to go to university. The whole process, from figuring out where to apply, completing the applications for admission and financial aid and scholarships, waiting for answers, and finally picking just one to attend, is often overwhelming. For my son Alexander, the whole thing was relatively painless. He decided what school he wanted to attend, applied early, and got in. My son Eliot had to wait but found himself with several excellent and very different schools from which to choose. He wasn't stressed, but he still had a deadline of May 1 to decide.

While it would be Eliot's decision in the end, my wife, Helen, and I had our own perspectives, and he was open to hearing them as he sorted it all out. So we used a spreadsheet.

I realize that last line sounds too businesslike for a personal decision like where to go to university, but hear me out.

Where do I want to go to university? Where do I want to live? Where do I want to work? Big questions many of you will ask. Maybe you try to answer them by listing the pros and cons of each option. Or maybe you compare your options based on what they offer. Maybe you turn to family, friends, and other people and ask what they think—or maybe they are already telling you their opinions, trying to influence your decision. All those maybes can lead to an answer but can just as likely lead to uncertainty, confusion, and fear of making the wrong choice. Overthinking everything, you may find yourself unable to choose, racked with the dreaded analysis paralysis or regret after making the decision.

Big decisions are usually a debate between the head and the heart. Paying attention to the weighting, not just the score, honors both sides. Your head lays out the categories. Your heart tells how much each matters to you. Creating a list of pros and cons is not enough. A really important pro can outweigh a bunch of cons—and vice versa. You need to ask how much each matters to you.

Without weighing what matters, we fail to gain understanding and perspective on our choices. Without paying attention to the weighting, we stay fixed in how we value things and ignore the fact that the passage of time, more information, and even the place we are located can impact each factor in our decision.

That brings me back to the spreadsheet. The way we handled Eliot's decision was to list all the important factors, score them, and then weigh them on our own, based on what we felt. First, we made rows of categories that were important to us like academics, grad school/job prep and placement, internships, college life, extracurriculars, range of majors, reputation, campus, support systems, distance from family, and cost/financial considerations. Next, we made columns for Eliot, Helen, and me to score each school in every category on a scale of one to ten. When we finished, we asked ourselves how much each category mattered to us and then scored them on a scale of one to one hundred. When we were done, we multiplied the two scores for the categories and added them up to give us a total score for each school.

Doing this exercise helped each of us articulate what mattered to us *and* how much it mattered, which impacted our choices in the spreadsheet table before we brought them to the dining table for discussion. We could confront our own biases and blind spots by changing a ranking in one category from one to five or a weighting from ninety to fifty and seeing how that made us feel. Looking over each other's rankings and weightings, we clearly understood one another's perspectives and priorities. For example, Eliot ranked the academics high at all the schools and distance from family very differently than Helen and I did. But because he weighed both those factors lower than we did, they did not affect his score as much. He ranked culture very high, and thus any change in rankings there would make a big difference.

And in the end the college that scored highest that night was . . . not the one Eliot attended. But that initial score wasn't the point of our exercise; it was understanding the importance of weighting and creating a record in that moment. That gave us and Eliot something to reflect on if things changed. And things did change for Eliot. He made the spreadsheet before he had visited all the campuses. After the visits, a different college was on top. Then an unexpected and unusual scholarship offer came in. That offer made him feel great and cemented that college as his top choice. None of this reconsideration was in spite of the spreadsheet but because of it. He simply changed his weighting and ranking of cost/financial considerations.

Lessons three and four are relevant here: writing it down and going meta are two fixed lessons that help you create an important record of your thinking to reflect on. This lesson prompts you to use those skills to adjust your weightings and scores over time as you gain experience and gather information and as circumstances change.

That is not overthinking. That is *thinking*.

We tend to value things differently as we leave home, meet new people, have new teachers and coaches, and add new categories to our "spreadsheets" over time, like the best place to raise a family or cost of living. The key is checking and changing the weighting after you do your first assessment to test and understand what you value and need to focus on, as well as what might not be as important. This unearths your implicit values very quickly, pushes you to see beyond what others tell you, and makes any decision more intentional. In fact, as Marshall says in his comment, weighing how much something matters to you may reveal you shouldn't have wasted your time with that decision in the first place.

Does that intentionality mean Eliot made the right decision? Perhaps this is the wrong question. The point is he decided in a meaningful way. Whatever comes next, the act of deciding mattered in and of itself.

And what if a decision turns out to be wrong? Whether you have a bias for action and go with your gut, make the familiar or safe choice to avoid conflict, or take my approach to important decisions using factors and weightings, you still retain optionality afterward, no matter how consequential the decision may seem.

Most of all, don't worry. Worry is the hobgoblin of overthinking, and regret is its henchman. According to research from the World Economic Forum, you'll potentially have at least twenty jobs and seven careers in your lifetime. Choose wrong, and the only bad decision is not moving past regret like Sanyin Siang did in the last lesson: pivot and realize that maybe you failed to weigh what mattered to you.

COACH'S CORNER
LINDSEY POLLAK
"OVERCOMING DECISION FATIGUE"

I was at a nail salon, and I had to pick a color for my manicure. There must have been at least four hundred options, so I narrowed it down by asking for a light pink—and there were still more than fifty shades to choose from. I am embarrassed to tell you how ridiculously long it took me to make this decision.

Nail polish color is pretty much the definition of a low-stakes decision, but it illustrates how often we're confronted by an overwhelming number of options. Particularly for perfectionists like me, this can easily lead to decision fatigue. You can only imagine how difficult choosing a major or a career path might be for someone who can't even choose between "Sugar Daddy" and "Mademoiselle."

LINDSEY POLLAK

If you sometimes struggle with decision fatigue in your life or career, here are some suggestions:

- *Find your own perspective*: Remember that people will always give you advice based on *their* perspectives to influence yours. What I love about Asheesh's lesson with his son is it helped him see his and his parents' perspectives individually, not collectively.

- *Make any decision*: Indecision is the real enemy to your well-being. As a perfectionist, I *hate* this advice. What I hate even more is that it works.

- *Iterate until you get it right*: There is no perfect decision, nor is there any wrong decision you can't get out of, learn from, or discover something good from. Do your very best and iterate from there.

Understanding the last point is essential to having the flexibility you need not only when deciding but *after* you decide, especially when you are young and figuring things out. Sometimes you are not going to know where a decision will take you. And as Asheesh says, as your circumstances and environments change, your perspective and expectations—personally and professionally—will change both your weightings of what matters and the things that matter to you. New opportunities and possibilities come from each decision and iteration.

That's what happened to me in college. I didn't struggle with that decision as I did with my nail polish. I went to college sure I was going to be an English major, because my father was a high school English teacher, and he instilled a love of literature in me. And I admit I enjoyed the prestige of saying this was my major. But I didn't love my English classes after I got there. So after my sophomore year, I became an American studies major, which meant I basically studied pop culture. "AmStud" was way less prestigious than English. And I loved it.

By committing to my decision to make a change, I chose to follow my own path, which eventually iterated into the work I love to do today.

What my story shows is just how much we can struggle to find our own perspective before we make decisions. Our decisions and expectations (i.e., our perspectives) are influenced by our environments, circumstances, and the people around us—often too much. We need to break free from those influences to open ourselves up to what we want, make our own choices, and maybe even find some new and different ones.

That's how my nail polish saga ends. After seeing fifty shades of pink, I mixed two together to make my own shade! I combined the best of what I wanted and created a path forward for me—what Asheesh would call a flexible path between my individual desire and the seemingly fixed options in front of me.

When it comes to making decisions, my philosophy as a coach is just start somewhere. Asheesh and I both know there is no way to know what decision will be right. You still need to make the decision to move forward. My biggest concern is you not making *any* choice rather than the right choice. Some of that may be analysis paralysis in the face of hard choices and overwhelming options. But part of it is that making one choice and sticking with it doesn't seem smart and may even sound dangerous. So choose to diversify. But *choose.*

Lindsey Pollak (lindseypollak.com) is one of the world's leading experts on careers and multigenerational workplaces, consulting for hundreds of organizations including Aetna, Estée Lauder, GE, and top universities. She is the bestselling author of books like Becoming the Boss: New Rules for the Next Generation of Leaders *and* Getting from College to Career: Your Essential Guide to Succeeding in the Real World.

FROM MARSHALL
CHOOSING NOT TO CHOOSE

After every major reading assignment, my tenth-grade English teacher would have the class write an essay on any topic we wanted. The essay just had to relate in some way to the book, play, or short story we'd just finished reading. Our teacher called these essays "freestyles." In eleventh grade, our new English teacher set a similar drill, except he chose the topics. I asked him why he didn't give us freestyles, as our previous teacher had. He said, "I'm doing most of your classmates a favor. Students have complained for years that they don't have any ideas. Freedom to pick their own topic is the last thing they want."

I think about this when I hear someone say, "There's nothing to watch" or, "There's too much to watch" about the choices on their streaming services. Both statements are saying the same thing: *I can't pick.* Streaming services know this, which is why they work so hard on algorithms that reliably suggest other shows you might like based on another show you just watched or liked. In France, if you scroll for too long, Netflix will actually choose for you to try to make you stay on the platform.

My English teacher and Netflix know what Asheesh and Lindsey have laid out in this lesson: an abundance of choice leaves us feeling as though we can't choose at all. Yet only when we decide to decide do we make change or progress.

We easily make at least a hundred choices a day, without realizing we're doing it. We choose what to wear, what to eat, how to get to work, when to take a break, what to read, what to watch, when to go to bed . . . but most of these choices are automatic, instant, and unthinking.

To live any life, you must make choices. Our existence is dominated by them. Creating an earned life begins with a more conscious choice. It begins with sifting through all the ideas you harbor for your future (assuming you have ideas) and choosing to commit to one idea above all the others. This is easy to say and not so easy to do. So I am going to focus on just one way to get started: choose not to choose.

Following the advice from Asheesh, I'm leaning all the way in on the importance of weighing in a way that works for my own priorities. Some people love giving a thumbs-up or down to an acquisition, or the length of an actor's hair, or the specific shade of gray wall paint. I don't. Perhaps you don't either. Yet extensive research shows that the process of making a choice probably represents the biggest expenditure of your mental energy each day—and it leads to depletion, which can ultimately lead to bad decisions. So, when it doesn't matter, I opt to opt out.

When I need a new assistant, I hire the first qualified interviewee. When I'm at a restaurant, I ask my waiter, "What would you choose?" Over time, the avoidance of those small choices that don't matter to me has become one of my highest priorities. This isn't sloth or indecisiveness. It's a conscious practice of dodging any nonessential choice to save my brain cells for the consequential decisions that occasionally arise in a day.

If I asked you to keep a log of all the choices you made in a day, starting, of course, with the decision to accept or decline this request, then your choice of paper, pad, notebook, or digital device to record the choices, then when you start logging them . . . how many choices would you estimate you make in a day? I'm a choice-avoiding extremist, and on an average day I hit three hundred before 4:00 p.m.

Creating an earned life is first and foremost a matter of scale: go big on important things that keep you on message and small on things that don't influence the outcome. An earned life is lived at the extremes: maximize what you need to do with discipline and sacrifice; minimize what you don't.

13.

SEE EDUCATION AS AN INVESTMENT RETURN, NOT JUST AN INVESTMENT

One of my favorite JA initiatives is the International Trade Challenge. Typically hosted by a JA location in Asia and supported by corporate volunteers from FedEx, the experience brings students together from across many countries to address a business challenge or social problem that is far removed from their current location, encouraging them to do research and learn about another part of the world. The students don't know the topic in advance and are placed into groups with partners from different countries, and then they must use their entrepreneurial skills to generate ideas and solutions to the problem by working together. At the end of the day, they present their plans to a group of judges who decide which group wins. For example, I watched groups of students from China, Indonesia, Singapore, and other countries from across the Asia-Pacific region collaborate to design a business plan for a restaurant in Cuba. Their ideas were off-the-charts innovative and creative. One group realized that Cuba invests heavily in a health-care system and that as a result its citizens care deeply about their health. So they created a restaurant that integrated health screening as part of the food-ordering process to recommend the right things for diners to eat. Another group designed a restaurant that took advantage of Cuba's soil and climate to grow as much as they served on the roof so everything would be as local and fresh as possible.

But more than all the creative ideas I heard that day, I remember how much fun the students had engaging in the process of learning to create their plans. To achieve more and better, you must learn to value and enjoy education as a process. Like modern achievement, success and fulfillment come from the journey of learning, not *just* the attainment of prescribed educational goals and objectives—by yourself, the institution, and others like your family and teachers.

Seeing education as a process is essential to seeing it as an invest-ment return, not just an investment. Please note my intentional repe-tition of the words "not just." Education is an investment of your time and often your (or someone else's) money, and we all want a return *of* that investment—to get back what you put in, be it time or treasure. You should have goals and objectives for learning and see results from your efforts—those JA students would have failed the assignment if they never produced a plan. But seeing it only in terms of outcomes limits the value of your education. When I say investment return, I mean a return *on* your investment, getting back *above* what you invested—in quantitative measures like a degree, job, or higher salary but also in qual-itative measures like intellectual curiosity, connections, opportunities, the ability to think differently about problems, and the happiness and fulfillment you get from learning new things and meeting new people.

Simply put, the more you see all learning and your investment in it as part of an overall process of *investing in you*, the more return you get. That investment extends well beyond the "classroom." In school, that learning can come from internships, co-ops, enrichment classes, and experiential learning, as well as clubs and sports. After school, that learning can come from mentorship, networking, attending conferences, and learning everything you can about the business and industry you work in. But it should extend to what you do for yourself, like learning how to cook or dance, joining a group to play a sport or do an activity, volunteering for an organization, or starting a side hustle. Those investments in you help expand your world and develop new

SIMPLY PUT, THE MORE YOU SEE ALL LEARNING AND YOUR INVESTMENT IN IT AS PART OF AN OVERALL PROCESS OF *INVESTING IN YOU*, THE MORE RETURN YOU GET. THAT INVESTMENT EXTENDS WELL BEYOND THE "CLASSROOM."

perspectives, and they help you understand who you are and what makes you different from others.

Education, like any process, must be flexible to succeed. In an unpredictable world in which you will likely have many jobs and careers, no matter what kind of education you get in high school, college, or beyond, you will need to keep learning in new and different ways. The bigger question is why this needs to be a lesson at all, and it is the same reason many people lose long-term gains from their monetary investments: they overweight the need to see a return *of* their investment over *on* their investment—getting their money back instead of building the returns over time.

Consider the American higher education story. Colleges and universities in the United States are enormously expensive compared to the rest of the world. As a result, many students pick a STEM major like computer science or biochemistry. After all, STEM grads make more on average out of college than liberal arts majors. With a STEM degree, they can start getting a return of their (or their family's) investment, begin a life on their own, and maybe start paying back any student loans they have. That said, while it is true that students who major in STEM subjects earn, in many cases, more than double what liberal arts majors earn when they graduate, by the middle of their careers liberal arts majors catch up and then surpass STEM graduates in earnings. There are many reasons for this, such as the rapid development of new technologies (everyone—not just STEM students—must constantly learn and train to keep up) and automation (liberal arts majors often develop and value the soft skills that are hard to automate, make them better leaders, and give them the ability to look around the data).

No matter how you write your achievement story, I want you to understand how you value your education and learning overall. You always want a return on your investment. But overvaluing the need to get your investment back over the investment return often means devaluing what you love, and that has consequences. Consider the process when it comes to that education and see the investment return as you pursue your education and all your future learning, not only to be successful but to be happier, healthier, and a better citizen of the world.

COACH'S CORNER
MICHAEL BUNGAY STANIER
"LEARNING THE POWER OF CURIOSITY"

I've checked a lot of education boxes in my life: I'm a Rhodes Scholar with a bachelor's degree in English, master's in literature, and a law degree. What I learned in checking those boxes is that too often the cele-bration and recognition of these credentials equates being smart with having the right answers. That's what gets you the top marks and high GPA. Living in a world that fetishizes knowledge, answers, solutions, titles, and opinions leads many of us to have a constant need to demonstrate our value by proving how smart we are, which is ironic since our world makes knowledge, content,

MICHAEL BUNGAY STANIER

and information increasingly accessible, transactional, and less valued. Almost anything we know, Google and AI know as well and answer much faster. The idea that information, knowledge, degrees, and certifications we get from education are our superpower is a bit deceptive and can be dangerous to our success.

To be clear, I'm not anti-education, but I am wary of the ways academic credentials get translated in professional life. Your GPA can't be the most interesting thing about you. Awards and letters after your name do not make you smart or guarantee that you will achieve more. I think having questions makes you those things and curiosity is our underutilized superpower.

I came to this realization when I was in law school. I was pretty bad at getting that degree, and not just because I didn't have great marks or because one of my professors sued me for defamation. During my summer working at a law firm, I realized that what I was learning in law school wasn't relevant to what it meant to be a lawyer. The practical stuff I was learning was out of date. The minutiae were often useless, and the fundamentals weren't helpful. That's when my whole perspective shifted. I realized law school was a game I needed to figure out how to play to get the results that I wanted and learn to ask questions like a lawyer. And when you're asking about how a game is being played, figuring out the underlying dynamics and bigger picture, you're being curious.

I wanted to stay curious—to see curiosity as a process the same way Asheesh sees modern achievement.

Marshall says invest in your reputation for being effective: How about a reputation for being someone who figures out what's at the heart of the problem rather than proving how much you know and offering opinions and ideas? Too many of us work hard at trying to prove we are smart and to solve problems that don't matter that much. We get seduced by busy-ness and urgency and the idea that the first challenge we face is the real challenge. One of the best reputations you can have in an organization—not just as a leader—is being someone who is curious about what the real challenges are and embraces curiosity over taking action, offering opinions, and giving advice. What a powerful way to show up.

But it's not just in doing the work that curiosity has its ultimate power. It's actually in connecting to others with whom you work. People talk about culture and strategy as the twin DNA strands of a successful organization. So how do you create a great culture and execute a great strategy? Have the right people doing brilliant stuff. Staying curious when you coach and work with others gives them an opportunity to be seen, heard, and acknowledged as the brilliant, messy human beings that we are. If you build a reputation for this, you create safety to push, encourage, nudge, and challenge them. You bring out the best in them by bringing out the best in them.

So how do you start being curious? Start by thinking of everything you do in your education and the early part of your career as a series of experiments to help you figure things out. Then, tap the well of curiosity by asking, *Who am I?* in the context of where you are now and where you want to go as you grow:

Be curious about the job you have. *What is the role I am playing? What is its importance?*

Be curious about how the organization works. Where does the power exist? How does stuff get done? Where's the most interesting stuff happening?

Be curious about yourself: How am I showing up? How am I perceived by others? Am I "playing small" or embracing risk and willing to be uncomfortable? What are any strengths and weaknesses and what am I doing with that insight?

Moving from school to the workforce is a reset. As you achieve more, all the stuff you thought you knew will often be limited or inaccurate. Use that time to be curious! Remember, it's not often the stuff you don't know that kills you. It's usually the stuff that you know for sure that turns out not to be true.

Michael Bungay Stanier or MBS (mbs.works) is best known for The Coaching Habit, *which is the bestselling book on coaching this century. His books have sold close to two million copies, and one book written in partnership with Seth Godin raised $400,000 for* Malaria No More. *MBS's training company, Box of Crayons, has taught coaching skills to hundreds of thousands of people around the world. He's a speaker, a podcaster, and was a Rhodes Scholar. He received the 2023 Distinguished Achievement Award for Coaching and Mentoring from Thinkers50.*

FROM MARSHALL

INVEST IN YOUR REPUTATION

It's taken me a while to figure out why so many of us neglect our reputation. It's not that we don't care. It's that we often value our need to be seen as smart over our need to be considered effective by the world. We need to, as Asheesh would say, understand the investment return in the latter.

The need to prove how smart we are is drilled into us from our earliest school days, when we're graded, ranked, and bell curved. In high school, college, and beyond that need gets even more deeply ingrained because the competition to be smart becomes tied to where we go to college and what jobs we get. We then continue this competition into the workplace where we want our bosses and colleagues to admire our brainpower and give us good "report cards" in the form of praise, promotions, and paychecks.

But the need to be the smartest person in the room can lead to incredibly stupid behavior. It leads to dumb arguments, in which we fight to prove that we're right and someone else is wrong. It's the reason we feel the need to tell someone who shares valuable information with us that we "already knew that." It's the reason we fight hard to defend an opinion or decision that has worn out its welcome. It's the reason bosses can't resist improving a subordinate's idea by saying, "That's great, but it would be even better if you . . ." It's also one of the biggest reasons so many of us are such poor listeners: we're so invested in presenting ourselves as smart that we believe we don't need to hear everything that people tell us; we're smart enough to tune out people and still succeed.

Those who are willing to sacrifice the fleeting buzz of needing to be smart for the more valuable feeling of being effective—of delivering on time, of bringing out the best in others, of finding the simplest route to a solution—do not succumb to that stupid behavior as often.

Don't get me wrong. Just as Asheesh is not devaluing the importance of seeing education as an investment, I am not devaluing the importance of being smart. I am simply suggesting striking a balance between being smart and being effective. For example, let's say you're developing a product for your company and face the choice of doing something brilliant or doing something practical. You could show your brilliance by proposing a dazzling solution that will be rejected by the company because of costs and production difficulties, or just because no one will understand its value yet. Or you could offer a solution that takes the best of what you can do and can be accepted and produced. Do you want to be known as someone who builds elegant objects that never get made or as someone who provides practical solutions that always "ship out the door"? There's no correct answer. Some people won't compromise their talent or principles to be more effective; some people will.

What I'd like to suggest is that you shouldn't think of these decisions in terms of compromise. That suggests an inauthentic choice, something that's not true to your beliefs and goals. Instead, I'd like to posit that these choices are easier to understand and make if you have a clearer idea of the reputation you're trying to build for yourself.

I'm very clear about what I want my reputation to be: I want people to think of me as someone who's extremely effective in helping successful leaders achieve positive, lasting change in behavior. I don't want to be just good in my field. I want a reputation as one of the best. And to be considered one of the best, I don't have a high margin for error. Partly because of that reputational goal, many decisions in my career boil down to this: Will it make me look smarter or make me become more effective? I always vote for effective. I'm not looking to be known as the smartest person with the most sophisticated theory about helping people change. I want to be known as the guy who is effective at helping people change.

Remember this smart/effective distinction the next time you face a career decision and how opting for the latter may cement the former. Many of us fail to think about the long-term reputational impact when we make a decision the same way Asheesh says we think about all learning: overvaluing the short-term needs to show how smart we are. Learn that asking, *Am I smart enough?* blinds you from the value of asking, *Does this choice add or detract from my long-term reputation?*

14.

PERFORM SEQUENTIAL TASKING, NOT MULTITASKING

had just finished graduate school and started my job at the World Bank in Washington, D.C. when an offer came in from the University of Toronto for a teaching position. The timing and logistics weren't great since I was committed to the World Bank, but my heart and head wanted to do it: I grew up in Toronto, and the chance to teach students at one of the best universities in the country was appealing. I also really wanted to teach students about what I had recently researched at Oxford. With the condition that I would keep my job at the World Bank and teach as an adjunct professor instead of full time, the World Bank and the university agreed, and I said yes.

My initial plan was to fly from D.C. to Toronto every Thursday and grab a taxi to the university, which was an hour from the airport. A car rental would have been cheaper and faster, but I didn't have a driver's license! I had never needed one. Growing up in Toronto, I took the subway, and there was public transportation wherever I worked or went to school. My new need to drive led me to a new and better plan: I would book a driver's ed course, have the instructor meet me at Pearson Airport outside Toronto, and do my driving lesson on the way to the university—instead of taking a taxi or renting a car. I did that every Thursday until I put in my hours, passed my driving test, and got my license just before the end of term.

Getting my license and teaching that course while I was living in Washington, D.C. is a good example of sequential tasking, rather than multitasking. Each task took place in its own time and place. When I was at the World Bank, I was not focused on driving lessons or teaching. When I was in Toronto on Thursday evenings, I was not at all focused on my work at the bank.

As we learned in the opening lesson, the classic definition of achievement involves going deep on one thing for most of your professional career. In modern achievement, that is just not true—or even possible. Many of you will build portfolio careers during your achievement journey, monetizing your skills and building a career from many roles at once. Even if you work at a single organization, you will need to navigate many competing needs and priorities daily, which is exactly why you need to build the capability for sequential tasking.

Simply put, if you want to be a productive modern-achievement-oriented person, you are going to have to do a lot of stuff. Sequential tasking works *with* your brain to grab value and productivity without distraction and helps you do things well.

Multitasking works *against* your brain. Every time you shift your attention between tasks, you deplete your neural resources and lose focus. In fact, research shows that it takes almost thirty minutes to refocus your attention completely after it has been diverted. This makes you not only less creative and imaginative but less productive, and it decreases the quality of the work or enjoyment of whatever—*or whomever*—you're focusing on. So multitasking undermines not only valuable, meaningful work but valuable, meaningful *relationships*. Sequential tasking gives each task and each person your time and focus. That's why when people tell me I'm bad at multitasking, I take it as a compliment. Because multitasking is where achievement goes to die.

Yet the lure of social media, screens everywhere we go, and people and competing tasks demanding our time makes us think we must try to multitask—or unintentionally fall into the trap of it. As a result, our attention is being diverted more than ever: Between 2004 and today, the average person's attention span shrank from two-and-a-half minutes to around forty-five seconds. Thus, before you can successfully perform sequential tasking, you need to remove distractions and other obstacles to action—the barriers and impediments that make you shift your focus and that get in the way of achievement.

What's one simple behavior step you can stop doing that makes it easier for you to have some time or focus? Maybe delete games from your phone—or an app like TikTok, as my son Alexander did to meet one of his annual goals (see lesson three). Maybe you need to take a break to get started. Take that nap or stare out the window. When you get bored, you ignite a part of your brain that unleashes different and creative thinking. For example, when you are in the shower, walking to work, or just washing dishes, you start to focus and think more deeply.

I never would have been in the position to teach that course at the University of Toronto if I hadn't learned the lesson of sequential thinking on an extreme level when I needed to finish my doctoral dissertation. I had an ambitious plan to finish my doctoral degree at Oxford in three years, but the lure of rowing, student clubs, parties, and other fun with friends in England left me falling behind schedule after the first two years. To remove those pleasurable distractions and face the commitment of writing in my third year, I moved back to Canada. I met one of the professors at the University of Toronto who was on sabbatical, and for six months he let me use his office to focus on writing my dissertation. Every day I worked in his office until 3:00 a.m., walked to my rental apartment in darkness, and slept until noon. Within six months, this focused routine helped me finish my dissertation with no distractions. No rowing, no parties, no student clubs.

We all have tasks we need to get done. So to get started, use lesson three and, on an index card, write down three of those tasks you want to accomplish tomorrow. It doesn't matter if they're personal or professional or how big or how small, just that they matter to *you*. Carry that card with you the next day until you complete them. Then, start the process again. My guess is you'll begin to understand not only what and who matter most to you but what's standing in the way of making them priorities.

And for the most part, like so much in these lessons on modern achievement, what's standing in the way is you. The key is to face whatever the difficulty is and remove the distractions before little problems or small tasks become big ones. Stop putting off anything simply because you think you can't do it, it won't be good, or you will fail. You might hate facing bad news, answering emails, making phone calls, or going to meetings, but facing what must be done sequentially and with focus and determination builds your ability to get things done and done well, one thing at a time.

SEQUENTIAL TASKING WORKS WITH YOUR BRAIN TO GRAB VALUE AND PRODUCTIVITY WITHOUT DISTRACTION AND HELPS YOU DO THINGS WELL.

COACH'S CORNER
WHITNEY JOHNSON
"FOCUS"

Like many high achievers, I struggle with anxiety. For me, that anxiety is most pressing as my brain darts around everything I have and want to do. I need to do this and this . . . oh, and I must do that and . . . and they need me for this . . . and . . . one day, as my anxiety overwhelmed me, I heard a voice I very much trust—God—say to me, *You need to do one thing and do it well and then move to the next thing.* I needed to hear that advice and learn how to focus. Only then would I learn to emotionally manage what I needed to do, relieve my anxiety, and move forward productively.

I didn't need to hear those words when I was just starting out. There were fewer distractions. No email. No social media fueling my fear of missing out, being left out, not doing enough, or thinking I'm failing at every turn as I'm bombarded with images of success. I went on a mission for my church in Uruguay in the 1980s, and all we could use to communicate were letters, except on Christmas and Mother's Day when we traveled to a phone bank to speak to our families. Today, when we can message anyone from almost anywhere at any time, I sometimes long for that inability to communicate again.

I do remember having some anxiety later when I graduated with my degree in music and had no idea how to navigate the workplace, let alone Wall Street. I also remember being aware that it was going to be different for me as a woman. Until I came across Carol Gilligan's *In a Different Voice* and

Sally Helgesen's *The Female Advantage*, all the advice I got was developed for men, by men.

But I digress. The anxiety I have today happened later in my achievement story.

Your journey may be just beginning, but the words I heard can serve you at any point in your career, whether you believe in God or not: *Do one thing and do it well and then move to the next thing.* Train yourself to focus—get started and keep practicing. I began by setting a fifteen-minute timer on my phone to focus on a single task. That helped me understand how it felt to focus and to identify what distracted and prevented me from focusing even for fifteen minutes.

I also focus on prioritizing: I decide what my top priority is, do that one thing and do it well, and then move to the next thing. I become more productive, and my anxiety has also dissolved. My ability to achieve comes at a lower cost. My life becomes mine again—more expansive and spacious. An unintended but happy consequence.

WHITNEY JOHNSON

Part of what has helped me focus is a simple visual tool we have developed at Disruption Advisors called "S Curve of Learning," which maps out what growth looks and *feels* like. It shows how learning is slow and effortful at my "launch point," or the start of a curve. But as I acquire new skills and overcome setbacks, I accelerate and hit my "sweet spot," where it is easiest to focus. I stay in my sweet spot until I move into "mastery," and the S-curve flattens because there is little left to learn.

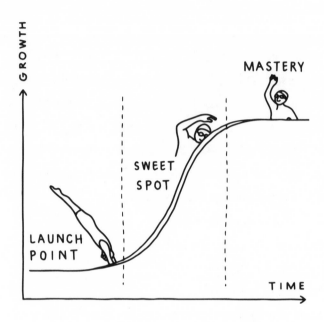

THE S CURVE OF LEARNING

To help me focus, I've added in yoga and meditation. I'm doing Positive Intelligence work, in which I am focusing on how I use my body to be present in the moment and get whatever I am working on done. I'm also using an app called I Am Streaking, which is a twist on Marshall's daily questions [see lesson three], in which I am learning to consistently do things every day (e.g., eat a piece of fruit or do some exercise) or behaviors I want to maintain (e.g., I feel good about what I ate today or I want to finish work by 8:00 p.m.). I get "streaks" for the number of days in a row I do these things. This helps me set goals and crystallize what's important to me, like writing my next book or becoming more of the person I want to be. And if I am performing as the person I want to be, the things that I want to do will happen.

While I can't say what causes you anxiety or what tools will work best to help you focus, I know not focusing on focusing will only let your anxiety grow and stand in the way of the person you want to become. Yet even as I have learned to focus, I need to be flexible as new opportunities present themselves and my priorities shift. It's harder to understand what your priorities are when you are starting out and are understanding your "why," wondering whether what you do will matter and whether anyone will care, and when your purpose for being on this planet is evolving. Your priorities should change and evolve as you grow, your circumstances change, and you gain experience and move into leadership. Priorities are not static: What are the things you want to get done this year or next, this month, this week, and this day?

But to get started, focus on this question: What is it meaningful for you right now?

A former award-winning stock analyst on Wall Street, and cofounder of the Disruptive Innovation Fund with Harvard's legendary Clayton Christensen, Whitney Johnson is now the CEO of Disruption Advisors (thedisruptionadvisors.com), where they activate engagement and growth in people, leaders, and their teams. She is also a Wall Street Journal *bestselling author of* Smart Growth: How to Grow Your People to Grow Your Company *and hosts the popular* Disrupt Yourself *podcast.*

FROM MARSHALL
LET IT — AND THEM — GO

Research shows that successful people have a strong need for self-determination, meaning they do what they do because they choose to, not because they have to. When you do what you choose to do, you proactively commit to achieving more for yourself and others—you focus on making a greater contribution in everything you do, which leads to more fulfillment and success. People who are doing what they have to do are compliant. They are putting in time for money—transactional in most aspects of their lives.

Of course, the impact of self-determination on success is not measured only in money. When you were a student, could you tell the difference between teachers who were teaching their classes because they loved teaching and those who were teaching only because they needed to collect a check at the end of the month? Committed people have a drive that comes from the inside. They don't give up when times are tough. They try even harder both in what they do and in the relationships they have.

The problem is that while your personal commitments usually lead to more success, they can make it extremely hard for you to change. The more committed you are to a strategy, the harder it is for you to realize it is the wrong strategy. You have heard the line "winners never quit!" Well, sometimes it is time to quit, time to resign, time to leave, time to stop certain behaviors.

I worked with four CEOs who needed to leave their companies. In all four cases I suggested, "Leave. Leave now. It is over. Don't humiliate yourself and the company. Leave with dignity." I failed in all four cases. All four were forced to leave. Two ended up being featured in national magazines, embarrassing themselves and their companies.

CEOs are not the only ones susceptible to this behavior. Maybe you tried to change the mind of a parent, significant other, colleague, or friend who had no interest in changing. Usually, it leads to lots of wasted time and effort and almost no results, because the other person was successful and didn't see the need to change.

My mother was a fantastic first-grade teacher. In her mind, the entire world was populated by first-graders. I was always in the first grade. My dad was in the first grade. All of our relatives were in the first grade. One day, when Dad was eighty years old, Mom was still correcting his grammar. He looked at her lovingly, smiled, and said in his shaky voice, "Honey, I'm eighty years old. Let it go!"

While you think about what behaviors, distractions, and tasks you need to let go of to focus on the things you need to get done, look back to the classic connection in lesson two and ask *whom* you might need to let go of.

How much of our lives have been wasted in trying to change the behavior of people who have no interest in changing? What is our return on this investment? Think of it this way: the time we waste on the people who don't care about changing is time that is stolen from the people who do. My guess is that you have little time to waste. You are as busy today as you have ever been in your life. So invest your time only where you are going to get a return on your investment.

Don't waste your time on a road to nowhere. Spend your time with people who sequentially work every day to be better at who they are and what they do—even if that requires a radical change—because they are the ones who will help you do the same and live a more successful and happier life.

15.

EMBRACE
THE MESS

When I was raising money for my first company, CircleLending, I pitched Jeff Bezos of Amazon from a pay phone hanging on the wall of Capitol Grounds Cafe in Montpelier, Vermont. That wasn't my plan.

After three meetings with a member of Jeff's investment team, I had finally scheduled a call with Jeff himself. As it turned out, I was asked to pitch another group of investors in Vermont on the same day. I was sure there would be cell phone reception in the state's capital that would allow me to keep my phone meeting with Jeff. I was wrong. So there I was in the café, at its old-fashioned pay phone, laptop perched on top, scrolling through my slides, and doing my twenty-minute pitch for one of the wealthiest men in the world loud enough for everyone to enjoy over their lattes. Still, Jeff liked what he heard and said he wanted to meet me the following week at Amazon's headquarters in Seattle.

At the time, Amazon was housed in an old hospital, and Jeff gave me a tour before we sat down. He loved the wide hallways of the converted hospital, where Amazon's leaders and staff could interact for impromptu meetings; he believed that was where the real work got done. When our conversation shifted to CircleLending, he understood the business model in less than five minutes and shifted the conversation to me. Not what I expected.

For more than an hour, Jeff asked me about my life: immigrating with my family from India to Canada when I was six, growing up in

Toronto, going to university in the United States, doing my doctoral degree in the United Kingdom, and coming back to the United States to work. He probed my story for examples of how I was able to pursue and capitalize on opportunities and whether I was ethical, persistent, and aggressive enough to manage his investment to fruition.

At the end of the meeting, Jeff decided to invest $400,000—the largest amount I had received from angel investors at that point. When CircleLending was acquired by the Virgin Group, he made a great return on that investment—its founder, Sir Richard Branson, one of the most famous billionaires in the world, effectively paid Jeff Bezos, the future richest man in the world, for stock in my little company!

That day in Seattle, I also made a great return on my investment. Not the kind measured in time or money but *in the acceptance of the messiness of modern achievement in which success is a process, not a destination.*

Our lives are always in motion, and we're lucky if things go according to script as circumstances change and obstacles force us to change and adapt. The more you show resilience and embrace the messy and imperfect moments, understanding that every step is something to build on and learn from, the more prepared you are to push forward with confidence.

I was prepared to succeed with Jeff Bezos in large part because I had already been rejected by at least seventy-five individuals and organizations after making my investment pitch. I didn't see those seventy-five nos as failures. Failure is having something not turn out the way you want and *not* learning from it. If you learn from it, it is just part of the messiness—part of your achievement process and story. I embraced the mess and reframed those rejections and all the things that went wrong in the moment as things that would lead to things going right in the future with continuous improvements and refinements. Dealing with failures and setbacks gets easier with experience. Lack of cell service in a state capital while pitching the future richest man in the world? I did what it took to push through.

That's the optimism that gives you the confidence to keep going through the messiness of life.

Note I said confidence, not certainty. No matter how much you believe in the path you are on, everyone's futures are unwritten. But more than ever, the setting of any long-term goals are leaps of faith in a world where you can expect to have seven careers and twenty jobs. Anyone who proclaims certainty is less prepared to reposition themselves and deal with gains and setbacks. They will struggle to find inspiration in any step they take and create the opportunities for success and their futures.

In fact, this entire lesson was a test of my ability to be flexible and embrace the mess.

This lesson used to be titled, provocatively, "Be Aggressive." Calling someone aggressive often implies that person is disruptive, loud, unfriendly, and unhelpful. Jeff Bezos did not mean it—and I didn't take it—that way. When Jeff wanted to know if I was aggressive enough to manage his investment, he was looking for someone ambitious, assertive, bold, energetic, and confident—who vigorously believed in himself as much as anything he was pitching. Because to him, what I was pitching was *me*. The best JA students understand this on some level. When they pitch their businesses to judges, the ones who do it with confidence and project strength—who say, "I'm going to make this happen, and here's the evidence as to why"—*and* do that in a likable way are inevitably more persuasive than the ones who are cautious and tentative. Having attended dozens of student entrepreneurship competitions all over the world, I can say that it is universally true that ambition and confidence are rewarded, particularly when balanced with honesty and kindness.

But when I spoke to Julie Carrier and asked her to add her comments and experiences to "Be Aggressive," she acknowledged the importance of the lesson but saw something bigger in what I was saying—not just in the examples I gave but in my whole life journey.

Julie is the world's top-ranked coach for young women, according to Leading Global Coaches. She strives to bridge the gap between girls' success in school and their lack of leadership positions in the workplace. To help close the leadership and confidence gaps that research shows emerge for girls in adolescence, she has created a curriculum called "The Leadership Course," which brings evidence-based leader development and coaching to support high school girls in developing the leadership skills needed to succeed outside the classroom, including resilience, confidence, and teamwork.

Julie reframed the entire lesson in terms of my achievement story and hers. She helped me more deeply understand that what I called "aggressiveness" can be seen as the perseverance, resilience and belief in yourself to navigate, push through, and embrace the messy middles of the journey. To realize that it's more than the goal—it's about how we learn, grow. and show up as our best selves and push through when unexpected and inevitable setbacks come along the way. More than "doing," success is the process of being—it's who we become in those messes that ultimately impacts more than our achievement of a goal—it impacts the trajectory of our whole lives.

"When I was young, I thought that once I finally 'arrived,' I would be happy and see myself as a success," Julie told me. "I was wrong. I worked hard, strived, and overcame so many obstacles to finally achieve every major goal that I had by the time I was twenty-seven: teaching leadership at the Pentagon, having my own company, traveling around the world as a leadership speaker on a non-stop schedule reaching thousands of young people, writing a bestselling book. I was devastated when I checked that last box and was not suddenly perfectly happy and fulfilled. I had practiced feeling 'less than' for so long—basing my worth on external things and reaching accomplishments that when I finally did arrive—I wasn't able to feel the feelings of happiness and fulfillment because I hadn't practiced them along the way. I hadn't learned to see life as one long journey of growth that includes valuing and appreciating messy middles on the path to reaching 'success.'"

What Julie came to understand aligns perfectly with what we call the process of modern achievement: That real success means building the skill set to appreciate all parts of the journey—including the successes and inevitable messes that happen along the way.

"Having the perseverance to embrace the messes that are ultimately part of the successes can be harder than ever," Julie says. "I see young people constantly compare themselves to picture-perfect highlight reels of success from social media that make them feel less than, left behind or make them want to give up on their dream. Rather than embrace the mess, they are being led to believe that if they don't already have all the answers or if the journey is hard or 'messy' it means they should quit or not start to begin with. Real achievement means embracing the mess—recognizing that uncertainty, mistakes, confusion, setbacks, and lessons learned are not roadblocks, they are the steppingstones to reaching your goals, and more importantly, learning how to become your best version of you along the way."

I hope Julie's words and her story that follows have the same power for you as they did for me. She helped me not only reframe this lesson but see how I had embraced the mess to get through the numerous obstacles that are part of my entrepreneurial leadership story. When I could not afford to build a prototype for CircleLending, I embraced the mess to do a deal with my employer at the time, global consulting giant Monitor, to spend half my time on my work for the firm and half developing the prototype in exchange for equity in the company. When I had been rejected by enough investors who had been burned by business-to-consumer dotcoms in the tech meltdown of 2000, I had to embrace the mess of how to finance my business by finding employees who did not need a salary. This willingness to embrace the mess led me to Jeff Ma—who was a math whiz able to beat casinos at blackjack worldwide and was the inspiration for the main character of the book *Bringing Down the House* and movie *21*—who agreed to be my first employee, even though we had nothing but an idea at the time. Without Jeff's technology skills and willingness to work primarily for equity, the company's first beta product would never have been built.

I also learned to embrace the mess through the years that followed the 2008 financial crisis—through the aftermath of Virgin Money acquiring CircleLending and then deciding to leave the US to buy a bank in the UK, through the tumultuous stock market when serving as CEO of Covestor, and through the pandemic when JA Worldwide needed to cut costs while simultaneously driving digital transformation to serve young people when schools were closed.

There is a self-help line I love and often quote that has been mistakenly attributed to both Winston Churchill and Abraham Lincoln: success is moving from failure to failure with no loss of enthusiasm. But I realize now from this lesson that it is best said differently: life is moving from mess to mess with no loss of confidence.

LIFE IS MOVING FROM MESS TO MESS WITH NO LOSS OF CONFIDENCE.

COACH'S CORNER
JULIE CARRIER
"YOUR MESSES CAN BECOME YOUR SUCCESSES"

When people see me on stage speaking to a conference of ten thousand people, many of them think confidence is something I was just born with. They have been led to believe that you are either "confident" or you are not. But, like most skills, confidence is a skill that I had to learn! I started high school with a growth disorder and felt super awkward with crippling anxiety. One creative outlet that I had was art, and I loved making polymer clay beads. My parents thought they were good enough to sell if I wanted to. *Me? A businessperson selling my art?* No. But my parents kept encouraging me until I went into a local craft store and asked them to buy my beads. The woman at the front desk laughed, patted me on the head, and told me I was cute. Then she told me they only buy from "real" artists who are adults.

JULIE CARRIER

Frustrated by the idea that you had to be a certain age to be a "real" artist, I pushed through my nerves and anxiousness, made more beads, put them in a nice display box, and went back. The woman laughed again and said the owner would not be interested. But I was determined. I had my mom get me a suit altered to fit my very small frame, and I went back to the store delivering the words I had rehearsed: *Hi, I'm Julie. I'm a bead artist, and I want to sell my beads at your store.* This time, the front desk person went back and got the owner, who told me to come to the back. She opened the display box and was so surprised that she bought all the beads. $64.75!

My entrepreneurial spirit carried me confidently into college, where I promptly became lost about what to major in, let alone what I wanted to do when I graduated. Political science, animal science, communications . . . I changed my major five times. My parents wondered if I was going to be a professional student. By my third year, even the college was wondering what I was doing. My life wasn't just messy; I was a mess!

By my fourth year of college, I had the opportunity to study abroad in England with a Rotary Ambassadorial Scholarship, and that was where I finally asked myself, *What is the job I love so much that I would do it for free but could potentially get paid to do?* In reflecting on the best and most fulfilled times of my life, I realized that I love leadership. When I got back to school, with the support of four amazing professors, I petitioned my university to create my own major in leadership studies. We put together an amazing curriculum with a mix of my previous courses, new ones, and independent study of cutting-edge leadership research that wasn't available in typical classes.

With a first ever degree in Leadership Studies from my university, I was offered a job opportunity before I even graduated with a specialized leadership consulting firm in Washington, DC. The company president brought me to interview with her newest client before I was formally given my role. Only when we pulled up in the parking lot did I realize where we were: the Pentagon.

I freaked out. *Who am I, this twenty-something, fresh-out-of-college-student, to do leadership development at the Pentagon?* My confidence disappeared. Then, I remembered words from my dad that gave me the courage I needed: "It's never about how old you are but how you can serve." They hired me on the spot as a senior management consultant in leadership development as the youngest member of the team who was also responsible for managing a team of people, some nearly twice my age.

This was the first time I understood that confidence is a learned skill that comes from practicing courage. Young people think that if they don't have confidence, that means they're not ready to step out into bigger things. But the reverse is true. You just need to practice courage. Courage means you feel the fear and move forward anyway. Courage is what develops confidence.

One of my favorite quotes I created to remember this is: "*Fear* knocked, *courage* answered, and no one was there. Then *success* showed up and *confidence* arrived."

It must happen in that order.

As I was at the Pentagon seeing the incredible successes and impacts of our cutting-edge leadership programs for executives, I kept thinking back to that awkward girl that I was in high school and wondered what would happen if I brought the same type of evidence-based, world-class leadership development programming I was doing at the Pentagon and brought it to young people, especially young women, who were struggling just like I was in high school? Sparked by this vision, I knew that my life's purpose was to help develop young leaders to know their inherent strength and worth. I knew I could do this by serving as a youth leadership speaker and consultant who specializes in bringing the same world-class leadership development best-practices and coaching normally reserved for adults to help girls and youth. After a lot of self-doubt, worry, and fear about making such a radical career change, I finally left my job at the Pentagon to start my own company doing best-practice leadership development for youth and young women—it was one of the happiest days of my life! I knew I was living my purpose.

Purpose is not a profession. You don't need a singular driving career statement. A profession can be an expression of your purpose, but your core purpose is much broader and deeper than your job. So, when I say my purpose was to help develop young leaders to know their strength and inherent worth, that takes many different and evolving forms from speaking to large audiences to talking to a young person in the checkout line at the grocery store. Showing up as my best self in the service of something greater than myself is a powerful way to overcome those obstacles, including internalized lack of confidence.

The day I resigned from the Pentagon—leaving a secure, high-paying job to launch my new venture—I was also terrified. I quickly went through my life savings. My lowest point was looking in my couch cushions for loose change to take the Metro train in DC to meet a potential client. But I embraced the mess, reached out and asked peers for help, learned the new skills of how to be an entrepreneur and run my own company, and—little by little—started getting calls and speaking at larger conferences. (Even though it wasn't about the money, by the next year, I was amazed at how the hard work paid off—and I made more than my salary at the Pentagon.)

I think you get the point: there will always be messy middles in your achievement journey—both between and within the jobs you do. Those messes can let you springboard into bigger things if you don't give up. Embracing the mess is about mindset. It doesn't always work that way in the short term, but they add up in the long term, as they did for me.

That's what I would say to my twenty-something self today: how you show up every day is practicing how you want to show up in the future. You can't just expect to switch your whole mindset when you check a box. Embrace the mess, the success, and that courageous, amazing person you are building along the way!

Julie Carrier (topspeakerforgirls.com) is a trusted authority on leadership development and confidence for girls and young women everywhere and is leading a movement to empower those who empower girls and empower girls to empower each other. She is the founder of the Leadership Development Institute for Young Women, an award-winning speaker, a consultant for leading girls' schools, colleges, and organizations, and the bestselling author of Girls Lead. *She received the 2023 Ideas into Practice Award from Thinkers50 for her trailblazing work bringing evidence-based leader development and coaching to develop young leaders in high school.*

A FAILURE OF IMAGINATION CAN HOLD YOU BACK

What I love most about Asheesh's and Julie's stories is how they show you the power of pushing yourself past your self-imposed beliefs and limitations in order to make your goals bigger and create the future you want. Unfortunately, too many of us fail to practice this lesson and suffer from a failure of imagination.

I know a coach whose first task for his clients is to have them draw up a list of their goals and dreams. "I told them to 'shoot for the moon!' and 'dream big!'" he told me. "Way too often I got answers like 'renovate a bathroom' or 'buy an extra car.' I told them that these are nice wishes to have, but they're not real dreams or goals. They're not life-changing."

This coach must work hard to coax his high-achieving clients into believing that they are capable of much more than they currently believe. He gives them *permission* to use their imagination so that they can challenge themselves to create something big rather than something ordinary.

I get why that coach's clients struggle. On the one hand, choosing between two or three valid ideas for the life you want to lead can be a legitimate source of confusion. On the other hand, some people cannot imagine even one path for themselves, let alone two or three.

I used to think this lack of imagination was a lack of creativity, which I defined as taking two slightly dissimilar ideas and merging them into something original, such as serving lobster with steak and calling it surf 'n' turf. You add A and B, and you come up with C. Then a successful artist told me

I was setting the bar too low. Creativity is more like taking A and F *and* L and coming up with Z. The greater the distance between the parts, the greater the imagination required to make them whole.

Only a precious few of us are A-plus-F-plus-L-equals-Z creative. Some of us are A-plus-B-equals-C creative. But, sadly, some of us can't even imagine a world where A and B are in the same room. You need to be curious to be creative. Curiosity is how we fire up our imagination and picture something new from the messiness around us.

For most of us, the first opportunity we have or had to imagine a fresh start and seek an identity reboot—a new presentation of self that will improve your odds of earning your place in the world—is or was when we applied to college. As Pulitzer Prize–winning novelist Richard Russo (*Empire Falls*) wrote, "College, after all, is where we go to reinvent ourselves, to sever our ties with the past, to become the person we always wanted to be and were prevented from being by people who knew better."

In fact, I'd venture to say that when we applied and chose where to go to college, it was the first time many of us felt we exercised some control over our futures. Sure, the process may have been rigidly shaped by our families and possibly a cartel of guidance counselors, testing companies, and college admissions officers, but we were nonetheless running the show. Once we got our decisions, we weighed the options, even if they were limited.

Every part of that college application story added up to a big lesson in embracing the mess: What do you *make* of it? How did you imagine your future? Did you try on new identities?

Pursue new opportunities? Think big about what you wanted and where you were going?

Or did you do the equivalent of renovating a bathroom?

As Russo suggests, you could accurately measure the success or failure of your college years by how recognizable you were at graduation when compared to the person who entered the scene four years earlier. Embracing the mess is your chance to see any choice as an opportunity to write a new script.

And if you haven't done that yet, now is the time to start.

As life goes on, many people let go of that expansive sense of possibility. They rein in their imaginations because they believe their paths are set, or they have accumulated obligations that force them to take certain actions. They lose the imaginative freedom of dreaming big. This doesn't have to happen. You can course-correct or change course. You can live bigger and be more fulfilled. But you must become aware of what matters to *you*.

Every day, every second, the world is open to you, because you always change. When you become aware of this, you will think bigger and take advantage of this knowledge that life is messy. Nothing stays the same—and this is a good thing.

16. THINK "AND," NOT "OR"

17. DON'T LET FEEDBACK GET IN THE WAY OF YOUR SUCCESS

18. LEARN TO BALANCE SIMPLICITY AND COMPLEXITY

19. LEAVE THEM WANTING MORE

20. MAKE OTHER PEOPLE'S GOALS YOUR OWN

CAREER

16.

THINK "AND," NOT "OR"

Often, life forces us to choose between two or more things: this *or* that. (Lesson twelve will help you make those choices when a decision must be made.) Yet too often, we turn things into binary choices that aren't choices at all. In a world that empowers us to write our achievement stories in color, we choose black and white—to be inflexible.

I have been susceptible to this limiting mindset.

Do I prioritize family or work? Do I want to make money or have a social impact? Those are questions I often asked myself in my early career, placing two things in opposition to each other by thinking they must be mutually exclusive. I learned to change my "ors" to "ands": *How do I balance my relationships and excel at work? How do I make money and have a social impact?* Rephrasing the questions in my mind to avoid binary choices helped me to stimulate more creativity and more freedom. Those "ands" empowered me and opened me up to new opportunities.

At CircleLending, I was passionate about creating a new global product category to provide affordable access to credit and bring informal credit transactions to the mainstream credit markets. We were pioneers in person-to-person loans. However, at the same time, I served as the founding board chair and helped launch Credit Builders Alliance, a nonprofit organization that convinced credit bureaus to accept data from nontraditional lenders such as nonprofit microloan organizations. This nascent nonprofit helped pioneer the powerful idea that your credit score is an "asset," just like your home, car, or college education. Doing both at the same time allowed me to connect the missions of the two organizations, including how we could convince the credit reporting industry to accept data on person-to-person loans and format the loan data in a way that was easily transmitted.

All that work took months of effort for both teams, but the impact went much deeper for me in defining what I wanted for my career: I wanted to have creative impact and help and mentor others around me to use their creativity. I wanted to share my own ideas and get the best ideas from those who worked with me. I wanted to be a good leader and nurture others to become great leaders. I wanted to build a nonprofit and a for-profit business. I wanted to make money and have a social impact.

That last "want" is something many of my students ask in an entrepreneurship course that I teach at the Fletcher School at Tufts University. Fletcher attracts bright and ambitious students who have double-bottom-line motivations, and they wrestle with how to make money and have a social impact. I advise them that the words we use are the choices we make before we make choices. Look for your "ands"!

Too often, we take the "or" approach. We limit ourselves by saying we could not possibly be happy or feel virtuous working for or with Big Company X or Industry Y or Person Z, by virtue of who they are and what they do. That having a financial *and* a moral compass at the same time is impossible. We miss the "and" opportunity because of assumptions around us—false assumptions that financial success is incompatible with doing good and being good instead of asking, *Why should we be good?* and, *How should we be good?*

These are the questions Gurcharan Das confronts in his book *The Difficulty of Being Good: On the Subtle Art of Dharma.* Das is the former head of Procter & Gamble India. He writes that he has entered what Hinduism calls the *sannyasa* phase of life—when a person is free to devote themselves entirely to spiritual growth. Das devotes himself to understanding how we can see the possibilities for good when we are young and how we can find a more fulfilling process of achievement—even when we believe the moral and ethical failings of people and companies have destroyed lives and brought the world closer to collapse. To answer those questions, Das turns to dharma, one of the core Hindu principles for living.

According to dharma, our thoughts and actions determine our lives: act righteously and morally and you will live virtuously. My parents taught me this from a young age. Dharma is not a test of virtue, like memorizing a list of vocabulary for an exam the next day. Das notes there are dharma *sankats*, or ethical and moral predicaments and dilemmas we will face. Sometimes, he argues, one doesn't know right from wrong. Of course, there are times one does know and still does the wrong thing. But then there are times when one thinks they know the path and limits themselves from having an even bigger impact with our actions. For example, say you want to promote sustainable energy for your career. Would you rather work for a giant "brown" energy company that makes most of its money from fossil fuels but is undergoing a slow transformation to add green energy businesses, or a smaller entrepreneurial company that focuses on solar energy. That "or" sets up a false choice, as if the two embody opposite truths. The pillars of dharma complicate the question: What if your work at the brown company could affect gradual change that made it greener and had a bigger impact over time on sustainable energy than the smaller company ever could?

Think back to Sanyin Siang in lesson eleven about the power of reframing. She immigrated to the United States when she was seven years old and came from a culture in which for something to be valuable, it had to be hard. There was no "and" in her achievement story. It was only a lost scholarship that forced her to reframe and connect her achievement dots in ways she never imagined that ultimately allowed her to use her "soft" skills to connect people and ideas and build a fulfilling career.

In a world where everything allows you to think "and"—from double majors in college to side hustles to portfolio careers—don't limit yourself. Take the meeting. Consider the offer. Listen to everything others have to say—even if it hurts.

In the end, the words that inform our choices can open us up or shut us down. Remembering you have choices and seeing different paths allow you to have the flexibility to see that achievement is not fixed, flexible, or freestyle but fixed, flexible, *and* freestyle. When work and life are so fully integrated in our lives, we must think abundantly about our choices and the impact we can have. You might say an opportunity "goes against my purpose." Maybe. Or is that thinking just a rationalization for not exploring possibilities and opportunities and reframing them into something bigger?

COACH'S CORNER
AMII BARNARD-BAHN
"GET GOOD AT DELIVERING AND LISTENING TO BAD NEWS"

I have more than twenty years' experience working with c-suite executives, and serving as one, in Fortune 50 companies, and when it comes to delivering bad news, I have come to this conclusion: most of us are allergic to it. We don't even like discussing how to deliver it.

IN THE END, THE WORDS
THAT INFORM OUR CHOICES
CAN OPEN US UP OR SHUT
US DOWN. REMEMBERING
YOU HAVE CHOICES AND
SEEING DIFFERENT PATHS
ALLOW YOU TO HAVE
THE FLEXIBILITY TO SEE
THAT ACHIEVEMENT IS
NOT FIXED, FLEXIBLE, OR
FREESTYLE BUT FIXED,
FLEXIBLE, *AND* FREESTYLE.

So how do you get good at delivering bad news? That's a skill Asheesh knows rarely gets taught in entrepreneurship programs or business schools, which is why I was excited when he invited me to speak to his students at Fletcher. Positive people, especially entrepreneurs, want to look on the bright side of things and not talk about what's wrong. But avoiding bad news turns small problems into big ones.

AMII BARNARD-BAHN

Delivering bad news is also not the time for reframing it as good news. I've been a chief human resources officer, chief compliance officer, attorney, and creator of compliance and investigation systems at global Fortune 50 companies. I've had to cut severance benefits prior to announcing mass layoffs around the December holidays. Reframing bad news like that as good news only makes things worse, costing you credibility.

So here are two more "ands" for your achievement journey: there is good news *and* bad news; you need to learn how to deliver the latter *and* listen to it. That's much harder than it sounds.

Behavioral science tells us that bad news messengers are not only viewed as unlikeable and less competent but are perceived unfairly as having ill intent. In fact, these messengers get subconsciously viewed as *enjoying* when bad things happen. Auditors, investigators, HR professionals, lawyers, and others are hired to put the brakes on an idea, evaluate best practices, and point out risks. Yet they are often distrusted, frozen, and vilified simply for doing their jobs. Crazy.

Set an example for them by speaking up yourself and creating a "speak up" culture. And when it is time for you to speak up, follow these six steps for delivering bad news:

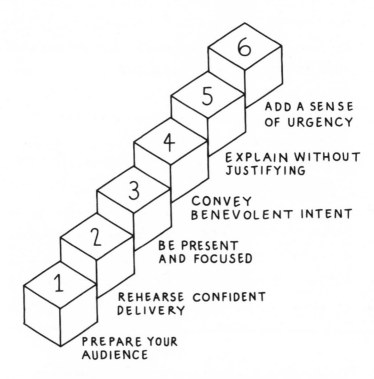

ADD A SENSE
OF URGENCY

EXPLAIN WITHOUT
JUSTIFYING

CONVEY
BENEVOLENT INTENT

BE PRESENT
AND FOCUSED

REHEARSE CONFIDENT
DELIVERY

PREPARE YOUR
AUDIENCE

6 STEPS TO DELIVERING BAD NEWS

1. *Psychologically prepare your audience*: Give a heads up! Prepare your audience for what's to come with a, "Hey, I wish I had better news." This reduces potential stress and distress as you speak and reduces resistance to the information you share.

2. *Rehearse confident delivery:* Be your best self and be pre-pared. Write down your key talking points in advance and review them before you speak. Practice increases credibility and reduces your stress level. Get in front of the mirror, listen to how you sound, and watch your body language.

3. *Be fully present and fully focused:* Talk to people directly in real time and respond immediately to emotional and social cues with empathy. Don't hide behind an email. Face-to-face is best, followed by video conference and phone. Then, circle the wagons. Check back in about what you shared and see if any relationships need repairing (especially if you/your team were the source of the bad news).

4. *Convey benevolent, proactive intent:* Counteract the bias we have against bad news messengers having malicious intent by sharing your good intentions, reinforcing your commit-ment to the person and/or organization, supporting them, and mitigating any impact to them while communicating necessary next steps.

5. *Explain without justifying:* Be direct and avoid excuses. Resist that urge to reframe bad news as a net positive. State plainly and clearly the facts and what happened and avoid blaming others. Do this well, and people will respect you, find you fair and reasonable, and view you (eventually at least) as a trusted advisor.

6. *Add a sense of urgency:* Frame it up: here are things that worked, here's what did not, and here's what we are doing about it. Give them a reason to act now and understand why.

Amii Barnard-Bahn (barnardbahn.com) is an attorney, executive coach, and consultant who specializes in helping leaders and organizations do the right thing. Working with c-suite executives, and serving as one, in Fortune 50 companies, she has more than twenty years' strategic experience in legal, compliance, and HR developing sustainable business models and healthy workplace culture. Her book, The PI Guidebook: How the Promotability Index® Can Help You Get Ahead in Your Career, *demystifies how to get promoted to the c-suite and beyond and what's needed to achieve career goals and personal satisfaction.*

FROM MARSHALL
YOUR PURPOSE IS DRIVEN BY "AND" NOT "OR"

In your career, you will have many different jobs. Within those jobs, you might need to fill the role of several different people every day. That doesn't make you a phony; that's being a professional.

Consider Telly Leung, whom I profiled in *The Earned Life*. For almost two years, Telly played the title role in *Aladdin* on Broadway. Every night, he took the stage and fell in love with the princess. Telly is gay. That princess was not whom he was going to fall in love with offstage. But you'd never know it from his performance. How did he do it? He told me that when he was eight, he went to a Broadway play and loved it. Every night, he thinks of that little boy and what that show meant to him. He's a professional! He needed to be who he needed to be for thousands of kids like him and their families in the audience. That was his purpose as an actor.

Acting is Telly's purpose, not the characters he plays. What matters in life is that you have a purpose and that your achievement is connected to that purpose—that you're doing something that you think is meaningful and love the process of what you're doing. Note the "ands" in that sentence. But also note two other words: "think" and "process." As Asheesh noted, the more openminded you are about the process followed to pursue your purpose, the bigger the possibilities are for your achievement story.

"And," to me, is about curiosity. Don't cut yourself off from what might be simply because you *think* it isn't true to who you are and won't be meaningful. You don't know exactly what you're going to love or where you will have the most impact. The start of your career is when you can write your story in different ways. Rejecting people, places, or jobs without pursuing them is self-limiting. Get offers and ask yourself three questions: Am I going to be doing something in which I can achieve more? Is it meaningful for me? Am I going to love doing it? The best answer is "yes." But there is power in "I don't know" too. Choosing that path shows curiosity. You might discover you are where you need to be, or you might find a path to your purpose that is new and different. You might find happiness, a better life, and more impact somewhere you never thought of or imagined.

17.

DON'T LET FEEDBACK GET IN THE WAY OF YOUR SUCCESS

Nothing challenges optimistic people quite like negative feedback. I will never forget the day a colleague of mine at Monitor, the consulting company where we worked, gave me negative feedback about a slide I made for a client presentation. He ripped into me, giving me a "three out of five" and saying my work "wasn't great." I was hurt and argued back to no avail. The rest of the day, instead of asking, *What am I not understanding?* and using the feedback to get better, I kept saying, *Who the hell does he think he is?* Worst of all, I started questioning whether he was right and whether I was good at anything I was doing. His words shook even my relentless optimism and made me think like a pessimist: Was there something permanently wrong with me? It didn't matter that no one else said anything negative. Only as I began to calm down did I wonder if maybe this guy knew something I did not—if maybe I should at least consider what he was saying. But mostly, his feedback and the way I took it damaged our relationship and slid me into self-doubt.

I grew up hearing the advice, "Listen to feedback; it will make you better." The reality is that very few people get better or change because of feedback received at work. OK, maybe I changed one thing right away and then a little more as I developed in my career. But the truth is that most feedback tends to be negative or critical, unsolicited, and ineffective, which is why most of us hate receiving it.

But feedback doesn't have to be this way. Think back to lesson four ("Write it down") and the way my family uses a framework called stop, start, and continue to approach the process of behavior change. There's a structure and a process and an open invitation to provide the feedback we give each other so it can be useful in helping us determine what we want to stop, start, and continue in the year ahead.

The solution is not to ignore feedback but to learn to invite it, listen to it, and use it to your advantage in the future. There is power in opening yourself to hearing something different or listening even to the people you dislike—all of which can lead to new possibilities or help you understand your own choices. Use the reframing skills you developed in lesson twelve to help you not only receive and process feedback but give feedback the right way, as an achievement accelerant.

Easier said than done. Unfortunately, there are no classes in high school, college, or graduate school on feedback—how to receive it or how to give it—which is why it is only in hindsight that I understand the important things I did wrong when my Monitor colleague gave me his feedback: I treated what he said as fact rather than opinion and did not say thank you.

Remembering feedback is opinion—not fact—is something Bill Carrier, who is the executive director of Marshall Goldsmith's 100 Coaches group and a highly regarded executive coach, drills into the senior executives and high-potential leaders he coaches. "The comments and feedback that I gather from others to share with leaders are opinions about a specific subject at specific moment in time, not facts," Bill says. ""Opinions cannot be true or false. Positive or negative, they are assessments and judgments. Often opinions from different people—and sometimes the same individual-- can be in opposition to one another. Some opinions may be irrelevant or occasionally incomprehensible--and some will be desperately important clues to the things you want to do in life. If you are not careful, some may make you feel like Asheesh did at Monitor. Your job is to take feedback and use it as a springboard into a conversation with yourself to learn more about the things that serve you in life."

That springboard is what saying "thank you" is all about. Marshall Goldsmith asks us to see all feedback as a gift, and what do you say when you receive any gift? *Thank you.* Saying "thank you" immediately shows gratitude when the gift of feedback is positive and lowers the volume in your head when it is negative by reframing the feedback as something useful. Marshall's whole feedback philosophy, as you see in his comment that follows, is feed*forward*—to focus feedback on the future as the giver or receiver: What do I want to get done in the next six months or year, and how can feedback from others help me? What do others want to get done in the next six months or year, and how can my feedback help them?

Whether the gift you received is an insight that helps you understand how to be better or a warning that you can take to heart—like to stay away from that person who uses his judgment of a slide to eviscerate you—use it to achieve. If I had just said "thank you" to the person at Monitor instead of arguing back and letting his feedback get to me, I—and my colleague—likely would have had a different, more productive interaction. Saying "thank you" would have also improved our relationship rather than harmed it.

The more you learn to reframe feedback when you are young, the better you will get at giving and receiving it effectively as you take on greater leadership responsibility.

THE MORE YOU LEARN TO REFRAME FEEDBACK WHEN YOU ARE YOUNG, THE BETTER YOU WILL GET AT GIVING AND RECEIVING IT EFFECTIVELY AS YOU TAKE ON GREATER LEADERSHIP RESPONSIBILITY.

You know you are not, and never will be, perfect. Asking for and receiving feedback by using the tools this lesson gives you shows you know you can always be better, helps you see what you might be missing, empowers the people who work with and for you to help make you better, and opens them up to hearing what you have to say.

Imagine if someone came up to you after a presentation and said, "Thank you for what you said today. This is so important for me to hear." Then they said, "But you know, this part did not work for me. I'm not sure why, but I didn't understand it." How would you receive that? Would you open yourself up with a "thank you" or shut down?

The best coaches I know live for those moments of feedback. In fact, this situation happened to me at Junior Achievement Worldwide with the young person we put in charge of growing our alumni community, Sarah Rapp, and helped me understand just how far I have come in my feedback journey.

Her manager, Erin Sawyer, and I had set some very ambitious targets for Sarah, one of which was to build a database of young JA alumni into a community that could rival those from established online alumni communities from places like Harvard, Oxford, and Stanford. Sarah was delighted with the challenge. But as she started the work, she questioned our approach. She believed we had things backward. When I asked her to explain what she meant, she gave me feedback about our approach to engagement: if we wanted to engage young people at scale, we should launch local alumni associations that meet in person to drive the network's database, not build the database in isolation. She understood that most of our young alums, like her, didn't want to join yet one more online community without the benefit of in-person gatherings.

After some encouragement from Erin to listen to Sarah's concerns and accept the feedback, I chose to support a revised strategy with new goals for alumni association engagement rather than just database growth, and the results they delivered were phenomenal: more than eighty JA alumni associations in regions, countries, and cities all over the world holding in-person events with regional JA alumni champions and growing the alumni database and online community to exceed the size of most universities in less than three years. It's your choice too: let feedback get in the way of your success or use feedback to drive you forward.

COACH'S CORNER
BILL CARRIER
"GIVING THE GIFT OF FEEDBACK"

I'm six feet three inches tall today and have always been tall for my age. When I was nine, I went trick or treating, and at every single house I heard, "Aren't you a little old for this, kid?"

Later, in middle school, I tried to play basketball, and expectations about my height got in the way again. I was terrible—and everybody told me so. *You're so tall, but you're terrible at this. You should be good, but you're terrible.* I thought they were right, and because I thought that, I never got better. Because I hated having my peers and coaches tell me how bad I was, I never even tried to play on a team again. *Believing* I was bad was my self-limiting factor.

My negative feedback journey peaked at West Point. Cadets get constant feedback from officers and other cadets, lots of it highly critical and negative. Those who called me names like "maggot" didn't make me want to follow them and improve. But the cadets and officers who said some version of, "Carrier, you're going to do something really important in the future, so I'm going to be really hard on you right now" made me want to do whatever they asked me to do and more. They were the coaches who helped me start my career as an officer and the direct supervisor of a combat arms team in high-stress training environments.

These stories are foundational to how I offer feedback today to the people I coach and others who ask for my help. I want the feedback I give to be useful and to help others uncover the life they want to live and understand how to be the best person they can be. Effective feedback does not mean beat them down, show how much I know, or prove I am better than them. Most of us understand this and want our feedback to be useful, but because we don't learn

BILL CARRIER

better ways to give and receive feedback, we accidentally resort to judging like Asheesh's colleague did at Monitor or wind up feeling resentful. Because his colleague was inconsiderately critical and because Asheesh was upset, the interaction they had was much more about the emotions that were triggered instead of the content of the feedback. Their relationship deteriorated, and the presentation didn't get any better. That's a feedback failure any way you measure it.

Asheesh's colleague could have disarmed Asheesh's defensiveness by doing what my best coaches in the Army did and what I strive to do today: be clear with your intent. When you give feedback, make sure you offer up that you value the person and the future they're creating, and that's why you're offering the feedback directly. And when you're done, ask if they understood what you said. Most importantly, ask questions rather than make recommendations and give advice. Be curious! Imagine if Asheesh's colleague had asked a question that expressed genuine curiosity as to why he presented the slide the way he did.

Start the question process by asking the person if they are even open to feedback before you give it—and to ask for feedback before someone gives it to you. For example, if today-Bill could go back to nine-year-old Bill and talk to him, I'd empathize with him first. Then I might say something like, "Because this seems important to you and we might learn something that can help you with basketball, would you like for me to ask you some questions?" If younger Bill agreed, I'd continue with "Why is your height so important? I wonder, do you think maybe they have some fear about your height and that maybe you would get better at this than they are? Because they've all been playing for much longer than you, what would happen if you gave yourself some time to practice and get better?"

Those are versions of questions I might ask one of my leaders I coach—questions designed to offer ideas that they can explore and then choose to pick up on. I then give them a lot of space to decide if it is something that they want to do. Because that's an important truth about any feedback: you can deliver it, but you don't have the power to make someone act on it.

Bill Carrier (linkedin.com/in/billcarrier) is the president of Carrier Leadership Coaching Inc., which specializes in coaching senior executives and senior teams in leadership, executive presence, and organizational impact. He is the executive director of the Marshall Goldsmith 100 Coaches community, an association of the world's top leadership professionals. An executive coach and thought partner to CEOs and senior leaders, Bill leverages best-practice from neuro-science, ontology, movement psychology/somatics, and West Point leadership development.

FROM MARSHALL
TRY FEEDFORWARD
INSTEAD OF FEEDBACK

Providing feedback has long been considered an essential skill for leaders. Yet most of us hate getting negative feedback, and we don't like giving it either. In addition to feedback's association with criticism and hurt feelings, it focuses on the past—*back* on what has already occurred, not *forward* to opportunities in the future. We can change the future and not the past, so feedback is often limited and static, as opposed to expansive and dynamic.

Why not build on the advice in this lesson and focus on what's next by turning feedback into feedforward? Feedforward can cover almost all the same "material" as feedback. Better yet, people tend to listen more attentively to feedforward than feedback, as it focuses on what is possible.

Consider the following exercise in which I ask a group of leaders to play two roles. In the first, they are asked to provide feedforward: give someone else suggestions for the future and help as much as they can. In the second, they are asked to accept feedforward: listen to the suggestions for the future and learn as much as they can. (The entire process of both giving and receiving feedforward usually takes about two minutes. The entire exercise typically lasts for ten to fifteen minutes, and the average participant has six or seven dialogue sessions.)

1. Pick one behavior you would like to change. (Change in this behavior should make a significant, positive difference in your life.)
2. Describe this behavior to other participants. (This is done in one-on-one dialogues. It can be done quite simply, such as, "I want to be a better listener.")
3. Ask for feedforward: Two suggestions for the future that might help you achieve a positive change in your selected behavior. (If you have worked with someone in the past, they are not allowed to give ANY feedback about the past, only ideas for the future.)

4. Listen attentively to the suggestions and take notes. (You are not allowed to comment on the suggestions, critique them, or even make positive statements, such as, "That's a good idea.")
5. Thank others for their suggestions.
6. Ask them what they would like to change.
7. Provide feedforward to them.
8. Say, "You're welcome" when thanked for the suggestions.

I have observed more than thirty thousand leaders participate in this exercise. When it is finished, I ask them to provide one word that best completes this sentence: "This exercise was _____." The words provided are almost always extremely positive, like "energizing," "useful," and "helpful." One of the most common words is maybe the last word that comes to mind when we consider any feedback activity: "fun." Yes, fun.

Feedforward does not mean that we should never give feedback or that performance appraisals should be abandoned. The intent is to show how feedforward is often preferable to feedback in day-to-day interactions. Effective and efficient communication between and among achievers at all levels is the glue that holds organizations together. A culture of feedforward can dramatically improve the quality of communication in any organization, ensuring that the right messages are conveyed and that those who receive them are receptive to their content. Sounds like fun.

18.

LEARN TO BALANCE SIMPLICITY AND COMPLEXITY

S oon after I finished my graduate work and started my job at the World Bank, my boss asked me to write a paper on industrial clusters that would be published and distributed. Industrial clusters are regions like Silicon Valley, an interconnected group of companies, vendors, and other institutions "clustered" together, attracting people to the region and generating wealth and economic growth, not to mention efficiency and global competitiveness. The World Bank wanted to understand how it could support the growth of industrial clusters in places like India and Nigeria to promote economic growth and reduce poverty. My paper was intended to contribute to that understanding.

I felt the pressure to deliver. Every part of my paper needed to be up to World Bank standards and demonstrate strong economic reasoning. My Oxford courses and doctoral degree had prepared me for that. I was less prepared, though, to make my research, analysis, and any ideas simple enough for an audience not well-versed in development economics to understand how these clusters might address poverty.

Note that I did not say *solve* poverty. There are many principles for using simplicity in complex problem solving, like Keep It Simple Stupid (KISS) or Occam's Razor (choose the hypothesis with the fewest assumptions and cut out improbable options). This lesson is about *understanding*, not solving.

KISS may be good advice for solving some problems and making some decisions, but it's bad advice for the process of modern achievement and the complex problems we face. As I said at the start of this book, our biggest and most stubborn social and economic problems stretch across global boundaries and evolve even as we confront them. Climate change, economic inequality, racial injustice, cybercrime, world hunger . . . there are no simple or singular (that is, fixed) solutions to these problems. We must embrace their complexity. That said, complexity can often be a barrier to understanding. Balance means being flexible enough to embrace complexity and present it simply enough to engage your audience and get their buy-in.

To be clear, the simplicity side of the equation does not mean "dumb down." Balancing simplicity and complexity means finding a way to present problems and ideas as simply as possible, which requires both thoughtfulness and effort. Remember, the goal of this process is not to come up with a solution but to generate understanding that allows you and others to iterate your way to success by embracing the process of creating and designing solutions together.

You don't have to be dealing with an intractable problem like poverty to understand the need to balance simplicity and complexity to create understanding. The Fixed-Flexible-Freestyle framework for this book and the one implemented at Junior Achievement are my attempts at balancing simplicity and complexity. In the case of JA, I was dealing with a global and challenging landscape both internally and externally. Rather than making multiple changes to our cumbersome and legalistic operating agreements, we needed a simple way to collaborate across locations and explain it to a global board and six regional boards. The framework allowed people and teams in different regions and countries with different needs to understand how we wanted to work with them and empowered them to design local solutions to

BALANCING SIMPLICITY AND COMPLEXITY MEANS FINDING A WAY TO PRESENT PROBLEMS AND IDEAS AS SIMPLY AS POSSIBLE, WHICH REQUIRES BOTH THOUGHTFULNESS AND EFFORT.

grow the organization. Similarly, I want *you* to find balance between the three dimensions of the framework as you approach the complex task of writing your achievement story. In both cases, the framework offers a shared language to own and find your path to success, both alone and with others.

In other words, by making Fixed-Flexible-Freestyle your own, you can use it to simplify complex issues for others and yourself and build the alignment around solutions and goals that is essential to modern success. (See lesson twenty.)

Or consider the case of CircleLending. When we launched the company, person-to-person lending was new. We iterated our way to success using the money from angel investors, and we built a prototype and website, then kept building better ones again and again to attract more customers and new investors. That iterative experience is essential to an entrepreneurial mindset, but those customers and investors would never have signed up if we showed them how the proverbial sausage gets made. We had to do a lot of complex work with everything from data to contracts. We had to convince the credit bureaus to accept data on our loans, as they do for bank loans, so that on-time or late payments had positive or negative effects on credit scores. No one had done that before, but it added more value and consequences to the transactions. We had to develop protocols for intrafamily mortgages and intrafamily reverse mortgages, which allowed relatives to transfer real estate to each other. We had to work with real estate authorities in each state to record the transactions legally. Meanwhile, we had our own internal discussion about taking a rules-based approach to our loans or an adjustment-based approach to meet the needs of everyone. And . . . you get the point.

Although the work to set up CircleLending was nuanced and detailed, none of the complexity was important to most of our customers, investors, board members, and potential employees. We needed to engage them on the idea and help them understand it and its potential. We needed to have the judgment to know when to broadcast the simplicity and when to add in the complexity based on the audience and circumstance.

You might be confronting an organizational issue; creating a new business model, product, or service; building a team culture; or trying to get an investor, boss, or potential employer to buy in to what you offer. Those are often complicated things to do. Finding the balance between simplicity and complexity draws people to you and allows you to achieve more for yourself and others, which is what the tools in Alex Osterwalder's Coach's Corner help you develop.

COACH'S CORNER
ALEX OSTERWALDER
"SIMPLE TOOLS FOR COMPLEX DISCUSSIONS"

What I am most passionate about and have been working on my whole career is simplifying complex challenges that today's leaders face and making tools like the Business Model Canvas that facilitate communication around complex issues.

After business school, I worked with Yves Pigneur, a computer scientist and professor of management information systems at the University of Lausanne in Switzerland, to create a computer-assisted design tool for businesspeople to generate business models like architects do for buildings. Architects can't talk about building without making drawings or prototypes. When you have that model, you can ask questions specifically around and about it: Why are we using space this way? We don't like that window there—why? Architects and design professionals are not the only ones who rely on prototypes and models. Asheesh built them in developing CircleLending. In medical school, doctors and students use physical and graphic tools to understand the physiology and anatomy of a human body. But when it came to the physiology and anatomy of business and entrepreneurship, it was very rare to have tools beyond napkin sketches to create a business model.

We don't really learn to make a business model tangible in business school. Sure, we *talk* about business models. But if I have a business I want to create and get others' buy-in, just explaining it with words is often inadequate. What if I have a diverse group of people from marketing, tech, and operations with different experience and perhaps global differences and language barriers. How can I represent what I am talking about? How can I help them understand and contribute to what is being discussed when they sit down together and align their understanding beyond verbal communication?

Working with my professor, I understood the need for tools in business and leadership to make intangible ideas tangible. Every organization faces complex challenges trying to create a business model. Same goes for things like its value proposition and organizational culture. These challenges need tools. So we worked to create the simplest, most tangible, understandable, and actionable tools we could. The first being the Business Model Canvas, followed by the Value Proposition Canvas and Culture Map. (You can download the Business Model Canvas at *strategyzer.com/library/the-business-model-canvas.*)

To illustrate what I mean by an artifact to make things

tangible here on a broader level, consider *ikigai* and an artifact someone created to help us articulate what we wanted at our company. *Ikigai* is Japanese for "reason for being," and we use it to align our professional and life goals. We want people in our company to be able to do what they love, what they are good at, and what the world needs—and we can pay them for it. Otherwise, they shouldn't be working at our company. Héctor Garcia and Francesc Miralles's book *Ikigai: The Japanese Secret to a Long and Happy Life* helped us understand *ikigai* in words but gave us a simple yet powerful tool for discussing a complicated process.

IKIGAI

Simply put, we have a lot of analytical tools for data, but we don't have thinking tools that allow us to ask the right questions. And if you can't ask the right questions about something, how are you going to work on it? Too many leaders give answers. They are prescriptive with rules and instructions, not descriptive to design potential solutions. You might realize many are wrong, but from that, you design one that is right. In innovation, ideas don't actually matter; iterating the idea until it works is what matters.

ALEX OSTERWALDER

Of course, we were not the first to create tools like the Business Model Canvas. But those that existed were too complicated to be useful. We created visual and intuitive tools and packaged them in ways that got people excited by balancing the simple and the complex. That is what I like about frameworks like Fixed-Flexible-Freestyle for achievement. They allow you to ask big questions of yourself and others, like the following: Why are things the way they are? Could we take a different approach? Could this organization be designed differently? Could *I* be designed differently? You need the right tools to ask the right questions to understand the contexts and iterate your success.

Alex Osterwalder (alexosterwalder.com) is a speaker, author of several books—including Business Model Generation—*and the cofounder of Strategyzer, which provides technology-enabled innovation services to companies like Colgate-Palmolive, MasterCard, and Merck. He invented the Business Model Canvas and other practical tools with Yves Pigneur, which are used by millions around the world.*

FROM MARSHALL

AREN'T I SMART, AND AREN'T THEY STUPID?

If I were to give you a productivity-enhancement tool that would help you align your goals with the goals of others, save time, cost you nothing, build self-awareness, *and* increase your efficiency in dealing with even the most complex problems, would you use it?

I've asked more than one hundred thousand high achievers and others I have worked with from around the world this question: What percent of all interpersonal communication time is spent on people talking about how smart they are, listening to someone else do that, and talking about how stupid others are, or listening to someone else do that?

The answer? Sixty-five percent! Two-thirds of our time is spent satisfying the need to advertise how smart we are, how dumb someone else is, and/or spending time listening to someone else do this. Now here's the kicker: we spend twice as much time talking about how stupid others are. Kind of makes you feel differently about when someone says, "keep it simple, stupid," huh?

I get it. Many of you are busy and under more pressure than you've felt in your whole lives. Asheesh's lesson about balancing simplicity and complexity is so important to achievement and iterating your way to success. But while finding that balance and iterating success can be fun, it is also hard, which is why so many people waste time talking themselves up and others down.

So here's the productivity enhancement: knock it off!

How much do you learn talking about how smart you are? Nothing. How much do you learn listening to somebody else do that? Zip! How much do you learn talking about how stupid others are or listening to someone else do that? Absolutely zero.

If you want to be a great leader, you'll have to watch what you say and observe how you act for the rest of your career. Start by doing this. Before you speak, breathe. Ask yourself, *Is my comment really going to improve anything, or am I just trying to prove I'm better and smarter and just love to hear the sound of my own voice?*

Next, stop pointing out why others are wrong and you are right—or even thinking in those terms! If you can stop yourself in these seemingly minor moments with someone who works closely with you and presumably knows you well—in other words, nothing is at stake, and you don't have to flex your "I'm smarter" muscles—you have the skill to stop telling the world how smart you are.

19.

LEAVE THEM WANTING MORE

launched CircleLending with one employee, $30,000 in seed capital from family and friends, and $350,000 from my first investors. In our first year, we had fifty clients and generated $2 million in loan volume—proof of concept, but we needed more funding to drive growth. In 2002, I raised a new round from angel investors. Followed by another. And another. For the next two years, I spent most of my time on company financing. I got used to being on the road and hearing "no" a lot. So much so that when I walk around New York City today, I frequently walk past office buildings that I got rejected in and can remember the emotions that I felt when visiting each office.

In the end, before venture capital firms provided institutional funding and before the Virgin Group reached out to me to acquire the company, I raised a total of just over $6 million from Fortune 500 bank CEOs and other high-profile individuals like Jeff Bezos at Amazon. But not one of those investments happened after only one meeting or only one phone call. In some cases, I was lucky if the partners or other decision makers who could say yes were even *in* the first meeting, which is why, whenever I made it inside, I lived by these words: the goal of a first meeting is to get a second meeting.

Whether you're pitching potential investors, clients, or partners on your business or potential employers on you, if the stakes are high enough, few if any will say yes to you after the first meeting—or even expect to. Many will come in looking for a reason to say no to you.

WHETHER YOU'RE PITCHING POTENTIAL INVESTORS, CLIENTS, OR PARTNERS ON YOUR BUSINESS OR POTENTIAL EMPLOYERS ON YOU, IF THE STAKES ARE HIGH ENOUGH, FEW IF ANY WILL SAY YES TO YOU AFTER THE FIRST MEETING—OR EVEN EXPECT TO.

You can present yourself well, be prepared to answer tough questions, show an understanding of yourself or what you have to offer, and overcome objections and concerns. All that still won't get you to "yes" . . . the first time.

What you need to do in that first meeting is make people want to talk to you again, and the best way to do that is to leave them wanting more. Notice I said *want to*, not *need to*. Whether it is a position that needs to be filled, a job that needs to be done, or money that needs to be invested, every meeting starts with a need. The need is a given. You don't get in the door unless they think you can fill that need and then *want* to take the next step with you more than with someone else.

Wanting is a feeling. You can fail to generate that feeling by being unprepared, not researching what the needs of the people you are pitching to are, or failing to read the room. But too often you fail to make people want you because you leave them wanting less. You try to do too much by showing how much you know, proving how smart you are, overpromising, and talking, talking, talking. You pack as much as you can into the time you have and leave no time to ask or answer questions—making it all about you, which leaves them wanting less.

Leaving them wanting more broadcasts confidence that you have much more to offer and talk about. For example, when I pitched CircleLending, peer-to-peer lending was new, and investors were still feeling the sting of the dotcom bubble. I knew I needed to show we could deliver on our promises when so many online startups had failed. As a result, I never showed a slide with milestones that were years down the road. Instead, I laid out our milestones, with the first one already checked off and the additional milestones just weeks away. The second one was done, too, but not checked. The third one I was 100 percent sure was going to happen. The remaining milestones were medium-term aspirations.

I did not leave that second box unchecked to be deceitful. I left it unchecked to generate anticipation and to assess when to hold the next meeting, before or after completing each of the subsequent milestones. Some investors needed more progress and wanted to wait until the third milestone, while others were ready to decide more quickly. I needed to communicate the things I was getting done when I followed up; help them get past any lingering doubts, fear, or concerns; and make them want to hear more. I wanted them to know I could deliver on my promises—*hey, this guy follows through*—and get that second meeting. (The goal of the second meeting was to get them to agree to a phone call with an existing investor, which would hopefully begin to close the deal.)

When you're pitching to people and making connections, don't try to show everything or think you need to. Shoot your best shot, but leave room for them to see themselves in you and to want to see what is next. Make them keep wanting more until they can't resist what you have to offer. Use the rest of the time to ask—and ask for—questions to learn what you don't know or need to do.

When dealing with people one-on-one, be sure to heed Marshall's advice and ask, *Do I need to say any more?* You can't leave someone wanting more if you shut them down or never give them room to speak! Keep something in reserve for your follow up to move the proverbial needle and ensure that second meeting.

MARK C. THOMPSON
"BE INTERESTED"

The contexts of Asheesh's lesson and Marshall's comment are different, but they are connected. Marshall talks about bosses shutting down people who come to them with great ideas. These leaders are so anxious to prove what they know and add value to those ideas that, even with the best of intentions, they suck the air out of the room, leaving none for the people who came in with the ideas. Asheesh echoes the need to demonstrate deeply that you are listening to people, in his case the ones you are pitching to. Make those people you want the second meeting with the subject of your focus so they feel understood and heard—and want more of *you*.

At the core of Asheesh's and Marshall's words is a principle I call the Virgin Effect: the only way to be interesting is to be interested. That's a big way to leave them wanting more: *be interested*.

The principle is named for Richard Branson, the British business magnate and founder of the Virgin Group. I have built entre-

MARK THOMPSON

preneurship centers with Richard for years and consider him a mentor. I have seen him in every meeting show everyone in the room he is interested in them by taking notes in his leather notebook. You don't carry something as substantial and permanent as that notebook, let alone listen that intently to take substantial notes, if you're feigning interest in someone and just want to make it all about you.

You don't need to have a world-famous billionaire in the room to know how it makes you feel when *anyone* shows interest in what you have to say and makes you feel heard and understood. Being understood is high among things that make us feel great. That's why it's one of Stephen Covey's legendary *7 Habits of Highly Effective People*: seek to understand before seeking to be understood.

You also don't need to wait until you're a leader to work on being interested to achieve better and more. I don't see a long line of people waiting to be interested in others in a substantive, contextual, and genuine way. If you can be interested in others like that when you're a "nobody"—actively listening to what your teammates, bosses, and clients say—you've demonstrated a belief in them that they can feel. They'll never get that feeling from you if you're just ass-kissing your way to the top. But being interested on this level goes way beyond just showing up and taking notes. You need to prepare to be interested—do your research and homework and learn about whom you are listening to and what they care about.

You can turn your curiosity into interest by using what you learned to ask good questions. People love talking about themselves. They don't want to see you a second time if they don't like you, and they'll like you because you heard them deeply in seeking to understand.

The additional benefit of being interested in others is you don't have to try so hard to be interesting yourself. And let's face it, talking about you is probably not that interesting when you're starting out. So how do you get started? Don't wait to be asked. Prepare to be interested.

I ended up being recruited by Charles "Chuck" Schwab at Stanford when Schwab was a fintech disruptor. I came across him when the company set up at a counter at school. Chuck was trying to disrupt Wall Street, and what he said clicked for me. He had a moral objection to brokers. He wanted to replace commissions with fees. Chuck wanted to hire people with a passion for investing, not pedigree, and I fit the bill. I didn't come from money. I struggled in school and almost got kicked out of Stanford twice because a disability left me unable to read until I was a teenager, and I couldn't complete the English requirements. But I was also well informed about how stocks and brokerages worked. I never had any money, so money was interesting to me, and I learned about it in my own scrappy way. I showed my interest (and excitement) by asking questions about what Schwab was doing and how and why. Chuck saw this and said, "Kid, you love to invest? Why don't you jump on the other side of the counter and get started?"

I was able to jump over that counter because I was already interested. If you get an opportunity to be interested, will you be ready?

After serving as the CEO for Schwab.com, Esurance, Rioport, and Interwoven, Mark C. Thompson (markcthompson.com) became a leadership coach for the world's fastest-growing, most innovative companies. He was a cofounder of the Stanford University Real-time Venture Design Lab, along with Sir Richard Branson's Entrepreneurship Centres and the JFK Institute for Entrepreneurial Leadership. His New York Times *bestselling books include*

Admired: 21 Ways to Double Your Value *and* Success Built to Last: Creating a Life That Matters. *In 2023, he was named a Coaching Legend by Thinkers50 and inducted into the Coaching Hall of Fame.*

FROM MARSHALL

DON'T LEAVE THEM WANTING LESS

Did you ever try to prove you were right in a conversation with someone you love and then get angry before realizing it was all trivial, meaningless, and not worth the energy? Too often our urge to win trumps common sense, and we keep piling on evidence and arguments. The goal shifts from informing to convincing to conquering.

Consider this scenario: Imagine you want to go out to dinner with your spouse, partner, or friend. You want to go to restaurant X. They want to go to Y. You have a heated debate about the choice. You point out the bad reviews Y has received, but you yield and end up going there anyway. Experience confirms your misgivings. You wait thirty minutes past your reservation for a table. The service is slow, the drinks weak, and the food tastes like ripe garbage. You have two options as this painful experience unfolds: critique the restaurant, point out to your partner how wrong they were, and state how this all could have been avoided if only you had been listened to; or you can shut up—write it off and enjoy the evening.

I have polled my clients for years on this scenario. All of them agree they *should* shut up and have a good time. But 75 percent say they would critique the restaurant. Even when they know what they should do, they do the wrong thing and try to win by proving how right they were. We all face this urge, but as the title of one of my books says, *What Got You Here Won't Get You There.* If the goal was a pleasant dinner, speaking up gets you further from that goal and hurts the person you are spending time with.

Now, let's imagine that you're my boss. I'm young, smart, enthusiastic. I come to you with an idea. You think it's a great idea. But instead of just saying, "Great idea" and asking if I want to talk about it or how you can help, you say, "Well, that's a nice idea. Why don't you add this to it? Why not think of it this way?" The problem with this is that while the quality of the idea may go up by 5 percent, my commitment to execute may go down 50 percent. You got so wrapped up trying to improve the quality of my idea a little that you damaged my commitment a lot.

You left me wanting to do less.

One of my coaching clients, JP Garnier, the former CEO of the drug company GlaxoSmithKline, helped me understand why this happens, especially when you're the leader. He said, "My suggestions become orders. If they're smart, they're orders. If they're stupid, they're orders. If I want them to be orders, they're orders. And if I don't want them to be orders, they're orders anyway." Understanding that anything he said was an order, JP became a better and happier leader by learning a lesson from me: to just shut up. You can't give an order if you don't open your mouth. JP told me, "Before I speak, I stop and breathe and ask myself one question: 'Is it worth it?'" Like JP, I'm sure you'll find the answer is most often "no."

20.

MAKE OTHER PEOPLE'S GOALS YOUR OWN

talked myself out of my job as CEO at Covestor to get one of the richest people in the world to buy the company.

Covestor launched in 2006 as a social networking platform that gave users the ability to track their own brokerage accounts, share them, and mirror trades of other users through its partnership with Interactive Brokers, a large online brokerage. When I joined as CEO in 2011, my job was to reposition and grow the company. My ultimate goal for the venture capital firms on the board was to make Covestor a target for acquisition, and as we became a leader in the wave of disruption in asset management and online investing, potential buyers emerged. One of them was our partner, Interactive Brokers, owned by the Hungarian American billionaire businessman Thomas Peterffy. So I flew with three of my c-suite colleagues for a meeting with him at his mansion in Florida.

I thought it was just a sit-down meeting, but apparently we were having lunch, which is why the butler frowned when he opened the door and saw the four of us. All dressed in a white uniform straight out of central casting, he silently turned to get Peterffy, leaving us waiting at the door confused.

"I'm sorry, Asheesh," Peterffy said as he joined us at the door. "We only have space for two at the lunch table. Your colleagues can't come."

I made a quick calculation and asked Peterffy if we could speak for a moment alone. I apologized for the misunderstanding and told him he didn't need to meet all of us, but he would want to meet my chief technology officer, Bimal Shah. Bimal wasn't the most senior person of the three people I brought, but I knew Peterffy built his early success as a computer programmer and had designed some of the brokerage industry's best financial software. Bimal was the rock star, I told Peterffy. He agreed to let Bimal stay, and I sent the other two disappointed team members away to get their own lunch.

That's when I started talking myself out of my job.

I spent our lunch explaining to Peterffy that I was the wrong person to run my company. Covestor's technology was what had real value to Interactive Brokers, not me. "The reason this business isn't even bigger is because I am not the guy to run it," I said. "You are. Look what you've done with your amazing business. Imagine what you could do with our technology."

Our conversation carried over to a post-lunch walk in his gardens, just Peterffy and me and the gardeners—*so many gardeners*—we passed as we strolled. He told me about his goals for using the technology of the company, and we discussed how to align goals. He wanted to know if I was genuine in my desire to leave the company and asked me to explain all the things I was not good at. Once he was satisfied, we rejoined Bimal, and Peterffy delved into asking technology-related questions. He said he would have his tech team do a proper testing of Covestor's technology capabilities and would then make his decision. A few weeks later, he bought the company. As of the publishing of this book, Bimal is still there.

Remember the first lesson of this book: modern achievement is a hybrid—a mix of approaches that allow you to both thrive and align your way of achieving with the goals of others. *The more you balance your need to empower yourself with the needs of others, the higher and better you will climb.* My explaining to Thomas Peterffy why I was not

THE MORE YOU
BALANCE YOUR
NEED TO EMPOWER
YOURSELF WITH THE
NEEDS OF OTHERS, THE
HIGHER AND BETTER
YOU WILL CLIMB.

the right person to run Covestor, and why he should still buy it, is an example of aligning goals: my own, Peterffy's, and the company's.

This may sound a bit self-serving coming from a CEO negotiating the sale of a company. But as Marshall says, successful people become great leaders when they shift the focus from themselves to others.

Learning this lesson early in your achievement journey is not easy. When you are starting your achievement journey, you tend to be focused on your own goals more than the goals of others. You're building self-efficacy by mastering new skills. But this lesson is actually a test of just how strong your self-efficacy is.

I learned the value of this lesson as a young achiever trying to balance my growing entrepreneurial spirit with the needs of the company I worked for at the time. In fact, my first company, CircleLending, might never have come to be if I hadn't convinced my employer, the global consulting firm Monitor, to share my goal while I achieved theirs as an employee.

When I started my first job at the World Bank, I had no desire to start a business, but a few months after I moved to Boston and started work at Monitor, I did. I had been inspired by a chapter in the book *Future Wealth* by Stan Davis and Christopher Meyer, which argued that the future would enable people to invest in each other, rather than just investing in companies. After all, most businesses fail, but most people succeed. I spent months outside work researching the potential of and developing a business plan for the peer-to-peer lending market that managed person-to-person loans for businesses, education, real estate, or whatever the need. I called the company CircleLending because the money would come from someone's circle of family and friends and other relationships.

When the time came to turn this side hustle into something bigger, I approached Monitor. I hoped they would see that the idea of CircleLending and investing in great people was exactly what I hoped they would do with me. I gave Monitor two options: if they were interested, they could invest, and I would leave to pursue it alone (which I did not want), or I could spend half my time consulting for them and half developing CircleLending in-house in return for part of my salary, office space, access to some market research support, and giving them right of first refusal to buy equity in my businesses in the future. Specifically, they would receive equity in CircleLending and the right to invest in any other business that I created before the age of forty, just in case the first business did not work out!

I'll never forget the feeling I had when they agreed. They believed in me to deliver on the promise I made and potential I offered. CircleLending was such a new idea that no one knew if it could work. They believed in me because I had shown I could see their goals as my own. So cool.

Truth is, my entrepreneurial spirit was far more likely to be recognized at a company that prided itself on supporting innovative ideas like Monitor, which had subsidiaries like Monitor Ventures and Monitor Marketspace. My spirit might have been swallowed whole by the bureaucracy of the World Bank, where my work had the potential to make a big impact, but I suspect I would have needed to be there fifteen years to have any authority to execute my own initiatives or launch new ventures. Still, I could have found a way. Because making others' goals your own is not about the scale of those goals but about having the flexibility to see them as an essential part of your achievement story.

When you are just starting out somewhere, you may think your flexibility is limited to the choices you make in regard to where and how you work. But from the energy you bring to what you do to how you react to people and situations, you have opportunities to make others' goals your own.

How are you showing support of others in your investment of others' goals?

How does your investment in others' goals manifest in your day-to-day behavior, not simply your words?

How do you respond and react when your ideas are not the ones chosen and you need to buy in to a different direction?

Asking questions like these builds self-awareness and opens you up to possibilities you may not have considered before. Moreover, when you align your goals and performance and the goals of the people and places you are working for and/or trying to pitch, you create a team environment in which everyone has a stake in iterating success. Finding alignment by making others' goals your own can be the ultimate difference-maker for you in your personal and career development. This skill can get you noticed, even promoted. Better still, it may lay the groundwork for where you go next. It might even turn you into a leader who helps people do that for themselves.

Today, Monitor is not so exceptional. There are companies and bosses like me who are delighted to let you pursue opportunities for yourself—whether it's a side hustle or just investing in education to get a bigger return on where you are going. Just don't let your job get in the way of achieving the goals of the team/company. Keep aligning your goals and performance with the goals of the people and places you are working for once you earn that right.

COACH'S CORNER
DAVID BURKUS
"BE UPWARDLY MOBILE BY MAKING YOUR BOSS'S GOALS YOUR OWN"

Before I started my first post-college job as a pharmaceutical rep, I attended a three-week training where I made sure to show off how brilliant I was. After I was done, my boss received a report on me filled with scores and notes on my strengths and weaknesses. Across the top of the report, it said "Too smart for his own good."

What a slap in the face. Even after I went on to become a professor, author, and speaker, I would never forget those words.

The note wasn't for my benefit but the team's: if I thought I was smarter than the room, I wouldn't be able to work on a team, which matters deeply in a business in which the clients, not just the employees, need to see you as part of their teams. Ironically, smart as I was, I wasn't smart enough to understand that my experience was a perfect example of how many young achievers and leaders feel the need to prove how smart they are as they enter the workforce and struggle to serve. I had not yet learned how to collaborate and move from what Heidi Grant and E. Tory Higgins call a "performance prove" mentality to a "performance improve" mentality.

Part of the reason for this struggle is that our education system, for reasons both obvious and important, instills a "performance prove" mentality, focusing on and celebrating individual achievement and results, not development and growth. But then we graduate and get dropped into team-based

environments and systems. Our performance is filtered through the team and boss, and our results and successes are determined not by our smarts or talent first but by others and the resources we have access to. "Individual" performance reviews are now based on how well we perform with others.

That's why when people ask me, "What do I do with star performers who are not good members of the team?" I tell them it is a trick question. If they are not good members of the team, then they are

DAVID BURKUS

not star performers. Part of their job is to support the needs of the team. A better strategy than thinking you are smarter than the room and talented enough to change the world by yourself—what I call the "lone creator myth"—is to put the needs of the team over the needs of yourself and *make your boss's goals your goals.*

If you're not going the entrepreneurial route and want to go further faster, you'll shine by helping your bosses and teams achieve their objectives and making them look good. That's what makes you indispensable and relevant to their continued success—and makes them want to bring you with them when they move up or on. That's what I missed when I started out and tried to prove how smart I was.

I get this approach might seem off for young achievers looking for inspiration (knowing how your behavior and role serve others and the world) and purpose (your "why"). Research shows most people derive more meaning from and get better at what they do from prosocial motivation. Of course, that research does not ask whether you get that sense of meaning and satisfaction from making your *boss* happy, yet that is usually the best path to a larger prosocial benefit: you see your impact by directly helping another person and the rest of the team achieve their goals.

This is true regardless of where you work or what you do. Too many of us cut ourselves off from opportunities because we think we—or anyone—cannot achieve prosocial goals in places not immediately aligned with our goals and dismiss them and the motivations of the people who work there.

For example, I live in Tulsa, Oklahoma, the natural gas capital of the United States. There are a lot of people here working with fossil fuels, deriving prosocial motivation and purpose from the fact that they keep air conditioners running in 105-degree heat and the lights on for hospitals. A lot of those people also care deeply about the environment and know even small changes made from the inside of a big power company could have more prosocial impact than any startup or they alone could ever achieve.

Regardless of what those people believe, their "power," like yours, will come through people they answer to—looking for opportunities to serve up to those people and their achievement goals. By making your boss's goals your own, you also force yourself to think a little more systematically and to see the thirty-thousand-foot view of the impact your work has—or can have.

Dr. David Burkus (davidburkus.com) is the bestselling author of five books about business and leadership, including his newest, Best Team Ever. *Since 2017, he has been ranked multiple times as one of the world's top business thought leaders. A former business school professor, David now works with leaders from organizations across all industries, including PepsiCo, Fidelity, Adobe, and NASA.*

FROM MARSHALL
LISTEN TO CONNECT, NOT CRITIQUE

Alignment is essential for living what I call an earned life: to succeed in having that life, you must have alignment between your aspirations, ambitions, and day-to-day actions while enjoying the journey, regardless of outcomes. But we all have behaviors and habits that get in the way of having alignment, and perhaps the limiting one is poor listening.

"My [boss, coworker, direct report] doesn't listen" is one of the most common complaints I hear in my work. People will tolerate all sorts of rudeness, but listening holds a special place in their hearts, perhaps because it's something all of us should be able to do with ease. After all, what does it take to keep our ears open, our eyes looking at whoever is talking, and our mouths shut? Apparently a lot. And bad listening often speaks volumes:

I don't care about you.
I don't understand you.
You're wrong.
You're stupid.
You're wasting my time.

No one wants to hear any of these. But when you fail at listening—especially as you move into leadership—you're sending out every one of these negative messages. It's a wonder people ever talk to you again!

An easy first step toward better listening and alignment is to *look* as though you are listening. No drumming your fingers, having side conversations, or checking your phone while someone is talking. Now ask what you're doing on the inside: Are you downloading your reply? Finding fault with what is being said? If so, you are not listening to understand.

In thinking about this lesson, I recalled a conversation I had with my friend Judith Glaser about conversational intelligence, which is also the title of her wonderful book. I asked her, "How can leaders find people who have the potential to be doing more than what they are? Maybe they are doing a good job, but you feel they could be more than what currently they are?"

Judith answered, "A lot of times, you are critiquing people to see if they are good enough. Other times, people fall off and you say, 'Well, I saw that coming.' We get in the habit of critique and limit rather than support and elevate. When you have it in your mind to look for and notice people who have more to give, something magical can happen. That's what it means to have an expanding mindset, not a limiting mindset."

According to Judith, a good way to start to shift your mindset is to do what I suggested in lesson eighteen: breathe before you speak. But it's what comes next that is what she calls one of the most important parts of conversational intelligence: *listening to connect, not judge or reject.*

As Judith told me, too often we listen to see what we are going to say or where we are going to speak next, or we judge the other person (whether we express that judgment or just think it). Instead, she suggests starting to observe how you can connect with others. Look at them as they speak, watch them as they listen to others, look for facial cues, reactions, and body language as an entry point to connect to what you see and hear from them. Don't just focus on what you want to say.

That's as positive as listening gets! It creates a connection between you and the other person that is essential for alignment.

F reestyle lessons are about designing and innovating *you*. They compel you to think creatively about your unique strengths. They encourage you to build your passions, understand your values, embrace differences, and connect your strengths and stories to others. Think of freestyling as if you were an athlete on a team: How can you individually *and* collaboratively maximize your potential as you grow to lift yourself and the team (i.e., others) to success at the same time?

Like fixed and flexible, the first set of lessons focuses on your life (self), and the second set of lessons focuses on your work (career), and each of them features the designer Ayse Birsel, who has taught millions of people to design the lives they love and created the illustrations for this book. But where the fixed and flexible sections featured a comment from a coach or connection to a classic person or text, six of the lessons in freestyle feature a story from a young achiever who I have met through JA and the universities and schools where I have visited and lectured. They talk about how they are navigating modern achievement as aspiring leaders—as they live it. Can't get any more modern than that!

The penultimate lessons in each set of freestyle lessons feature stories from multiple current and past Junior Achievement leaders and alums worldwide, who reflect on the power of the lesson in their lives. Finally, the last "lessons" in self and career honor the idea of freestyling you. They ask you to write your own modern achievement lesson that has helped you achieve success in your life and then offer you the chance to share it with us and our online community!

PART 3
FREESTYLE

21. EMBRACE YOUR INEXPERIENCE AND CLUELESSNESS

22. CREATE PROTECTED TIME

23. DO IT NOW

24. EXPERIENCE DIFFERENT

25. FREESTYLE YOUR "SELF"

SELF

21.

EMBRACE YOUR INEXPERIENCE AND CLUELESSNESS

W hen I was in Oslo for a JA board meeting, I was invited to present awards for Norway's best social entrepreneurs at the Ungt Entreprenørskap (JA Norway) startup competition for university students. One of the award winners was Akrida, a company run by Norwegian university students that strives to reduce carbon emissions and waste by introducing more sustainable food made from insects. Insects! While meeting all the competitors and seeing their products, I had a chance to sample Akrida's snack packs made from crickets. High in protein! After the ceremony, I spoke with one of Akrida's founders, Mikael Frølandshagen. He told me they saw potential in a relatively unestablished market outside Asia: "Not a lot of people outside of Asia ate sushi fifty years ago, and now supermarkets in the United States alone sell more than forty million servings a year."

That unestablished market included Mikael and everyone at Akrida. Before they started the company, none of them had eaten crickets or any type of insect before, let alone produced flour or fried food from them, and they had no idea how to source them. But they were undaunted by their lack of knowledge and experience with this new product category. "Once we got past our own hesitations and biases that insects are ugly or disgusting and tasted some products, we were pleasantly surprised. We thought if people didn't have to look them in the eye, we could sell products made from them," Mikael said. "And even if we can't figure it all out in the long term or it stays just a small part of my life, I will never regret this experience. I'm learning more about myself and how far I am willing to go."

Mikael's words took me back to my story from my summer internship at a fashion magazine in New York City that started the first lesson of this book, when my cluelessness and inexperience with food made me look foolish in front of a bowl of intentionally cold tomato soup. I was embracing my inexperience with reviewing gourmet restaurants to learn something new to inform my own journey.

Remember, modern achievement doesn't lend itself to a singular, goal-oriented, linear path to *the* career, *the* job, *the* salary. It is a dynamic and evolving approach to your future that requires an ability to evolve yourself and adapt to ideas. You can't embrace that kind of nonlinear approach to achievement without embracing your own inexperience and cluelessness along the way. That's what opens you up to thinking creatively and differently about yourself. That's what starts to build self-awareness. That's what allows you to think differently about the people you surround yourself with and the relationships you make.

In fact, most of my achievement story is an exercise in embracing inexperience and cluelessness to drive innovation. I knew nothing about online lending when I started CircleLending. I knew nothing about asset management when I became the CEO of Covestor. I knew nothing about running a global nonprofit when I started at Junior Achievement Worldwide. But, in each case, I believed I could bring an innovative lens to the organization or to the industry. At times, I would even call my inexperience and cluelessness an advantage that heightened my optimism for what could be achieved: I had no idea I *couldn't* do something, so I believed I could push the proverbial envelope.

I call this quality "naïve audacity." You can be audacious when you are inexperienced and clueless. You can be bold. At CircleLending, I didn't know how much money it would take to build a new product category in financial services, so I became its evangelist to get others excited about the idea of person-to-person loans online, talking about it about on the radio, on TV, in newspapers, and in books (one of which came with an introduction from Richard Branson). At Covestor, I didn't know that asset management was a closed club of professional investors, so I helped build and reposition a technology company that aimed to democratize access to investment management talent in an online marketplace (which was rebranded as Interactive Advisors after its acquisition in 2015). At JA Worldwide, I learned the limitations of my experience when it came to global diversity and non-profit governance, so I learned about, refined, and implemented the Fixed-Flexible-Freestyle framework to help board members and staff understand how we could balance global, regional, and local priorities while moving forward together.

Does naïve audacity have limitations? Of course. Every lesson in life has its limitations, especially if you overweight it. You can't navigate a nonlinear path to achievement just by being clueless, and you can't use cluelessness or inexperience as an excuse for continued ignorance. At the internship, I had not done my research about gazpacho before taking the assignment, and that left me too inflexible to consider that soup could be cold. At CircleLending, I learned over time that while the market potential for person-to-person lending is large, the product line and price point have to be customized for each segment of the market, such as mortgages, education loans, and business loans. At Covestor, I had to surround myself with some very experienced people to teach me about investment management, trade execution, and online marketplaces. And at JA Worldwide, I have learned substantially from my colleagues about how nonprofit structures, motivations for volunteering and donating funds, and educational priorities vary in different regions, countries, and local communities.

But it was only after I started writing this book that I understood how embracing my inexperience and cluelessness, and indeed all freestyle lessons, is about more than *creating the life I wanted*. They are about *designing the life I love*.

Design the Life You Love is the name of a book by Ayse Birsel (subtitle: *A Step-by-Step Guide to Building a Meaningful Future*). Ayse created most of the illustrations that appear in this book. She is the cofounder

AYSE BIRSEL

of Birsel + Seck, an award-winning New York design studio that brings simplicity, systems-thinking, and humanism to the complex problems of life and work. She believes that if you have the desire to explore your life from a new point of view, think about it proactively, and change it creatively, you can design the life you love. For her, "design your life" is a freestyle methodology for imagining the life you want.

According to Ayse, design is a problem-solving methodology, and designing your life teaches you how to problem solve. "That's the difference between the business school mindset and the designer mindset," she says. "In business school you're taught to do research and come up with the one solution and execute it. In design school, you're taught to generate multiple solutions, permutations of ideas, and then see which one of those ideas works. You might do quick prototypes to see what works without investing too much in them. Freestyling is solving problems to generate multiple solutions—generating multiple yous from permutations of ideas from which you choose one to pursue as you keep growing and collaborating with others. Because freestyling is both individual and collaborative. It has to be for it to work. Just like a product is no good if it is designed just for you."

Simply put, modern achievement is about both life and work—self and others. As Ayse says, "Achieving just the work or intellectual side is not enough anymore. You need to think about achievement the way a designer thinks about a product: holistically. You need the human-centered emotional, physical, and spiritual sides, too— to think about what gives you joy. That is where freestyle comes in. Fixed and flexible help you find solutions intellectually, but what makes freestyle most interesting is it shows you can have a process for generating multiple ideas about you, not just your career."

That's exactly what this lesson in embracing your cluelessness and inexperience allows: exploration of who you want to or could be, imagining the life you want, and building connections to others. But it is not just embracing your cluelessness and inexperience that allows this: *everything* you embrace combines to create what Ayse calls our "ready-made purpose."

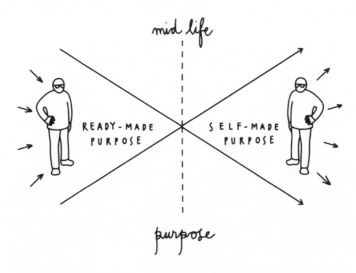

TRANSFORMATION OF PURPOSE

IN A WORLD WHERE YOU WILL HAVE MANY JOBS AND CAREERS EVEN AFTER YOU BECOME A LEADER, EMBRACING YOUR OWN CLUELESSNESS WHEN YOU ARE STARTING YOUR ACHIEVEMENT JOURNEY AND OPPORTUNITIES ABOUND PREPARES YOU FOR AN UNCERTAIN FUTURE FILLED WITH NEW DIRECTIONS AND CHOICES.

In *Design the Long Life You Love*, Ayse notes how we all start life with ready-made purposes. For most of us, that ready-made purpose is shaped by some combination of our families (those we are born with and those we create), schools, places of worship, friends, employers, colleagues, and other influential relationships. This purpose guides our goals as we start to achieve more in life.

What you should do as part of your freestyle approach to achievement is take that ready-made purpose and use it to design a future you love. But your ready-made purpose does not define you forever. As you hit midlife, purpose defined from the outside is not enough, and your ready-made purpose or what life expects of you transforms to a self-made purpose or what you expect of life. You create that self-made purpose through learning and teaching, leading and serving, and standing for what you believe in. But, as Ayse notes, "Perhaps the most powerful tool for self-made purpose is creativity"—creativity that starts with choosing how you design your future when you are young.

Pursuing any future is a leap of faith. In a world where you will have many jobs and careers even after you become a leader, embracing your own cluelessness when you are starting your achievement journey and opportunities abound prepares you for an uncertain future filled with new directions and choices. Keep putting yourself in environments that allow you to learn about yourself and look for the possibilities for designing you, even when the choice to move up and on is not yours or the steps do not create a linear path.

Of course, your steps may not be as nonlinear as mine. You may *know* you want to be a doctor or a teacher or an accountant for the rest of your life. You may want a job with consistent hours of work. You may never want to be the boss. You may want more than one side hustle or none at all. But within any part of your achievement story, there are choices and chances to embrace your own naïve audacity to learn and explore more about life and work.

As the title of Ayse's TEDx Talk asks, "If your life is your biggest project, why not design it?" You have the power to freestyle, no matter what your achievement story throws at you. Think of it as mapping you in your own life and work road trip. The road trip of the past is not the achievement map of the future. Even if your destination is always the same, landscapes and destinations have changed and will keep changing. There will be traffic as you go, detours, and unexpected obstacles and joys. You will need to follow laws that govern the roads and places you visit. But you still have the freedom to decide where to go based on your values (see Ayse's exercise on finding your values in Marshall's moment)—and keep deciding throughout your journey.

You probably have already started mapping your journey and designing your life, which is why Ayse told me that if she had to do anything over, she'd call her book "Redesign the Life You Love." Our lives are always in motion. The road trip has begun. It's about the journey, with multiple stops along the route, not just the destination.

YOUNG ACHIEVER STORY
HOWARD (YIQ ZHENN) LEONG
"DON'T LET IMPATIENCE GET IN THE WAY OF YOUR DESIRE TO EXPLORE"

Until I was twelve, my family owned a steel manufacturing business in Malaysia. Then the company went bankrupt because of mismanagement. We went from eight people living very comfortably in two big houses to all of us in one eight-hundred-square-foot house. I watched my parents struggle to keep us housed and fed, pay our bills, and provide for our education.

My mom pushed us through those tough times. While she, like so many Malaysians, measures success in material wealth and prestige—which we no longer had—she never let us give up. She made sure I believed I could still do whatever I wanted and never let us lose hope. She instilled in me the optimism I have in creating myself.

The problem is, my mom wants me to achieve her kind of success— wealth and prestige. That's her ideal life for me. I want those things, too, but that's not my ideal life right now. Not that I lack ambition. I have dreamed of being a neurosurgeon (because it looked cool on a TV series about doctors), studying at a top institution, and becoming

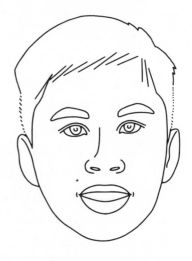

HOWARD LEONG

a Fortune 500 CEO. But I have also dreamed of doing social good and wondered how I can best contribute to the nonprofit world. I want to learn and pursue all I can, and even if I have no experience with the subject or any idea how to do something, when I see an opportunity—like building an e-commerce site for JA student-run companies or spearheading an investment app in the United States trying to democratize value investing—I want to seize it.

This approach to achievement makes my family impatient with me. But it is not their impatience that gets in the way of my embracing this lesson and my cluelessness and inex-perience; it's mine. Their expectations make me even more impatient about achieving and making it "to the top." Because I do have the fear of falling behind.

Often, I feel like I'm in a tough spot when I am pursuing something that makes no money or is just about exploring opportunities. I feel a lot of pressure on me to keep achieving stuff, no matter what I do. At JA conferences, I have to be the Howard who makes things happen and has an impact. Then I come home and wonder, *Should I continue on a different path? Am I leaving some opportunities on the table if I am not hungry enough? Not proactive enough? Should I do what my mother expects and is the social norm for so many high achievers? Get more intern-ships? Get into big tech companies, consulting companies, or maybe investment banks, even though I don't enjoy investment banking, but a lot of people encouraged me to do it because I will have an "easier" life down the road?*

As a result, even though I'm not thinking small about my achievement, I frequently find myself in a position in which I rationalize or justify my own actions just to feel better. In my head, there is a war between the choices that meet my family's and others' definitions of achievement and my own. I feel I need to be a hero for everyone and sometimes lose myself in the process. In my effort to try to please everyone, I failed to please anyone. What I need to do is to try to be more patient and stay grounded and not feel lesser for what I am doing. I know that piling on success after success and all the goals and achievements may not lead me to where I want to be. That's just what others expect of me. It is much better to focus on what I want to achieve first and explore. I don't want to limit myself, even if I have to "fight" myself when I do it.

I have also learned to advocate for myself and get others to support me, which has built my self-efficacy. That's how I ended up getting my professors and department to support my attending a three-week AI program at the University of Oxford in England. Because of my childhood experience, which was situated at the receiving end of senseless convictions that led to family bankruptcy, I see a growing need to fuse economics and AI to optimize decisions and outcomes. Though I may not have the prerequisites, I applied for it and asked for a recommendation from one of my professors. He was confused at first, but when he read my personal statement, he understood that this was my chance to get into AI, which is a senior-level course in computer science. I wanted to show that learning pathways can be nonlinear and that you don't need all the prerequisites to do or learn something as you follow your curiosity.

When my professor asked me how I was going to pay for it, I told him I'm working two jobs and had some money saved. He told me he would sponsor £1,000 if I got in. That gave me a huge confidence boost that led to more grants.

Following the AI program, I'm now better positioned to answer intricate problems in economics. That would not have been possible if I hadn't taken the chance on myself, regardless of my experience, which is what I did when I was building JA Malaysia Mall (I had no software engineering background) and when I was building the investment app (I had no trading experience). But everyone saw how hungry I was.

Because I *am* hungry. I *do* have ambition. I just don't feel the need to be one thing right now, or maybe ever. Sure, I often find myself emphasizing prestige and social status and having a kind of contradictory worldview. I'm curious about how life might be if I were to choose the other path. There is always a contrafactual. Those moments get louder in my head when I feel the most clueless and least in control about my direction as options become abundant. The question of "what if" creates anxiety. And then I start getting impatient.

Still, I know if I explore—embrace my inexperience and cluelessness—I will achieve more and reach many "tops" in the long run. I have that self-efficacy. I am always trying to elevate myself. I think achievement is a factor of work, not speed. I could get there faster, but what would I miss? I believe at any time I could choose to achieve as an investment banker if I wanted to. In five or ten years, I think I will laugh at my concerns and be grateful I moved forward doing what I felt was right for me. And maybe my impatience can even become an asset—by creating my own vision of success and driving my resistance to others' expectations.

Howard Leong (howard-leong.github.io) is an alumnus of JA Malaysia and JA Asia Pacific and is now the Global Alumni Ambassador at JA Worldwide, building new JA alumni chapters around the world and strengthening the network. He is majoring in economics at the University of Calgary and studied AI and machine learning at the University of Oxford in England. He is the architect of the JA Malaysia Mall, an organized online marketplace of JA's student-run businesses, for which he won Global Student Prize 2021, a global award.

BE MORE LIKE YOUR HEROES

When Asheesh connected with Ayse for this book, it was a full-circle moment for me: I might never have met him if it hadn't been for her.

In 2015, when Ayse was launching her "Design the Life You Love" program, she had only six people signed up for one of her first outings in New York and asked if I could bring some people. I brought seventy.

If Ayse was nervous or intimidated by the big crowd, I couldn't detect it. But I also knew that talking for an hour or more to an audience of several dozen strangers requires a little more projection of personality than talking to six people does. Six people are a dinner party; six dozen are an audience. So I decided to help raise her energy level. I prodded participants to be bolder in deciding what they wanted to do next. At one point, one of those participants turned the tables on me and asked, "If you think it's so easy, what's next for you?"

I went blank.

Ayse, a master problem solver, tried to help. "Let's start with a simple question," she said. "Who are your heroes?"

That was easy. "Alan Mulally (former CEO of Ford), Frances Hesselbein (former CEO of Girl Scouts of the USA), Paul Hersey (cocreator of Situational Leadership), Peter Drucker (father of modern management), Bob Tannenbaum (UCLA professor), Warren Bennis (a renowned leadership expert), Richard Beckhard (a world leading organizational development consultant), and of course Buddha."

"OK, why?" she asked.

"Well, I'm a Buddhist. And Drucker, who became a mentor late in his life, was the greatest management thinker of the twentieth century."

"OK, but what's 'heroic' about them other than the fact that you like their ideas?"

"They gave away everything they knew to as many people as they could so others could pay it forward. Even though Buddha's been dead twenty-six hundred years, and Peter Drucker died at age ninety-five in 2005, their ideas survive."

"Why not be more like your heroes?"

Before I could answer, Ayse repeated her "heroes" exercise with the audience. She had us write down the names of our hero or heroes and why—what we found most heroic or admired about them. Next to each of my names I wrote, "Extremely generous, great teacher."

Then, Ayse asked us to cross out our heroes' names and put in our own names.

I wrote, "Marshall Goldsmith—extremely generous, great teacher."

"That is your heart's desire—to be an extremely generous, great teacher like your heroes," Ayse said to me. "This is the kind of leader you want to show up as."

That was the moment Ayse made me realize I could do more than admire these people who were my heroes. I could adopt their ideas and what I valued most in them. I could aspire, however modestly, to become what most impressed me about them. How to go about it didn't gel with me right away, but Ayse had planted the seed. And it grew, which is how I "accidentally" formed my small community of like-minded people known as 100 Coaches, which is then how I met Asheesh.

We place our heroes on pedestals too high to reach, rarely considering them as role models to emulate. Ayse's exercise corrected that error for me. Whether you are a leader or aspiring to be one, her heroes exercise can help you be the person you want to be by finding your values as you navigate your way through the process of modern achievement.

Don't worry if you struggle at first with the exercise. Ayse knows it is hard. Most people give pretty standard answers without thinking or talking about what their heroes have done, like I did, not why they admire them. Once you let go and open yourself up to the exercise, the answers become personal and show you what you value most.

As Ayse says, "Once we know our values, we can see our choices." But she also notes you might need to repeat this exercise as you design and redesign your life: "Our values are not fixed. Some are like honesty or directness. But then things change. You get married and start a family. You become a leader. You move, maybe to a new country. The heroes exercise focuses you on what you value most as you change to keep designing the life you love. Values are our inspiration."

AYSE BIRSEL'S HEROES EXERCISE

- Write down the names of your heroes. Who inspires you?

- Write down short descriptors of the values and virtues that endear them to you—why they inspire you.
- Cross out their names.
- Write your name in their place.
- Start and keep designing a life you love around what you see. What would you do to be more like your hero?

22.

CREATE
PROTECTED
TIME

n 2007, Richard Branson's Virgin Group acquired a controlling stake in CircleLending, the pioneering online person-to-person lender I founded six years earlier, and rebranded the company "Virgin Money." At the launch event in Boston's Copley Square, Richard told the media that Virgin Money would hire five thousand people in the city, making headlines and leading to a deluge of resumes and calls over the next few weeks. He and I then went on a media tour, flying to New York on his jet and speaking on all the morning shows. We sponsored a transatlantic voyage on Speedboat, a ninety-nine-foot sailing yacht that was among the world's fastest. Richard also invited my wife, Helen, and me to Necker Island, his home in the Virgin Islands, to spend time with the leaders of other Virgin businesses, discuss our annual strategic goals, and build friendships with each other.

As it turned out, 2007 was a great year to sell my business and to grow a new financial services company in the United States. With the benefit of a strong balance sheet, unique product line, and great marketing, my little company grew rapidly after the acquisition, tripling in less than a year. Richard encouraged us to expand Virgin Money beyond the niche of person-to-person loans to launch Virgin-branded student loans for college students, business loans for start-up entrepreneurs, and mortgages for first-time homeowners. The future looked bright!

The following year, 2008, was a different story. In September, financial institutions such as Bear Stearns and Lehman Brothers collapsed.

Lending institutions froze credit. By the end of the year and into 2009, the Great Recession's financial crisis spread to the UK. The government had to nationalize British banks including Northern Rock, one of the well-known chartered banks in the UK. This created an opportunity for Virgin. Rather than trying to market a Virgin-branded student loan or business loan as Virgin Money, a non-bank lender, it was now possible to buy a bank and collect deposits from customers to then lend out. This was much safer and smarter than trying to just sell lending products during a credit crisis. But it meant we would need to raise more than $1 billion in capital and bring in a new management team of experienced bankers who knew how to buy and run a chartered bank.

As this shift to buying a bank happened, one of the senior executives at Virgin asked if I wanted to move to the UK and work for the new entity or at the corporate office. I thought about it. But I knew it was time for me to leave. I was in my early thirties, and I wanted to do something different. It was challenging and painful to think about letting go of the company that I had built and run for more than eight years. I was concerned that it would all change after I left. And it did. Virgin completed the acquisition of Northern Rock and shut down the US operation completely about a year after I left so it could focus on banking in the UK. Virgin transferred all the loans and clients from the original person-to-person lending business to a specialty lending company and exited the US mortgage business altogether. (Shortly after Virgin left, one of the ambitious young sales executives whom I had recruited decided to set up his own competitor business, National Family Mortgage, to focus on serving the market niche that was the most profitable part of CircleLending's product line.)

My last day at the company was terrible. We had a board meeting in the morning, and I was out by the end of the day. Since Virgin was not yet public about its plans to become a bank, I was not able to share this with my colleagues or make a speech thanking them for coming on the incredible journey with me. I just went around the office, shook hands, and did my best to express gratitude without saying anything about the future. The next morning, I received a nice note of thanks from Richard Branson, but I desperately wanted to go back to the office and tell everyone what lay ahead.

The financial crisis was a crazy time for me. I had lived through the peak of the crisis with sleepless nights and stressful mornings, feeling responsible for the welfare of my colleagues. I was exhausted. My wife, Helen, and pretty much everyone I knew told me I should take some time to breathe and reflect. But to the surprise of no one who knows me, my first instinct was to think, *What's next?*

As you know, if you read "go meta" (lesson four), I kept that promise and resolved to create some extended protected time and take a beat before starting something new. I took the first few weeks of my time off to reflect on and explore what I was good at, what I enjoyed, what I had always wanted to do, and what drove me. I tried to come up with a systematic way to look at these things. Then, I started focusing my time on planning our family's great adventure: a six-month sojourn in India. We had already traveled a bit, but when Helen and I talked with people who had traveled around the world with their kids, we got really excited. We knew this was the perfect moment for us to do something special because our twin boys wouldn't be starting kindergarten until the fall. Once the kids started school, we wouldn't have the same kind of opportunity for extended travel. So we took advantage of the opportunity.

The trip was everything we imagined.

My protected time during this year propelled me forward in my career. It recharged me. It might be a stretch to say I might not have found success without it, but I surely would not have enjoyed and understood the process as much and probably never would have written this book. It wasn't that I didn't know how to reflect or that my protected time was all about reflection and going meta. What I realize now is that the power wasn't just in how much time I protected or how I *used* it but that I *created* it—that it was intentional, it had a purpose, and I dedicated myself to it, whether I had minutes or months.

Too often, we conflate protected time with focus and productivity. Stories abound about using a good old-fashioned hourglass or kitchen timer for time management to reduce distraction and to complete tasks and/or understand how long a particular task can take. One of the most famous is Francesco Cirillo's "Pomodoro Technique," where you do up to thirty minutes of focused work and then take a five-minute break or longer depending on how many repetitions you do. You focus until the timer goes off and then rest and repeat. It is called the "Pomodoro Technique" because Cirillo is Italian and used a kitchen timer that looked like a tomato (*pomodoro* is Italian for "tomato").

I love that technique for focusing to get work done, but protected time is about so much more than getting work done or just going meta to reflect. At the start of my career, I used it for making time for my most important relationships, such as making it a priority to meet Helen every two months after college when our careers put thousands of miles between us. I used it for journaling what I wanted to achieve. Today, I use it to ask my "daily questions" (see lesson three) or just to let my mind rest and run free by taking a long shower, which triggers creativity, ideas, and curiosity.

You may find the same effect staring at the ocean or a lake—or walking in a park or another natural landscape. The act of protecting time is an investment in thinking about you—not only where you have been, where you are going, and what you might do but how you are caring for yourself mentally, emotionally, and spiritually to design the future you love. You don't need months, days, or even hours to do this. Even if you create time to escape for a few minutes every day and be still, you are being intentional with your time and making the creation of protected time a habit that benefits your well-being.

Most of us have not had a chance to do this since high school or college. That's when you have the most opportunities to create protected time to explore classes in different subjects, participate in clubs or student government, volunteer, and try new and different things and even new identities. You could choose to take internships in what interests you for your career or just for exploring what might interest you. You could also choose to protect your time with a gap year. Gap years before and after college, as well as during your career, are now commonplace and need no justification, particularly if they are about your mental health and wellness.

Of course, not everyone can afford a full year off, so as you start your career, you can use time between jobs to create a little protected time, not just to search for or leap into the next job. Think of this time the way an athlete does: an offseason. You can see your offseason as a sabbatical for your mind (to relax, step away, decompress, or be a little clueless so you can jumpstart your creativity and curiosity) or as a chance to invest in some education or skills you need to grow. If you have been in a job for a while and have no intention or desire to leave, you can still ask for time to learn, explore, destress, open your mind, or even pursue a side hustle. You'd be surprised how flexible your boss or employer can be if you've earned the right to ask for these things, if they know how important it is to you, and if they see it will help retain a valuable employee.

Again, the key is creating the protected time to empower you both on an ongoing basis and when the need or opportunity arises to empower—and take care of—*you.*

EVEN IF YOU CREATE TIME TO ESCAPE FOR A FEW MINUTES EVERY DAY AND BE STILL, YOU ARE BEING INTENTIONAL WITH YOUR TIME AND MAKING THE CREATION OF PROTECTED TIME A HABIT THAT BENEFITS YOUR WELL-BEING.

MAYA RAICHOORA
"IT'S OK TO BE SELFISH TO PROTECT YOUR TIME AND ENERGY"

I was a very high-achieving young girl. By the time I was fifteen, I was a top student in England, studying for my Advanced Level qualifications, or A-Levels, and training for the Olympics in badminton. Then I was diag-nosed with ulcerative colitis, an incurable irritable bowel disease. I endured crippling physical, emotional, and mental pain for which I took sixty to seventy pills a day and still had to go to the loo dozens of times. Sometimes there would just be blood. It was dehumanizing.

MAYA RAICHOORA

I could have had my colon removed, but I refused. I still wanted to win—to achieve what I had been working for. I did my A-Levels but mostly from hospital because I couldn't walk. I was losing hope.

During one of my hospital stays, a nurse asked me, "What would you be doing if you weren't here?" I told her she was being rude and to get out of my room. But then I thought about her question. I knew what the answer was; I wanted to walk again. I mentally rehearsed myself walking every day. I knew immediately something had worked because I felt a bit more hope. I then focused on my pain. I described the pain as having piranhas in my gut, so I used my imagination to go in there and kill them all. I then turned to my body. I learned how to walk again by first mentally rehearsing each step—in my room, then the hospital hallway, then outside, then hiking, then running.

I didn't know it at the time, but I was practicing visualization. I hadn't yet read the work of people like David Hamilton (*How Your Mind Can Heal Your Body*) to know that visualization is often used in medicine, from cancer patients to stroke victims, to change their mindset and create changes in their brains and bodies, similar to the way I used it to manage my pain.

Note I said managed, not *cured*. I changed the chemistry of my body and my mindset, but I still had an incurable disease. I literally sh** my pants when I was presenting on stage at the JA finals in Berlin. I couldn't go straight to uni because of how unwell I was. I would never play badminton at the Olympics. But I kept visualizing and eventually made it to uni, where I studied design thinking and systems approach, learned about the neuroscience behind visualization and the link between emotions, stress, and disease, and began to build the company I run, which is dedicated to helping others visualize.

Simply put, visualization saved my life, and I wanted to help others learn the technique as part of their mental-fitness routines. I want them to train their minds the same way they go to the gym to train their bodies. I share how my visualization practice has evolved—and become more intentional—since my hospital days. I use it not just for my health but to tap my potential. I use it for pitching, presentations in business, visualizing for outcomes, process, and creative thinking. If I can see and feel it in my mind, I can make it happen.

Few of the people I work with suffer from a chronic illness

like me, but they suffer just as much from the pressure of achieving. They may not know it yet, but the stress is making them sick. It still makes *me* sick sometimes. The world makes it really hard to protect my time and energy daily for my visualizations and, on a larger scale, for my mental fitness. There are so many distractions and demands on my time, from running my business to being with the people I love and who depend on me. I haven't let go of my high-achieving spirit; I have the same drive and fire and passion I had at fifteen. Sometimes I don't have a choice but to be "on" and perform constantly.

That's OK. I just have learned to separate my self-worth from what I do and balance performance and well-being. I draw all the extra energy I need to keep going from the people around me. But I always ask myself, *What am I doing to achieve balance? How am I surrounding myself with who or what drains my energy and who or what radiates it? How am I resting and not letting productivity anxiety force me to just keep doing?*

That's why I say it's OK to be selfish when it comes to protecting your time and energy. I think a lot of people don't know how or why they need to protect their energy. Time is easier. Just say "no." But sometimes I do have the time for people but don't have the energy for them. I need to say no then too. Those boundaries are never easy and are often uncomfortable. Some people take it personally, but I need to remember it is personal to *me*.

In fact, I have learned that being selfish now and then with my time and energy is essential to being selfless, because if I can't show up for others, then I am not doing anyone any good. This time goes way beyond my daily visualization. I use that longer protected time to "date myself" but also to visit family, devote myself to a relationship, heal from an injury, and learn something new—and never to avoid dealing with stuff.

When I am protecting my time and energy, I make sure to tell people what is happening—that I need to disappear for a bit. I don't justify; I just let them know I won't be on my phone or going out much. I've learned solitude and loneliness are not the same thing, just as activity and action are not. Our teachers thought something was wrong if we went off alone. But we don't always have to play with someone. We need to be able to spend time on our own and not give into FOMO or the fear of missing out (the perception that others are having more fun, living better lives, or experiencing more fun things while you're alone). I choose to replace the fear with joy and embrace JOMO, the *joy* of missing out. Everything in life has an opportunity cost. I prefer growing joy over fear.

I find it helpful to think about each of us as athletes. Athletes understand the intricate balance between peak performance and maintaining well-being. They know training the mind or actively resting is not a reward for the work; it's part of the work. We can and need to apply the same principles to our lives and businesses. Be proactive in staying agile and prepared!

As CEO and founder of Remap Mental Fitness, Maya Raichoora (mayaraichoora.co) is on a mission to make mental fitness as common as physical fitness and to help working professionals become mentally fit through the power of visualization. She hosts mental fitness events, coaches individuals, speaks globally, and works with global brands like Nike, Lego, and Barclays. She delivered the TEDx Talk "Dare to build the future you deserve."

A SIX-SECOND SIX PACK?
THERE ARE NO QUICK FIXES

One Saturday morning, I found myself channel surfing and was amazed by the number of ads/infomercials I saw about getting in shape. One ad proclaimed I could have a "six-second six pack." Another would turn my "flabby abs into that sexy six pack." My personal favorite was the one that claimed "visible results" could be achieved in two three-minute sessions! All of them shouted how incredible the product or program was, with "customers" calling it a "miracle." "It feels terrific!" one spokesperson declared. "Let us show you how easy it is!"

If you want to know why so many goal setters don't become goal achievers, you can pore over a bunch of enlightening academic studies about goals, or you can watch these ads for fifteen minutes. Where did we ever get the crazy idea that getting in shape is supposed to be quick and easy? Why do we think that there will be almost no cost? Why are we surprised that working out is arduous and healthy foods don't always taste that good?

I see the impact of this delusional thinking all the time. Take Mary, an executive vice president for human resources who reached out to me about a job. She was dealing with the integration of people and systems after her company acquired another. Her CEO had been hearing some serious grumbling about the CIO.

"The CIO is fifty-six years old and has great experience. No one else in the company can match it. Unfortunately, he wants everything to be done 'his way,'" Mary groaned. "There are some brilliant people in the company we acquired who have their own ideas. Several of their top people, including the new COO, are expressing concerns about our CIO. The CEO wants this issue resolved now!"

Mary told me the CEO wanted to see a dramatic change in the CIO within a couple of months and had suggested that she hire an executive coach. But she knew the CIO was busy and impatient. He wouldn't work with a coach that was going to waste his valuable time.

"Do you think that you can help us?" she asked. "When could you start?"

Mary wanted the coaching equivalent of a six-second six-pack: change the CIO—immediately! But this wasn't Saturday morning TV, and there was no "miracle." I pointed out that the CIO was fifty-six years old. His behavioral habits took years to develop and wouldn't go away in two days, two weeks, or two months. During the next year, that CIO would be barraged with competing goals that would distract him from his efforts to change. He needed to realize that lasting development change of any kind, but especially leadership development, is a lifelong process, no matter how old you are. A temporary change in behavior to "look good" in the short term only creates cynicism if you don't stick with it in the long term.

If that CIO was interested in investing time, working hard, making his change a high-priority goal, and maintaining his changed behavior through the aftermath of the acquisition and for the rest of his career, then I could help him. If not, hiring me would probably be a waste of everyone's time.

We all set goals to get some aspect of our lives in shape. All too often, they don't come to fruition. The changes I help people make are generally very simple. However, they are never easy. Just as with diet and exercise, in order to change behavior, you must put in the effort to overcome the four main challenges to goal achievement.

1. **Time.** (I am already busy and don't have or make time for the little things filling my calendar. How do I have or make time for the big changes?)
2. **Effort.** (So much of what I do is already hard. Why is it worth changing, especially if I am already successful?)
3. **Competing goals.** (I am consumed with so many urgent things. I'll worry about this later.)
4. **Maintenance.** (I need things to change for good and stay that way. What am I supposed to do? Keep working on the changes for the rest of my life?)

These are the same obstacles to creating protected time. To achieve meaningful goals or create protected time, you'll have to pay a price, and that starts with you. If you want to invest in creating a better you and becoming a better person, a better professional, and a better leader in the future, look in the mirror—not just at how you look but at who you are. There's no product, no diet, no exercise program, and (I hate to admit it) no book or executive coach that can make you better if you don't want or think you need to be. Only you can make you better.

If your source of motivation doesn't come from inside, you won't stick with it, and you won't get the job done. This is bad news for you if you believe in the possibility of a six-second six-pack but great news for you if you are striving for real change and earned achievement!

23.

DO IT NOW

have been visiting Babson College in Massachusetts for years to give guest lectures, serve on advisory boards, and attend events. I love the vibe of the place. Rather than teaching entrepreneurship as a separate course for students, Babson has attempted to infuse an entrepreneurial mindset into all its academic departments and challenged faculty from English to data science to introduce a bias for action into coursework for students. Babson understands that a mindset that leans toward action and iteration rather than deliberation and paralysis in a world that is rapidly changing is necessary for your success.

But that mindset is one we all struggle with in designing our futures.

Imagine you are designing a product. You have visualized what the product looks like, but instead of starting to design, build, and test versions of your product and iterating toward success, you are stuck thinking about planning, avoiding mistakes, forecasting for what you believe is to come, and accounting for all the dependencies involved in bringing your product to market. As your overthinking continues and constant concerns and fears about future unknowns consume you, they hold you back from focusing on what you need to do to get started on the product.

Now imagine the product you are designing is you. No matter what you visualize or how well you plan, the future is moving quickly and getting more and more uncertain. According to the World Economic Forum's *The Future of Jobs Report*, 23 percent of today's jobs and 44 percent of workers' core skills will change in the next five years. You can't get stuck worrying about what might happen and thinking about a future that is full of unknowns. You need to act now to design, build, and test versions of *you* that you put out into the world. Sure, you will make mistakes and missteps as you do. But you will do more than learn from them and this process overall. You will build the resilience and confidence you need to keep iterating to success.

You will "learn by doing," which builds self-efficacy.

In the first lesson of this book, I quoted Marshall's line: "Self-efficacy is borne from personal responsibility." Now is the best time to embrace that responsibility. *So what stops you from taking an action-oriented approach to your achievement story and learning by doing?* The answer, like the one to many questions in these lessons on modern achievement, is *you*. Specifically, fear and all the negative emotions associated with confronting and pushing through the barriers and setbacks. Designing the future you love requires acting, even if that action makes you uncomfortable.

We all put off things we associate with negative emotions instead of anticipating the positive moods that come through effort, exploration, and accomplishment. Emotions rule our behavior, and research (and experience) shows we are wired to avoid things that are hard or cause us discomfort or pain. We prefer safety (flight), which leads to comfort, over confrontation (fight), which makes us uncomfortable.

Negative emotions are a big reason so many young people—because of pressure from family, friends, or other authority figures, or just self-imposed beliefs—get stuck in thinking about the end of their achievement story. It is far less confrontational and much safer to avoid difficult conversations and do what they think they must or have been told to do, rather than to take a risk now and explore other possibilities, opportunities, and things that they love, or test their assumptions. Better block all that out and focus on following one career path—an engineer, a doctor, a banker—to certain long-term success. But what good is that path if that future is uncertain or if it feels inauthentic to you?

Research on negative emotions also extends to procrastination. We naturally procrastinate to avoid doing what makes us uncomfortable and instead gravitate toward what gives us pleasure or allows us to check a box more easily. For example, Dr. Piers Steel, professor of motivational psychology at the University of Calgary and author of *The Procrastination Equation: How to Stop Putting Things Off and Start Getting Stuff Done*, has shown that procrastination has less to do with being lazy than it does with your mood.

Instead of avoiding negative emotions, harness the power of those emotions you are feeling and channel them into productivity and positivity. When we master our emotions around positive thinking, we not only effectively remove distractions, barriers, and other obstacles that compromise our focus (lesson fourteen) but also draw people to us.

Consider how to approach anger as an emotion, turning something seemingly negative into something productive. "Asheesh, you need to get angry at people when they screw up!" and "How can you remain calm at this time?!" I have heard these lines too many times to count, and they are connected. No one *needs* to get angry, especially in urgent, important, and tense situations. In the age of doom scrolling, it is easy to go down that rabbit hole. Of course I feel anger, but it is my choice as to how it manifests, and I try my best to choose a calmer approach. I'm not saying anger isn't warranted. Psychologists will tell you anger can be a productive motivator in certain situations, especially in the short term. Sometimes anger is just a manifestation of our fears.

Either way, its long-term effects can be damaging to you and others. Like any emotion, it is best not to deny it but to understand it, master it, and harness its power by channeling its energy into action—ideas, solutions, and success for yourself and others.

You could even turn this mastery into one of your greatest strengths, like one of the most action-oriented people I have ever met, Bill Schwabel. After four years as a captain in the US Army, Bill spent nearly two decades at Gillette, the company best known for its razor blades, traveling the world to build international businesses and alliances for the company. Bill jokes that he had made five mistakes each morning before his competitors had breakfast but discovered that his willingness to embrace those mistakes was actually one of his competitive advantages: a bias for action. This mindset helped Bill build more than thirty successful businesses after leaving Gillette.

Bill joined the Global Council of JA Worldwide after having served for many years on the board of the Greater Boston chapter and encouraged me to move faster in executing our global strategy, particularly when it came to building partnerships with other organizations. For a large organization like JA, there is a natural tendency to avoid the risk of failure and stay in our comfort zone. Every time we meet for lunch (religiously followed by an ice-cream sundae), Bill pushes me to work faster and harder to build partnerships that modernize JA. Even if the rest of the organization is not yet ready for change and some of these partnerships will not work, Bill knows working with other organizations at a global level to build new capabilities and advance our mission starts with my willingness to act.

NEGATIVE EMOTIONS ARE A BIG REASON SO MANY YOUNG PEOPLE — BECAUSE OF PRESSURE FROM FAMILY, FRIENDS, OR OTHER AUTHORITY FIGURES, OR JUST SELF-IMPOSED BELIEFS — GET STUCK IN THINKING ABOUT THE END OF THEIR ACHIEVEMENT STORY.

YOUNG ACHIEVER STORY
HARSH SHAH
"ADVOCATE FOR YOURSELF WITHOUT FEAR"

In 2016, I joined a group of like-minded high school students who shared a passion for combating alcohol abuse and putting an end to drunk driving. There had been several high-profile drunk driving cases in the news in Canada, and some of us had been impacted personally by it. We wanted to find a way to change people's behavior and make a difference. Making money was secondary to saving lives. The idea we came together on was SpitStrips, a saliva-based blood-alcohol content indicator that could discreetly tell a person if they were over the legal alcohol limit and should not drive. Eventually, I became the president of the company.

HARSH SHAH

At Junior Achievement, I learned how to create, run, and structure a business. But SpitStrips took my education to another level. We got accepted into top university incubators, and I spent most of the summers of my junior and senior year of high school waking up early and heading to downtown Toronto to work on a business plan with our team, talk to potential customers, and develop the product and website for our 2017 launch. When we did launch, the media attention was huge, as was the support from many organizations, including the police.

While all that was happening with SpitStrips, I was also preparing to go to college and decided to apply for the most prestigious award from JA for all of Canada: The Peter Mansbridge Positive Change Award and Scholarship. It was a bit of a moonshot; only one student in all of Canada receives it each year. In the end, that student was me, and I was asked to speak at JA's Canadian Business Hall of Fame gala, where I was seated beside Asheesh. I had never met him before, and I used the opportunity to get to know him and asked if we could stay in touch. As you know from lesson nine, Asheesh is now one of my most influential mentors, and I strive to be what he calls a "good mentee."

What I realize today is that I might never have stepped up to help turn our idea for a business into reality, applied for that scholarship, and asked Asheesh if we could stay in touch without being willing to win the moment by advocating for myself—fearlessly—even if doing so made me a little uncomfortable.

Capitalizing on these opportunities has broadened my perspective and allowed me to reflect on new experiences I otherwise wouldn't have had. Conversations with mentors enabled me to reassess my decision criteria and make sure they were aligned with my goals. This gave me comfort with my decision to start my career in investment banking and to pursue my goal to help build critical infrastructure in underdeveloped countries, improving access to the internet, clean energy, clean water, and education.

I continue to take risks and build relationships with anyone who can help me reach that goal professionally and develop me personally. And I make sure to pursue those relationships when the opportunities come. For example, within the first week of starting my investment banking job, I arranged to have lunch with a vice president on the digital infrastructure team, told him I would like to work on his team at some point, and explained why. I was unafraid of rejection, respectful in my approach, and genuine in my ask. He took it very nicely, and when there was a chance to put a good person on his team, he chose me. That would have never happened if I didn't step up, ask, and be willing to stand out and advocate for myself and not wait—to just start now.

That's what I did the last time I spoke with Asheesh before he started this book. I told him I joined the digital infrastructure team at the bank and remembered he used to work at the World Bank and did some work on the impact of privatization and public-private partnerships in his doctoral studies. I asked what advice he had for someone who wanted to advance in this field. He then told me he had connections at a top fund that did investing in infrastructure globally. He knew I was not going to wait for this opportunity and advised me on how best to approach them given how young and inexperienced I was.

I am so grateful for moments like these, but I also know they will never come if I don't continue to do the good work that rewards others' faith in me. Just because I am fearless doesn't mean I can be selfish. I don't think I'm entitled to anything and try to pay it forward wherever possible. I'm never the loudest one in the room. I work hard to listen and be collaborative. And I always show gratitude and try to help others as fearlessly as I do myself. Because every relationship matters. I'll always continue to shoot for the moon, take advantage of opportunities that come my way, and make sure people remember me.

Harsh Shah (linkedin.com/in/harsh-shah-637158112/) is an associate at DigitalBridge in New York, a global alternative asset manager dedicated to investing in digital infrastructure. He was previously an investment banking analyst at Houlihan Lokey. He was the 2017 recipient of the Peter Mansbridge Positive Change Award and Scholarship and named one of Canada's Next 150. He is a graduate of Ivey Business School at Western University, where he also earned his BA.

FROM MARSHALL
A MARSHMALLOW IS CALLING YOU
-OR-
THE DELAYED GRATIFICATION COST OF AN EARNED LIFE

When I was twenty-six years old, I went out to eat at The Imperial Dynasty, a top restaurant in California. The walls were filled with pictures and endorsements from important and famous people from all walks of life. One of them caught my eye. It said, "This restaurant is so good that if your endorsement is on the wall, it is not a compliment to the restaurant; it is a compliment to you." I said to myself, "I'm going to become this restaurant." Not get on its wall—but to be the embodiment of the words I read. Today, if The Imperial Dynasty had survived, I would have earned that compliment. And if you are endorsing my books, like *The Earned Life*, or joining my group of coaches, I have my own "wall" of special people who endorse my work, have helped and continue to help me achieve and learn more, and do some epic stuff.

To do epic stuff, you need to pursue goals without fear—sometimes multiple goals at the same time and often in different directions. You need to pay the price to achieve these goals, but delaying them too aggressively in anything you do can have consequences too. Sometimes, you should eat the marshmallow.

Let me explain.

In the late 1960s, Walter Mischel, a psychologist at Stanford University, conducted his famous "marshmallow studies" with preschool children at the university's Bing Nursery School. Children were taken to rooms where they would sit alone at a table, facing a marshmallow and a bell. A researcher told them they could eat the marshmallow whenever they wanted. Ring the bell, the researcher would return, and the marshmallow was all theirs. They were also told that they could have two marshmallows if they waited to eat the marshmallow for a period of time (up to twenty minutes), until the researcher returned. It was a vivid choice between immediate gratification and delayed gratification.

Follow-up research on the children years later led Mischel to conclude that the subjects who waited for the two marshmallows had higher SAT scores, better educational achievement, and lower body mass index. He documented it all in his book *The Marshmallow Test: Why Self-Control Is the Engine of Success*. The book made the test one of the rare laboratory studies about human behavior to become a cultural touchstone.

Of course, later studies questioned the soundness of Mischel's test. Affluent kids with highly educated parents in the Stanford community were more likely to be brought up in an environment where the rewards from delayed gratification were more obvious than what lower-income kids with less-educated parents were used to. Affluent children were also more likely to believe that the authority figure (the researcher) would deliver the reward.

Still, the underlying premise was sound: to make smarter choices about when to pay the price and when to pass, we first have to resolve the tension between delayed gratification and instant gratification. Broadly defined, delayed gratification means resisting smaller, pleasurable rewards now for larger, more significant rewards later. Much of the psychology literature celebrates delayed gratification, linking it with what we consider "achievement." Thus, we are relentlessly bombarded with the virtue of sacrificing immediate pleasure to achieve long-term results.

In my dictionary, "paying the price" is synonymous with delayed gratification, and "not paying the price" is synonymous with instant gratification. They're both about self-control, and many of us face a choice between them the moment we wake up.

Say you want to get up early to exercise before heading off to work. When the alarm goes off, you pause, tempted by the instant gratification of staying in bed for more sleep. You weigh getting up against the benefit of your fitness routine as well as the psychic pain of starting your day with an episode of defeated intention, a galling failure of will and purpose. Now comes breakfast: Will it be oatmeal and fruit or the tempting eggs, bacon, and toast? Then comes work: Will you spend your first hour tackling the toughest item on your to-do list that will take most of the day or clear your desk of some easier items to feel like you've gotten something done?

The choices have only started, and it's not even 9:30 a.m. As I see it, there are only two times in your adult life when instant gratification isn't a choice that tortures your soul. The first is when you are just starting out. You have no sense of disappearing time, so you can be extravagant with it and all your resources because you have time to make up for lost ground. Paying the price is something you can delay till some time "later" (whatever that means).

The second time is late in life, when the gap between the "now you" and the "future you" narrows. At a certain age, you become who you thought you wanted to be or, if not, accept who you have actually become. You can legitimately feel you've paid enough—and should luxuriate, however briefly, in easing up on yourself. The marshmallow is calling you. So you cash in your chips. Book the expensive trip. Volunteer your time freely. Consume that quart of ice cream without guilt.

In the many years between these times, you will constantly be forced to choose delayed gratification. It's why the ability to experience delayed gratification is such a decisive factor in living an earned life, perhaps an even more reliable predictor than intelligence.

In the end, the most persuasive reason for paying the price is that anytime you sacrifice something for something else, you are compelled to value what you gave up more. Adding that value back to your life is a goal worth earning and makes paying the price feel good. There's no shame in falling short if you gave it your best shot. There's no regret either. Remember, regret is the price you pay for *not* paying the price.

This is why I like to think about the marshmallow test on an even bigger level. Imagine if the study was extended beyond the second marshmallow. After waiting the required minutes, the child was given a second marshmallow but told,

"If you wait a little longer, you will get a third marshmallow!" And then a fourth marshmallow . . . a fifth marshmallow . . . a hundredth marshmallow.

By that logic, the ultimate master of delayed gratification would be an old person surrounded by thousands of stale, uneaten marshmallows. Who wants to be that person?

I often strike this cautionary note about the marshmallows with my coaching clients. Sometimes they're so busy making sacrifices to achieve for the future that they forget to enjoy life now. My advice to them is my advice to you: there are times when you should eat the marshmallow.

So when a marshmallow is calling you—especially if it is one that allows you to experience pleasure while you are paying the price, explore something you have always wanted to explore, or do some epic stuff—ring that bell and eat it. Do it now, if only to feel or recover the thrill of instant gratification. Don't wait for some late-life glimpse of mortality to shake you up.

24.

EXPERIENCE DIFFERENT

W hile I worked at the World Bank in Washington, D.C., I also taught a class at the University of Toronto called Public-Private Partnerships. A core focus of the class was learning the impact of user fees versus taxes. The difference is this: when you pay taxes, you're paying for local, regional, and national services that benefit everyone; when you pay user fees, you are paying for specific services rendered to you, and that changes your expectations. For example, you have expectations about the cleanliness, convenience, and maintenance of the roads and highways you use, but you don't pull out of your driveway and say, "This road better be good, faster, and worth it for me." But if you are paying a toll for using a specific highway or road, you do have those expectations because tolls are fees directly paid by you to use specific roads; the other roads are paid for as part of your (and everyone's) taxes.

I could have just laid out that and other examples of user fees versus taxes on a whiteboard. But I had another idea. To help my students understand how their expectations would be different if they paid for the course out of their pockets (user fees) rather than as part of all services funded by their tuition (taxes), I convinced the university to allow me to conduct an experiment. Students would pay the tuition for the course only if, at the end of the semester, they found value in and were satisfied with the course and the services I rendered as their professor. The only condition was if they opted not to pay, they would have to explain why in the form of a detailed letter.

The students, the university, and pretty much everyone I told what I was doing looked at me like it was the strangest thing they ever heard, and it made me a little bit of an eccentric celebrity on campus. In the end, the risk paid off: the students felt I delivered the value they expected from the course, paid for it, and ranked it among the best courses at the university that semester.

I have reflected many times over the years on why I did what I did in that course. Some of it was my dedication to the practice of experiential learning (learning by doing). Some of it was my wanting my students to learn the subject in a way they wouldn't forget. Some of it was my desire to give students agency in their learning and a measurable stake in their success *and* mine: I had "skin in the game" the way no professor of mine ever had.

But *all* of it was because of my willingness to *experience* different—to embrace the unfamiliar in service of a greater goal.

How are you experiencing different? This is not the same question as *What makes you different?* That question is asking what makes you stand out or why you can do a job better than others who have similar skills, experience, and achievements. The question *How are you experiencing different?* is asking you about your own experiential learning of difference.

Experiencing different in everything you do instead of just your job empowers you to better understand yourself, others, and the world around you. Experiencing different makes you better at your job, attracting others to you and what you have to offer. Most of you will work with people who come from places you have never been to and have experience and experiences you do not have. How can you *know* what makes you different from them without experiencing different?

Experiencing different:

- Compels you to engage and understand people, opinions, and cultures you are unfamiliar or disagree with to learn about other perspectives and find points of understanding, agreement, and compromise.
- Gets you out of the "echo chambers" that reinforce your existing beliefs and ways of thinking.
- Opens your heart and mind to possibilities, beliefs, and points of view you had not considered.
- Prepares you for questions when obstacles arise, such as *Is there any other way to do this? Is there something else I can do? Is there something others see that I don't?*
- Empowers others around you to embrace experiencing difference too.

My willingness to experience different has allowed me to achieve more throughout my career.

I only found the Fixed-Flexible-Freestyle framework while having a job shadow experience in the offices of ManpowerGroup with its chairman and CEO, Jonas Prising, who was also JA Worldwide's vice-chair of the board at the time. In experiencing something different in his offices, I saw how this framework could be reworked for what we needed at JA.

That said, your willingness to experience different, embrace the unfamiliar, and use what you learned isn't always enough to lead others or attract them to your thinking if they do not believe you are 100 percent genuine in your effort. Too many times, our actions, especially when we become leaders, do not back our words; we say one thing and do another. That leads to distrust, which is often how we perceive difference in this world.

EXPERIENCING DIFFERENT IN EVERYTHING YOU DO INSTEAD OF JUST YOUR JOB EMPOWERS YOU TO BETTER UNDERSTAND YOURSELF, OTHERS, AND THE WORLD AROUND YOU. EXPERIENCING DIFFERENT MAKES YOU BETTER AT YOUR JOB, ATTRACTING OTHERS TO YOU AND WHAT YOU HAVE TO OFFER.

My experiment with my students would never have worked if they did not trust me to deliver and if I did not trust them to be honest brokers of the value of the course. Similarly, at JA, I needed board members and the key regional leaders to buy into the framework for it to help. The operational shift was subtle but important. For example, by introducing the framework and empowering the six regional offices of JA to be equals, it elevated the CEO of JA Africa, which was a relatively small operation at the time, to the same level as the CEO of JA Europe, who had been in the job for over a decade and supervised a region that generated tens of millions of dollars in revenue and served millions of students each year. I needed our leader in Europe to be willing to embrace and experience different by seeing her colleague in Africa as a peer and feeling connected to the mission of all of JA, rather than just Europe. She did—and was then promoted to the global headquarters team even though she was living in Belgium—which in turn has allowed others to open their minds to a different way of thinking about career paths at JA Worldwide, in which they feel part of one global organization with opportunities for promotion, regardless of where they live, rather than separate regional offices with opportunities for promotion limited by geography. This subtle but important operational shift has helped JA Worldwide to become more globally diverse, with staff from many countries.

> **Ask yourself: How can you better experience different in designing who you are and want to become? Audit how you spend your free time, the media you consume, whom you talk to, what you eat, and where you travel when you have the chance. All of them may bring you pleasure, but how many of those things are the same all the time? What might you be missing, or what might be cutting you off from learning?**

Just the act of considering what you could be experiencing different can tell you a lot about who you are and how others perceive you.

It never ceases to amaze me how seemingly small detours to experience different, especially early in your life's journey, can change your trajectory. For my wife, Helen, her study abroad experience in Kenya during her junior year of college prompted her to design an individualized major in international development at Penn, which in turn led her to work for CARE, the international relief organization, after graduation. After working with CARE, Helen went to India to do economic development work with Seva Mandir, a large NGO in Udaipur, India.

Without the confidence that was fostered by her living in Kenya, a country that was entirely unfamiliar to her, and navigating Nairobi on her own as a twenty-year-old, would she have been bold enough to move to India to do development work at twenty-four? Those experiences helped Helen identify her own unique strengths and refine her interests and passions.

STORIES FROM
JUNIOR ACHIEVEMENT LEADERS

"HOW I ACHIEVED MORE BY EXPERIENCING DIFFERENT"

In writing this lesson, Marshall and I realized I am surrounded every day at Junior Achievement with colleagues who have shared their experiences with different that led them to learn more about themselves and their strengths. So, rather than choose one young achiever for this, we thought it would be great to end this lesson with multiple stories from achievers around the world reflecting on how experiencing different as they started their achievement journeys influenced their lives.

I think the only thing I knew for sure when I graduated university in Canada was that I wanted to be out in the world somehow. I was hungry to experience different places and people. I never had a plan for X job or Y career. I was keen on languages, especially French, so I chose to go to Europe. This was in 1990, just moments after the Berlin Wall fell. The excitement and drama happening in Central and Eastern Europe was reverberating across the continent. I was in London, on my way to tour France and Belgium, when I met two young women my age, one from East Germany and the other from Czechoslovakia. They were desperate to go home and see their families but had no money for the trip. I offered to leave my tour behind and drive them in return for a place to stay. I wanted to go there and see the action.

That choice took me down a path I could never have imagined. I ended up teaching English in Bratislava, meeting people

I never imagined meeting. I learned to speak Slovak, which opened even more doors for me. I was there in 1993 for the "Velvet Divorce," when Czechoslovakia split into the Czech Republic and Slovakia. Like all the former Soviet republics, Slovakia was a transitioning economy, desperate to rebuild. A new frontier.

Because of those circumstances, my Western background and language skills paid off. I decided to stay in Slovakia but shifted away from English teaching when I saw the opportunity to set up a local JA chapter. Launching a nonprofit startup in those days was not for the faint-hearted, but the kind of education that JA offered seemed a perfect fit for a new Slovakia— and, as it turned out, for me. I had found a meaningful career at JA and left Slovakia after seven years to become the senior vice president and eventually the chief executive officer of JA Europe, a job I held for eighteen years until I became chief operating officer of JA Worldwide, the global organization that oversees the JA network. Now I work with people in countries around the world to help young people thrive.

All because, as the Robert Frost poem says, I took the road less traveled.

Caroline Jenner
Chief Operating Officer, JA Worldwide

I grew up with a strong sense of the value of quality education, but it's not necessarily where I thought I would spend my career. After initial stints as a middle school history teacher and a financial services job with Smith Barney, I joined Junior Achievement on the international side of the growing organization. JA combined all my areas of interest: education, business, and international economic development (which I had studied in college). I eventually became the president of JA of Georgia, focusing on improving the lives of young people in Atlanta, which led me on a deeply fulfilling and unexpected journey as a social entrepreneur.

JA's platform was unique, in my experience, in that it addressed entrenched systemic issues connecting education and economic mobility. After a few years of deepening partnerships with school districts in metro Atlanta, the opportunity arose to cocreate a new model for high school that leveraged JA's expertise in relevant, experiential, and real-world connected learning. This innovative school model came to be known as 3DE.

As a semi-independent subsidiary of JA, 3DE reimagines education to improve the high school experience and expand economic opportunity for student communities across the US. At 3DE schools, students learn academic concepts by using the case method to see the connection between school and the skills, mindsets, and behaviors they will need to thrive in the future of work. It's been invigorating to see 3DE work in practice and expand from Atlanta to many other US cities and school districts.

In the end, my career has been all about experiencing different, which led me to create something different. When I was young, my father advised me to be willing to step into the unknown and take full advantage of opportunities with humility and curiosity. For me, experiencing different jobs, roles, and people has allowed me to be a better leader and in turn to believe that change is possible, even in the often "stuck" narrative of public education—when approached in a collaborative and comprehensive but different manner.

Jack Harris
CEO, 3DE Schools

In 2016, when I was twenty-four, I left my consulting job in New York City and moved back to Nigeria to set up JA Nigeria. When we introduced the sixteen-week JA Company Program to secondary schools, we found that the boys would take the lead setting up the business. But by week ten, their attention dwindled, and the girls stepped up to lead, powering through all the challenges and getting the business across the finish line. Because of that, in 2001, I started a leadership program that would empower the girls who discovered their leadership ability. We created the Leadership, Empowerment, Achievement and Development, or LEAD, camp, a one-week program that would bring the fifty most outstanding girls from the company programs across Nigeria to Lagos for a week of projects that they had to start and deliver within the week.

The LEAD programs are extremely empowering for the girls. They meet entrepreneurs and leadership role models in the public and private sectors—all from different walks of life that they never even envisioned before. Many also learn about gender-based violence and sexual reproductive health.

By the end of the week, we have all these supercharged girls just raring to go home and enact change in their communities.

But there have always been at least one or two girls who didn't want to go back home, because going back home meant facing the gender-based violence we learn about. Maybe their father is raping them. Sometimes it is an uncle who is the financial sponsor of the family, and the family is powerless to act against the molestation. It broke my heart sending these girls back home, but I had no other recourse. We had them speak to our counselors, who would help them recognize their power to say "no," but I always felt like that just was not enough. I couldn't keep them in Lagos, and there were no organizations, social welfare, or government agencies that I could call to intervene.

So I created one. When I joined the African leadership program, they challenged us to think about how we wanted to change the world: If there was one thing that we wanted to change that was a source of pain to us, what would that be? I imagined a world where you had millions of girls across Africa in leadership positions, creating our policies and social safety nets that empower girls to complete their education and become whatever they want to be. We can bring together millions of Black girls from across Africa who are leading in their communities—who are thriving and building businesses that hire people—and together help develop policies and laws that change the way that girls and women are treated.

That's how 10 Million Black Girls or 10MBG was created. I called it 10MBG because I also wanted African girls to have a powerful network that looked like them across the world— that they can inspire and that can inspire them—a powerful network of women in leadership building businesses across barriers, across regions, across difference.

Simi Nwogugu
Chief executive officer, JA Africa
Winner of the 2023 African Education Medal

I have campaigned at the United Nations for proper investment in children's early years and spoken at the JA Americas conference about youth development. That I spoke on these topics would surprise no one. Youth development is my greatest passion. What surprises me is that I was even on those stages. Some of me is still the shy girl who didn't want to speak in public. I learned how to do it through helping others not like me.

Most people in Argentina did not grow up with the resources I did. In a country where 50 percent of children live under the poverty line, you become aware of your privilege, even when you don't have much. I knew I never had to struggle. At times during my education, studying was my only job. I got to travel abroad to compete in a geographic Olympiad for free on a scholarship when I was sixteen. That is not the reality for so many people in my country, where education is the way you move between classes.

When I came back from the Olympiad, I got interviewed by the media and was asked what I wanted to do next. I said I want other students to have the same opportunity I did. That's why I started working to build the JA alumni network in Argentina to support JA, as it is free for all students. That's how I came to focus on creating their volunteer networks to help more broadly with youth development.

At times, people have looked down on what I am doing. They would say, "Why don't you focus on your job? Your job is the way you grow professionally and get more opportunities." But investing time in my volunteer work has helped me grow as a leader and as a person as much as, or more, than anything I have done in school or at my jobs. In fact, I have my job because of all the work I did volunteering for JA. That's why I believe helping others is helping yourself and encourage everyone—no matter their age or professional status—to find a way to inspire, support, or uplift others. You can grow in ways that you wouldn't be able to by just going to school and getting a job.

Nelly Cetera
Staff member, JA Americas

25.

FREESTYLE YOUR "SELF"

F reestyle lessons are about designing and innovating *you*, so how are you designing and innovating yourself in the world?

What is your modern achievement story?

What are your unique strengths? How did you discover them? How have you leveraged them as an aspiring leader or as you start your leadership journey?

After you reflect on these questions, ask yourself: *Based on your experience, what is your favorite achievement lesson you would share with others?*

Now share it!

Sharing your story can help inspire others. So when you're ready to share your lesson with others, allow us to help you. Go to **modernachievement.com**, click on "share," and if we choose your lesson, we will share it with our community of achievers!

---

26. DESIGN YOUR PASSION

27. GO PLURAL

28. MAKE FRIENDS FIVE TO
    TEN YEARS OLDER — AND
    YOUNGER — THAN YOU

29. SHARE YOUR STORY TO
    INSPIRE OTHERS

30. FREESTYLE YOUR CAREER.

CAREER

26.

DESIGN YOUR PASSION

As part of a recent retreat, my wife, Helen, did the Enneagram, an assessment that identifies which of its nine basic personality types you most closely align with. Helen came out strongest in category three: "The Achiever." She was floored. She thought she would be strongest in category eight: "The Helper." In fact, she was sure in the past she would have been "The Helper." I have known Helen since college and admired her work in the nonprofit sector. I can assure you she is right: she is, has been, and will always be a helper. But I was not surprised "achiever" came out on top for her this time. She *is* an achiever. Her career may have focused on helping others, but her personality has shifted as she has gained experience and grown. That was an important and valuable recognition for her—and for me—when it came to this lesson.

If you haven't already done a personality assessment like Enneagram, Myers-Briggs, or *What Color Is Your Parachute?* at school, work, or just for your own career education, you probably will soon enough. These assessments—and similar ones for skills and strengths like StrengthsFinder 2.0—are valuable tools for employers but also for understanding yourself and designing a career you love. They are terrific for resolving current dichotomies (see Marshall's comment) and understanding who you are, where you are, what matters to you, and why you may not be maximizing or performing up to your potential now. It is thrilling to discover when something is different or has changed, as Helen did, to gain new understandings and insights. When I do assessments with my students, like from Amii Barnard Bahn's "Promotability Index," they are as floored as Helen was with the results, which lead to more self-awareness and self-knowledge.

But personality, like modern achievement, evolves over time, and very few people in my experience, including myself, treat these tools as a process. You take the assessments once, and then, even if you reflect on them years later, you don't go back and take them again. That failure does you a disservice.

Assessments are snapshots. Like a picture, they are trapped in time, while you are not. As you age, you won't just change physically; you will continue to learn more about yourself, others, and the world around us, which changes you emotionally, mentally, and spiritually as well. You should use any assessment or framework like Fixed-Flexible-Freestyle as a checkpoint to help you understand where you are now and make sure you are still designing the life you love. Assessments provide data for you to consider as you design your achievement story, and that design will need to evolve over time.

For example, thinking back to when I did Ayse Birsel's heroes exercise (lesson twenty-one), one of my heroes was Mahatma Gandhi. He might have been on my list throughout my life for various reasons. But I also listed Marshall as a hero, whom I met only in 2017. I admired them for the ways they use storytelling and rhetoric to move others—whether countrymen or high-achieving leaders—to act and change their behavior. That ties very much to my current work for JA Worldwide and less to my early career. Because as my jobs and careers changed and evolved, so have the qualities I aspire to in my work.

Ayse knows this evolution is a natural part of designing the life you love. We expect the products and services we use every day to adapt, change, and do different and more things, so why don't we expect

WE EXPECT THE PRODUCTS AND SERVICES WE USE EVERY DAY TO ADAPT, CHANGE, AND DO DIFFERENT AND MORE THINGS, SO WHY DON'T WE EXPECT THIS OF OURSELVES? OUR VALUES AND EXPERIENCES ARE NOT FIXED. YET THAT'S EXACTLY HOW MANY PEOPLE TREAT THEIR ACHIEVEMENT STORIES, ESPECIALLY WHEN IT COMES TO PASSION.

this of ourselves? Our values and experiences are not fixed. Yet that's exactly how many people treat their achievement stories, especially when it comes to passion. Most of us treat passion as something we create over time. We are told we should find our passion, implying that it will be fully formed when we do, and that it will lead to our happiness and fulfillment. But that is often not the case.

Simply put, "find your passion is awful advice." That was in quotes because it's the title of a 2018 article in *The Atlantic* by Olga Khazan. Specifically, she says that *developing* your passion embraces a "growth theory" of interests, while *finding* your passion embraces a "fixed theory."

Carol S. Dweck was the first person to delineate the difference between growth and fixed mindsets. In her book *Mindset: The New Psychology of Success*, she describes how a fixed mindset believes that success should be won without effort. A growth mindset believes success comes from your efforts, strategies, and help from others to discover your unknown and untapped potential. Khazan noted that Dweck was now working with Paul O'Keefe of Yale and Greg Walton of Stanford to extend that theory to passion and show that passions aren't a found or fixed theory of interests that are there from birth, waiting for you to discover them, but are developed or grown from interests you cultivate throughout your life. This delineation echoes earlier research, such as "Finding a Fit or Developing It: Implicit Theories about Achieving Passion for Work" (*Personality and Social Psychology Bulletin*) about how "fit theorists believe that passion for work is achieved through finding the right fit with a line of work" and "develop theorists believe that passion is cultivated over time."

Regardless of the terminology researchers used, their results all showed that most people believed in the fit or find-your-passion fixed theory. That is not what the iteration process of modern achievement rewards. Finding your passion is a fixed approach to your career. Designing your passion is about growth.

I admit to my bias here. I am not a "fixed" kind of person. When I started my career, I never thought I would end up leading JA. JA was something I did as a teenager, but I didn't see it as my future. I never thought I would end up working for the organization or even a nonprofit. Even when you have found your passion for a single career like law or medicine, you cannot stay fixed in your knowledge and experience, so why stay fixed in your mindset and stop exploring your passion for that career?

Failing to develop her own passion and following a predetermined career path was how Sanyin Siang in lesson eleven learned to "plan for serendipity." That phrase speaks to the fixed-versus-growth dichotomy of approaches to passion. You can plan for passion like you plan for outcomes and results, or you can plan for serendipity and embrace the process that opens you up to new possibilities and ideas.

Sanyin sees this as part of "diversifying your emotional risk" to keep perspective and stay emotionally invested in our careers and lives. "Just as we diversify our financial risk with a portfolio of investments, we need to also diversify our emotional risk when it comes to our jobs," she says. "Be emotionally vested in things outside of work, in creating opportunities for other areas of growth, such as through volunteering, mentoring, or personal relationships. When you diversify your emotional risk in your career, you can make better decisions, have better perspective, and be even better at your job."

The way Sanyin reframes risk is the way we should reframe passion and modern achievement: as an ongoing process for finding fulfillment, not a single destination. Do that and you will develop the emotional intelligence—the self and social awareness and empathy—that attracts people to you and makes for a strong leader.

What I am advocating for is an approach to passion that uses the same growth mindset that is essential to any entrepreneurial endeavor. A growth mindset encourages you to take an iterative approach to designing your passion and career as you would any product or service by doing the following:

- Valuing the process over the end results.
- Having a sense of purpose to keep the big picture in mind.
- Acknowledging and embracing your imperfections.
- Seeking learning over approval and results.
- Replacing the world "failing" with the word "learning."
- Rewarding actions not traits.
- Constantly creating new goals.

Can you succeed if you believe that you will find your passion? Of course! And I certainly believe you can learn to be passionate about something even if you don't start out that way. But I've seen too many people waiting for passion to land on their laps. My concern is what you may be cutting yourself off from by not cultivating passion over time—ruling out jobs, careers, or experiences because you think it is not your passion and therefore is irrelevant, uninteresting, or lacks value.

YOUNG ACHIEVER STORY
CLINT CADIO
"CURIOSITY DRIVES YOUR PASSION"

When I connected with Asheesh for this book, I had just won David Meltzer's *2 Minute Drill*. The show features five entrepreneurs competing for more than $50,000 in cash and prizes. We had just two minutes to deliver our pitches to four judges and then had to answer questions. I pitched a solar tech company, BumbleBee, which represents my mission to make an impact by empowering others through climate tech and sustainability. Our company increases the efficiency output of the standard solar cell so we can bring down the size of solar panels and make them more scalable at the commercial level. But BumbleBee can be more than just a source of elec-tricity; it can be a symbol of hope for those who have been left in the dark for too long, and it can continue to create a sustainable future for all.

CLINT CADIO

I loved every moment on *2 Minute Drill*. I felt prepared in my pitch and had done my research on what kind of hard questions they might ask, like, "Why don't you attack the inefficiencies of solar at the consumer level?" (Answer: Working with manu-facturers made much more sense to us at scale.) But I have no idea if solar tech is my future. My interest in solar energy and research in photovoltaics are only my latest passions to grow. At my heart, I am an avid software developer who loves to build projects in blockchain and AI. Just a year before the show, I worked as a researcher for iMining Inc., a blockchain sustainability company doing software development and engi-neering. Before that I was doing hackathons. It was only when I did some research on the energy grid in places like sub-Saharan

Africa and how they were relying on solar tech that my curiosity for climate tech grew.

Curiosity and creativity are my strengths. If I have a lot of passion, that's a good thing. I just want to follow my curiosity and find serendipitous opportunities that open me up to things I never knew I could be passionate about. I used to think passion was something that just comes to you. But as I started my achievement journey, I learned that the more you gain experiences and perspectives, the more you will find that different data points will lead you to more paths you might be passionate about.

Of course, my parents think I'm crazy. They told me I was going to be a doctor or engineer. They love me, but they put me in those boxes for achievement without even knowing what they meant to me. I need to respect my parents but then do the things that seem interesting to me to define what I might want. The more I try things out that are authentic to me, the more I will be able to pursue whatever I want and achieve. If I don't, I might be pursuing something I can achieve in, but how will it make me feel?

It's up to me how I let external factors define me as a person and what I pursue. For example, in school I excelled at math and science, but I only discovered I have a passion for philosophy and the humanities thanks to one teacher who helped me understand what reading could mean to me. This teacher told me to try out a book about philosophy because I might enjoy it, and I listened—and I loved it. I understood I didn't hate reading. Now I seek out the simple pleasure of sitting and reading a book, which keeps me off my phone and away from screens.

I realize now that not pursuing your passion is really about fear. I used to be scared to try out new things, thinking that I would not be good enough. But thanks to programs like The Knowledge Society and Junior Achievement, I learned you can pursue what resonates with you. The more I try things, no matter how many mistakes I make, the more I will find new opportunities and work to develop and grow them. Even exploring different aspects of something I love like AI or blockchain develops my passion so I don't get stuck focusing on one thing.

In the end, my parents just want me to have opportunities they did not. And that is what I am giving myself. I finished high school. I plan on eventually going to university. I will have opportunities and choices my parents never dreamed of. If I saw my path as singular, I would never have deferred my admission to uni and taken a gap year to pursue the company and wound up winning *2 Minute Drill*. University will always be there for me. This opportunity to pursue my new passion for solar tech will not.

So I say to you what I say to myself every day: keep building your passion and enjoying the process to find and understand what you love! I'm excited to see what happens, and I know it will be fun. I have just started scratching the surface of what I can learn.

Clint Cadio (clintceo.com) is a computer science student and a fervent advocate of climate tech and sustainability who aims to foster global connectivity by pioneering advancements in sustainable software practices. He is a student activator at The Knowledge Society and a reporter for JA Worldwide. He is an alum of JA Canada and JA Americas.

RESOLVE YOUR DICHOTOMIES AND BE THE PERSON YOU WANT TO BE

Too often in life, we get lost in results and the belief that somehow if we keep getting those results—paying the price and following a predetermined path, enjoyment be damned—we will "get there" and achieve a permanent state of happiness. But as the poet Gertrude Stein said about her childhood home which no longer existed, "There is no there there."

Only fairy tales end with the sentence "They lived happily ever after."

Instead, think of every day as a chance to start over or continue to build a new you. To enjoy what you're doing and to try to achieve something meaningful. That's not tied to the work you do. It's tied to a higher aspiration. Yes, you need your health, an income you can live and make a future on, and good relationships with people you love. But those are results that should come from doing something that you think is meaningful—that has a purpose. That's how we live our own earned lives instead of someone else's version of them.

If you don't feel you're being the person you want to be right now or that you want to be a better version of what you are, perhaps you need to resolve some dichotomies in your life.

In lesson twenty-one, we introduced you to Ayse Birsel's *Design the Life You Love* and her heroes exercise for discovering your values. At the same seminar where Ayse taught me that exercise, we talked about dichotomy resolution—a designer's term for resolving either/or dilemmas. She told me that her favorite part of product design was resolving these either/or decisions that the client left to her discretion, such as whether the design should be classic or modern, small or functional, stand-alone or expandable into a product line . . .

Ideally, a designer like Ayse creates a mash-up of the dichotomies—a classic design but updated with modern materials or a product that is high performance and affordable. That's very hard, but do it right and you create incredible value and growth. That said, it's not always possible. "When holistically designing something—including yourself—you need to consider your intellectual, spiritual, emotional, and physical sides," Ayse says. "But even designing something holistically, we still must make choices. That's when you need dichotomy resolution."

Dichotomies demand a choice rather than forced integration. Optimist or pessimist? Joiner or loner? Active or passive? Seeing the world as an endless string of dichotomies doesn't automatically simplify your decision making. You've merely reduced your many options to two. It doesn't matter if you see the world in black and white or in shades of gray. Pick one or the other—you can't be both at once.

Dichotomy resolution is especially critical at the start of the aspiration process. Unless you're hoping to flip your personality completely, your aspirations should not conflict with your core values, preferences, virtues, and quirks. They must authentically fuel your passion. As Clint said, it wouldn't do him any good to pursue one career path or passion within a single career if it felt inauthentic to him. So he has already resolved some dichotomies at this point in his life by choosing exploration over settling, creativity over the status quo, and multiple paths over one direction.

Not all of us can be as clear about our passions as Clint, but even if you think you are clear on where you are going, Ayse's exercise below will help you identify the dichotomies in your life and continue to grow.

AYSE BIRSEL'S DICHOTOMY RESOLUTION EXERCISE

- List all the interesting dichotomies you can think of on a piece of paper (e.g., optimist/pessimist, active/passive, joiner/loner, collaborator/independent, self-starter/doing what you're told, flexible/structured, small/big, start-up/established, leader/follower, noisy/quiet, marriage/single, family/no kids, salty/sweet). If you're stuck, ask partners or friends for their suggestions.

- Using a pencil, check each dichotomy pair that applies to you now.

- Using a Sharpie, completely redact each unchecked dichotomy that doesn't really apply to you. You should end up with a sheet of blacked-out words that looks like a redacted top-secret document.

- Study the remaining dichotomies and decide which half of each pairing reflects you. Cross out the other half with the Sharpie.

- Look at the piece of paper. The remaining unobscured words reveal your defining qualities.

You can't argue with the picture those qualities paint. You painted it. These qualities influence what you aspire to. (Bonus exercise: Share your finished sheet with the people who know you best and ask what they think.)

But before you move forward, remember that achievement is a process. You will grow and change like the world around you. That's why the world "now" appears in Ayse's exercise. Doing it once helps you understand where you are, but the path to success is never straight. You will encounter new dichotomies, value new things, uncover new opportunities, discover new strengths, and build new passions as you grow. Make sure you heed Asheesh's advice and return to this and *any* exercise you do over time to make sure you are still becoming the person you want to be and designing the life you love.

27.

GO PLURAL

"**G**oing plural" was a term I first encountered in England. It is associated with people, usually senior executives, who retire or leave their companies and take on several jobs instead of another full-time job to keep learning and unlocking potential, have more influence and less stress, and still generate income. People at the start of their achievement journeys might understand this as a version of a "portfolio career": an employee who takes on several roles within the same company or a young person who has side hustles, supplemental gigs, or several unrelated jobs to make ends meet or generate multiple income streams. Going plural or a portfolio career is certainly familiar, especially to entrepreneurs who always play a few roles and a few hands at once. They don't just bet on one project or business to succeed; they have multiple businesses and projects to hedge their bets.

For me, "going plural" is also a synonym for what I call a twofer. In January 2010, after I left Virgin Money but before I took my next career step, I was interviewed for a Harvard Business School case study and said this about my future goals for myself: "One of my central insights in life has been that you need twofers, threefers, even fourfers, ways to combine different parts of your life or goals. That intrigues me. It means that two things could be better separately, but I'd be willing to make a tradeoff to do them together."

Usually the term "twofer" refers to point-of-sale transactions where you get two items for the price of one, but I was thinking about trying

IN A RAPIDLY CHANGING WORLD OF MULTIPLE JOBS AND CAREERS — SOMETIMES AT THE SAME TIME — A DYNAMIC AND EVOLVING ENTREPRENEURIAL APPROACH TO SKILLS AND STRENGTHS COMES FROM YOUR ABILITY TO EVOLVE AND ADAPT TO IDEAS.

to have balance when work and life are so integrated. I was trying to design a life that combined my desire to make money with my desire to have a social impact while also spending time with my twin boys and supporting my wife on her achievement journey. I was going plural in incorporating all those things into the process of designing the life I wanted.

But going plural is not just a choice; it is also a skill.

In a rapidly changing world of multiple jobs and careers—sometimes at the same time—a dynamic and evolving entrepreneurial approach to skills and strengths comes from your ability to evolve and adapt to ideas. You are in control of your value and how you stay relevant, up to date, and prepared for the inevitable shifts in the way companies operate and business gets done.

The more you develop skills that help you anticipate change, live with uncertainty, see possibilities and opportunities, and stay focused through the noise, the more attractive you are to the people looking to hire you. And these skills are not found within the credentials on your resume, nor are they the ones businesses and graduate schools train you on.

According to the World Economic Forum's 2023 *The Future of Jobs Report,* four of the five skills that are expected to grow in importance the fastest are defined as cognitive skills ("creative thinking" and "analytical thinking") and self-efficacy ("curiosity and lifelong learning" and "resilience, flexibility, and agility"). The only technology skill to crack the top five was "technological literacy" at number three.

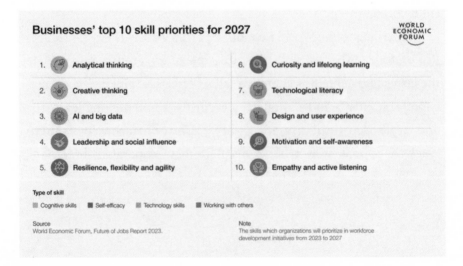

The report is based on a survey of a wide cross-section of the world's largest employers: 803 companies and 11.3 million workers across 27 industry clusters and 45 economies. Consider their list of skills on the rise against what they said their top skill priorities were for five years down the road.

The breakdown in the top five skills is the same with cognitive skills at the top—"analytical thinking" just swaps places with "critical thinking." The self-efficacy skill of "leadership and social influence" jumps into the fourth spot, bumping "curiosity and lifelong learning" down to number six, while "resilience, flexibility, and agility" stays at number five. Number three is still a technology skill, but "AI and big data" has replaced "technological literacy," which dropped to number seven.

The picture painted by the data around the need for cognitive skills is compelling and reflects "the increasing importance of complex problem-solving in the workplace," which businesses across the board are emphasizing the need for. The data around self-efficacy is more complex. Self-efficacy remains essential, but the skills vary in importance from industry to industry. Most companies recognize the importance of workers' "ability to adapt to disrupted workplace" today, but some industries see adaptability becoming less necessary if or as disruptions recede. A diverse range of industries—from insurance to research, design and business management services to chemical and advanced materials—will emphasize resilience, flexibility, and agility. Medical and health services and electronics industries will emphasize skills development in curiosity and lifelong learning. Infrastructure will focus its self-efficacy skills strategy on motivation and self-awareness.

Full disclosure: I am active in the World Economic Forum (WEF) and serve on the Stewardship Board for the WEF's Center for New Economy and Society, which collaborates with the group that develops the annual *The Future of Jobs Report*. The addition of self-efficacy in these reports is partly the result of my advocacy since I have seen it up close and personal among JA students who thrive in the new economy. But there is plenty of complementary research to confirm the data in our report. For example, the 2023 edX AI Survey of eight hundred executives for *Navigating the Workplace in the Age of AI* found that those executives think that in two years AI will render almost half of the skills used in the workforce today irrelevant, including their own! The same number of executives think they and their people are unprepared for the workplace of the future, which also aligns with our report.

Consider also the recent work of Adam Grant, an organizational psychologist at the Wharton School. In *Hidden Potential: The Science of Achieving Greater Things*, he shows how even the "underrated" and "overlooked" can maximize their potential through learning. Specifically, he stresses the importance of stretching beyond our strengths to get outside our comfort zones and achieve more: "Neglecting the impact of nurture has dire consequences. It leads us to underestimate the amount of ground that can be gained and the range of towns that can be learned. As a result, we limit ourselves and the people around us. We cling to our narrow comfort zones and miss out on broader possibilities. We fail to see the promise in others and close the door to opportunities. We deprive the world of greater things." Nurture of that kind requires the skills of creative and analytical thinking.

I want to be clear that I am not diminishing the importance of technological skills and training, but the top skills you need in the future will have little to do with knowledge and experience or technology. Many jobs and many of the basic skills needed to do them are becoming automated or obsolete, and anyone whose job or skills can be automated can be replaced. According to the WEF report, 44 percent of workers' core skills are expected to be disrupted or to change in the next five years. That doesn't mean they are in decline— the report showed no skills to be in net decline—just that the other skills have become more valuable. That doesn't mean companies are training on those skills. WEF found five of the top six skills that companies report to be increasing the fastest are "not always reflected in corporate upskilling strategies" (i.e., trainings that businesses give employees to keep up with industry and other changes to give them the tools they need).

Simply put, creative and analytical thinking are skills humans still value in humans, but most companies and graduate schools do not train on it. Marshall's comment provides a great set of tips to get you started on thinking about how you acquire those skills. Remember, the reason to grow your passion is that *you* will change. The reason to grow your cognitive and self-efficacy skills is that *the world* will change, and you need to think about and own your place in it. That's exactly why going plural is essential to ensuring everything you do from your main job or jobs to your side hustles and gigs combines to build and develop the most important skills you'll need in the future.

Money will always be worth less in the future. Cognitive and self-efficacy skills will not.

YOUNG ACHIEVER STORY
SARAH RAPP
"THINK GLOBALLY ABOUT YOURSELF"

I grew up in a protected, privileged bubble in a small town in Germany, which I never wanted to live inside. I wanted to develop my own bubble that could float out over the world. Junior Achievement helped me understand how much bigger that world was.

After doing the JA Company Program in my town, I traveled to Cologne for a JA Innovation Camp and realized how small my experience had been. All the students talked about going to the European finals—I didn't even know there were competitions—and my brain just exploded. Only one person had done JA with me in my town, so I became very active in the alumni network in Germany to connect with others, and I volunteered

SARAH RAPP

to be a coordinator and then the membership manager for the network. Then I became a project manager for the European alumni network, and when I was twenty-four, I took over as president of the European alumni network. That was crazy—twenty thousand members in twenty-four countries. And right after I started, they told me my first role was to speak to the European parliament. *OK* . . .

After two years leading the alumni network in Europe, I got fired. Not from JA—from my paying job in Malta, along with 160 others.

You see, JA was not my job. Everything I had done for JA since Germany had been volunteer work so I could stay connected to my goal of becoming and working as a global citizen. To be clear, I had wanted to do that in my other jobs. After high school, I got my BA in sports management while I worked for the German sports federation in Stuttgart. At nineteen, I got to do some big international events like the World Cup because I was the only one who wanted to speak English. I worked five and a half years there until I finished my studies, working in different departments, building communities, doing budgets, and arranging sponsorships.

My final event for the sports federation was leading all the delegations at the world championships in rhythmic gymnastics. That's when I said, *That's it. It can't get bigger than that here.* I had felt stifled for years. As in many German organizations, everyone followed the ways things had always been done. It was hard to push new ideas forward. So I quit and applied for jobs everywhere but in Germany. I eventually landed a job in sports sponsorship in Malta, creating campaigns for sports teams like Manchester City in the Premier League. I hadn't been there a year when the layoff happened.

The first thing I did after losing my job was reach out to JA and say, "Hey, here's my CV in case you know anyone who would need someone like me." A week later, Erin Sawyer, JA's vice president for people and events, called me and said JA was not going to forward my CV to anyone. *OK* . . . Then she said JA was going to hire me for a new paid position: global alumni community manager. Asheesh wanted to build a JA alumni community and networks around the world to mirror the success of the alumni networks in Europe and Mexico. My job would be to connect the wildly diverse programs from six global regions and one hundred plus countries.

My bubble was now the world!

Fast-forward to today, and JA has a huge alumni community and one hundred alumni networks and counting. I am now the director of alumni and people engagement and serve as a connector for the young JA graduates who want to change the world to older JA alums and other people, resources, and communities in our network. They connect through us. We also host alumni summits where we bring together alums from across the regions. I get to do everything from fundraising and events to partnerships and marketing. It feels like my own startup inside JA, which JA encourages—the exact opposite of my previous work experience. The work also inspired me to start my own brand.

In Germany, my job was to bring people together who were all in the same box. That isn't a global environment. At JA Worldwide, my job is to bring together all these cool different cultures and people with diverse values, beliefs, and understandings. *How do I help all these people connect to and understand one another?* That is global. Of course, the first thing I did was Google "how to be global," but that was no help. That's when I started building my own brand called "How to Be Global" and hosting the podcast of the same name. Four years and more than one hundred episodes later, I have also gone on to do keynotes and workshops on intercultural communication, global citizenship, and navigating a global world. I'm also involved with the UN Foundation's Equal Everywhere Campaign, and I am the head of PR at Nomad's Giving Back. Now I am working on building a hub for all that and more.

All these pieces of my career connect through me and are aligned with who I feel I am and want to be. They connect people and embrace the complexity of being a global citizen.

Sure, while I was building my brand, I was terrified to talk about it at JA because I didn't know what people would say. I shouldn't have worried. I had never let what I did outside of JA affect my work (just as I never let my JA volunteer work affect my other jobs). In fact, JA sees how my brand benefits everyone and supports what I do as long as I continue to do the job I was hired for! I have even started a scholarship program in Ghana with a JA global alum. What's even more amazing to me is that I now have people who *volunteer for me* working on my brand, and I try to empower them globally the way JA did for me when I was their twofer.

I want everyone to connect as who they authentically are. And you don't need to travel and be the kind of global citizen I am to be global. *You just need to think of yourself globally in what you do, who you are, and how you operate to achieve better and more.*

Yes, when I was in my twenties people questioned whether I had the capacity to do all this, but that's exactly when you are likely to have the capacity to pursue multiple paths with fewer demands on time, like a family and kids. If you are focused on what you are doing and it is right for you, let the judgers judge. Don't let "them" make you afraid to try it all. Just find the right balance and don't lose yourself in the process.

I realize now I became a successful global citizen only because I thought of myself as global—as more than who I was when I grew up. I tried to build the relationships and skills I needed to create more opportunities, like doing the JA volunteer work or speaking English. Because some of it was volunteer work or generated no revenue for me, it opened my mind, introduced me to new people, and built new skills. Not everything you do on the side needs to be a side hustle that (eventually) generates income. Those opportunities that develop you globally can be more valuable to your personal brand in the long run. You never know when they might become your ticket, not just to greater skills but to greater opportunities.

Sarah Rapp (sarahrapp.global) is the director of alumni and people engagement at Junior Achievement Worldwide, where she works to create opportunities for JA students who have graduated and want to stay involved with JA. She is the founder of the How to Be Global brand and podcast, which aims to connect the world by lowering boundaries to enable more interconnected human experiences and celebrating diversity. She is an ambassador for the UN Foundation's Equal Everywhere campaign and leads public relations for Nomads Giving Back and Nomads Skillshare. She has traveled to almost fifty countries.

FROM MARSHALL
"NINE TIPS FOR 'HI-PO'S' TO START THEIR CAREERS OFF RIGHT!"

No matter how strong the job market is, job security is largely a thing of the past. High-potential people, or hi-po's—people who not only achieve and get promoted but ascend into leadership—used to spend their lives at one company or in one industry. Now, the stories of people spending their lives at one company are fewer and farther between. Actually, most *companies*, no matter the size, won't last your working life, and as the World Economic Forum data shows, the jobs and industries themselves are changing. Like it or not, even if you start out in a large corporation, you need to think as Sarah and Asheesh do: be an entrepreneur for yourself.

While I realize we cannot all be entrepreneurial in the sense that we can't all start our own companies, we can all be entrepreneurial in terms of how we approach our careers. Below are a few suggestions for how to demonstrate the entrepreneurial spirit that you can implement as you start your career. Some of them echo what you have read in other lessons. Gathering them all here gives you a place to reflect as you consider how you freestyle your career.

1. Pick a path. This is critical! No matter how many jobs and careers your achievement journey will have, your path comes from the inside, so read about, reflect on, and research what you want to achieve in life now. Don't worry too much that you might take the wrong road. You can always change your mind along the way. Personally, I found my path as a university student in Indiana. I was nineteen and had spent all night thinking about what I wanted to do with my life. Dawn came. I looked out of the window and saw people waiting to go to work. I realized I didn't want to do that. I wanted to become a university professor, but through my course of study and jobs I took, I found my passion was in helping people become better leaders. I didn't start out in life thinking I would become an executive coach. I didn't even know there was such a job. In fact, I don't know if there was! It's evolved through the years as I've followed my path and sometimes changed directions.

2. Love what you do. Years of hard work (which generally precedes success) don't seem so hard if you are doing what you love. My friend and mentor Dr. Paul Hersey, upon receiving an honorary doctorate, shared one of his secrets for success with graduating students. He beamed at the hundreds of young people in the audience and said, "Looking back on my career, I don't feel like I have ever worked a day in my life. If you really love what you are doing, it all seems like fun!" Finding what you love to do may take some effort, but it is worth it.

3. Be curious. One of the greatest entrepreneurs I have ever known is Mr. G. M. Rao. He is the founder of GMR Infrastructure, which is now a large infrastructure company in India. When I asked his colleagues what Mr. Rao was doing right, they all marveled at his constant curiosity. One commented that "he travels through life, constantly observing. He makes notes on all kinds of potential opportunities, which most people might not even notice. He doesn't just observe—he acts! He immediately follows up with messages to staff that say, 'Please check this out.' While many of his observations do not turn into business opportunities, some do. This is one of the reasons that he is so successful."

4. Find your own market niche. In the same way that successful entrepreneurs provide innovative solutions to market opportunities, you can work to develop a special competency that differentiates you from everyone else. Be creative. Look for market needs that everyone else may not have considered. Anyone can do what everyone else is doing. Great entrepreneurs provide products and services that are better than or different from what everyone else is doing. You can also do this at your present job: What should be done that isn't being done?

5. Become a world expert. As intimidating as this sounds, achieving serious "world-class" expertise may not be as daunting as you might believe. If you pick a reasonably narrow area of specialization, focus on it, and learn as much as you can, you will start to accumulate serious knowledge within a few years. While you can never become the world authority on everything, you can definitely become a world authority on one thing. That is what Sarah Rapp did in thinking global, and she turned it into her brand (see number eight).

6. Learn from the best. As you ponder your career options, ask yourself: "Who do I want to be like in ten years?" or "Who are the world's experts in fields that are related to my desired area of expertise?" Try to learn from these people's lives. You may be surprised. Some may even go out of their way to help you.

7. Do your homework. While the role models you look up to may be willing to help you, respect the fact that they are very busy people. Their time is valuable. For example, if they have written books on a topic, read the books before you ask them questions. If they are executives in your own company, study their history—read their bios—and learn from their coworkers before you ask them to invest their very limited time in helping you.

8. Build your own brand. Peter Drucker, a visionary and influential thinker on business and management, once told me that companies should be able to "put their mission statement on a T-shirt." The same can be true for individuals. For example, my mission is to be the world authority in helping successful leaders achieve positive, lasting change in behavior. Your customers (or employers) will respect you more if you do not pretend to know everything about everything but instead have a brand that is uniquely you.

9. Pay the price. It is possible that you may just get lucky and become incredibly successful without having to work very hard. Don't count on it. Most successful people work very hard. The "luck" that they experience is often impacted by the years of effort that have prepared them to take advantage of fortuitous opportunities.

28.

MAKE FRIENDS FIVE TO TEN YEARS OLDER — AND YOUNGER — THAN YOU

The inspiration and foundation for this lesson come from Aman Ghose, a student in my entrepreneurship course at The Fletcher School at Tufts University in 2021. While putting together this book, we interviewed and asked for feedback from young achievers like Aman, and his suggestion to "make friends five to ten years older than you" for a lesson was a bit of a revelation. I began to ask questions of myself about how things might have gone differently for me and my career choices if I had heard and embraced this lesson back then. Would forming friendships with people five to ten years older than me have led me to stay at the World Bank or Monitor? Would my businesses have been more successful if I'd had older friends to guide my choices?

I did have friends who supported and pushed me (see lesson ten), but most of those were friends my age. I also had friendships with my mentors, but they were older, which is typical in most mentorships (in which the mentor is someone senior by a generation or more, who shares experience and wisdom with the mentee). Aman saw what I couldn't: a hole between those two relationships, and he understood the value of filling it. As he says in his story, "[These friends] help you through every situation because they understand things change so much faster than they did for people who are much older."

I will let Aman tell his story of how he came to understand the power of this lesson in the comment that follows. My contribution is its inverse: you need to make friends with people five to ten years younger than you, too. As Aman becomes more established in his career, he will be the five-to-ten-years-older friend others seek out, and these friendships, like all great relationships, must be reciprocal.

I have recently built a relationship with Martynas Kandzeras, who is about ten years younger than me. Martynas is from Lithuania and is building a venture fund to invest in start-up companies, started by recent graduates of JA Lithuania's entrepreneurship programs. After seeing so many bright and promising businesses seeking funding, he decided that it was time to raise a seed stage fund for young entrepreneurs—the first of its type in his country. Martynas's passion energizes me, and I am as eager to learn from him as he is from me. He is also thoughtful about how to build his relationship not just with me but with the dynamic community of entrepreneurs who graduate from JA programs each year. For example, we created a side letter with the entrepreneurs who receive funding to encourage them to "pay it forward" by donating back to JA when they succeed in their careers. This side letter is not a contract, but simply a moral obligation that builds a culture of philanthropy in Lithuania among future business leaders and a sustainable way to fund future activities of JA with financing from alumni.

In fact, part of the reason we have worked so hard to set up our global alumni communities at Junior Achievement Worldwide is that the older alums are often invigorated by what they learn from the younger alums. The younger alums help the older ones see and solve problems and feel empowered as they do. You might not be a JA alum, but chances are you have alumni networks from high school, college, work, and other organizations you belonged to in order to start finding and forging friendships with people five to ten years younger than you.

Meanwhile, at work, you can bridge that gap by asking for some reverse mentoring, in which younger employees teach you skills instead of vice versa. Making time in my schedule to have a reverse-mentoring experience is now on my to-do list, and I owe that to Karl Moore and his book *Generation Why*, which offers valuable lessons and leadership advice for unlocking potential in younger employees.

Karl taught management at Oxford and is now a business school professor at McGill University in Canada. What I love about his book is what I loved about him at Oxford: he was different. He was neither British nor a traditional academic. He had been an IBM executive who became a highly prolific management professor midcareer. Karl would assign me readings, even though he wasn't my primary dissertation supervisor, to spark my curiosity and improve what I ultimately wrote. But he was intellectually curious and wanted to continuously improve and learn too. Meeting for lunch or for walks in Oxford, we would talk for hours. He turned to students like me who energized him and thought about and taught him things he did not know. He was not insecure that we knew things he did not. He *valued* that.

The energy Karl brought to our relationship and his approach to it are exactly what you need when making friends five to ten years younger than you. You need to have the same curiosity Karl did and see that they can help you achieve as much as you help them. As you move into leadership, you will need to hire people to do the things you cannot. Your job is to collaborate with and empower them—give them the space and agency to run with the piece of the business that is theirs. For me, it has always been that the person who has the best idea should be able to lead it, even if they have no previous leadership experience. Empowering others empowers you.

EMPOWERING OTHERS EMPOWERS YOU.

YOUNG ACHIEVER STORY
AMAN GHOSE
"MAKE FRIENDS FIVE TO TEN YEARS OLDER THAN YOU"

My parents moved from India to the United Arab Emirates (UAE) for my dad's banking job when I was a kid and Dubai had just started its ascent to the global megacity it is today. I went to an international high school where my class was made up of sixty different nationalities. But while I had a diverse group of friends in school, the transient nature of the city meant families usually came to the UAE for a year or two and moved on. What I understood as friendship was skewed by this reality. I thought friends come and go.

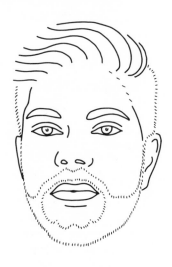

I stayed in the UAE until I went to Claremont McKenna College in California, where I studied politics, philosophy, and economics and graduated with absolutely no idea what I wanted to do. Diplomacy interested me, so I headed to D.C. and found a job with

AMAN GHOSE

the Confederation of Indian Industry (CII), India's largest trade association and advocacy group. At CII, I connected the Indian aerospace and defense industry to lawmakers on the Hill and governors of the various states, listened to deals getting done in Congress, and produced advocacy and policy papers. Despite the interesting nature of the work, I did not find it fulfilling, and my impact on the overall course of events was minimal. I had the urge to transition from government into the private sector.

Working at an organization like Boeing, Lockheed Martin, or Raytheon would have been my dream job, but that was not realistic as I did not have an engineering degree or MBA or any deep knowledge of the aerospace and defense industry. As I got rejected for roles at my dream companies, the president of CII encouraged me to move to India to gain a competitive advantage by understanding its aerospace and defense industry. People thought I was crazy to leave. Many of my peers from the Middle East and India who moved to the United States for school wanted to stay there. But I followed my heart and moved to India in 2017, where I cold called and promptly got rejected by all but one of the multinationals that were getting into aerospace and defense: the Aditya Birla Group, a $50 billion metals, mining, telecoms, and financial services conglomerate, which hired me in their new business ventures division.

My coworkers at the Aditya Birla Group were much older than me with families, and they preferred not to travel globally. Since I had no such commitments and was eager to learn, I found myself with the opportunity and trust of my company to conduct due diligence missions and business development negotiations with global firms at various air shows and production factories across China, France, the UK, Middle East, and Australia. I did that for two and a half years until I was twenty-six, but the nature and complexity of the industry meant that deals moved slowly, and I still didn't have much to show for my work except some transformational experiences and connections. That's when I really started to understand the value of personal connections and the art of building relationships.

During my time in India, I was introduced to a network of entrepreneurs, artists, actors, diplomats, journalists, and tech and banking professionals, largely by my cousin. This network happened to be, on average, five to ten years older than me. I immediately developed an affinity for them and their experiences and stories. Their willingness, patience, and kindness to impart key lessons, strategies, and guidance on how to navigate my early career was more connected to what I needed than any other relationships I had. They saw that I had the desire, focus, and potential to achieve my goals and helped me understand who I could be next, how to get there most effectively, and the value of staying humble but still hungry. I worked to understand all the wisdom they imparted.

It was one of these relationships with someone older, forged on a soccer pitch, that translated into a job at a private equity firm. When I first moved to India, I joined an amateur football league in a bid to both keep fit and socialize through sport. I quickly realized that I wasn't the most talented player in the league and had to find a way to maximize participation when I did not get minutes on the pitch. What I lacked in skill and stamina I made up for in effective organization of the team and in managing egos and expectations. My skills caught the eye of a private equity managing director who appointed me manager of his team in the league. We got to know one another, and what started as an owner-manager relationship ended up as a close friendship. Two years later, when I wanted to pivot out of my job, I relied on him and the friend group we formed around football for advice. While mulling over my next career move, he offered me a role at his private equity firm and gave me an opportunity to learn about portfolio management, insights into how to evaluate start-ups and founders, exposure to how private capital is deployed, and strategies for how to effectively scale a business.

I served as an associate at the private equity firm for six months as it navigated the downturn in the economy through the start of the COVID-19 pandemic. The experience deepened my appreciation for entrepreneurship, and as COVID-19 released its grip, I knew I had the entrepreneurial bug. That's when I enrolled in Asheesh's class on entrepreneurship at The Fletcher School at Tufts University and secured an internship at Mastercard working on frontier technologies like artificial intelligence, digital assets, biometrics, and cybersecurity. Eventually, the company created a completely new role for what I was doing and offered me the job.

But that's not the job I ended up taking and have today, which came through my network of friends who are five to ten years older than me.

It's fascinating how many job opportunities and offers happen this way. They never or barely ever get advertised. It's all referrals and endorsements from friends and peers in your network. In this case, my friend had become an early investor in Aquanow, a fast-growing start-up based in Canada that was expanding globally. He knew the company touched all the things I was interested in and thought it would be an ideal platform for me to launch the next phase of my career. So, when I was at his wedding, he introduced me to the CEO of the company. We started talking about my work at Mastercard and what I would like to do, and he started talking about their expansion into the Middle East and Turkey. Next thing you know, he hired me in a senior role with equity in the business to align incentives.

So I am back in Dubai, working for Aquanow, taking the risk of proving myself to people all over again in an industry where everything can and has gone "poof." The pressure is fierce in my current job, and the terrain is tough to navigate, given the constant ambiguity. But I relish operating in ambiguity and thrive on being able to find order within chaos. And I am once again relying on the lessons, wisdom, and guidance from my friends and network of peers who are five to ten years older than me to give me the confidence to follow my heart and overcome whatever life may throw my way. I may have passed on the stability, name recognition, and attractive pay at Mastercard to follow my instincts and begin my entrepreneurial journey, but I know I can always return to a large corporation if I maintain my friendships and relationships.

Today, I understand what I could not with my transient high school friendships: the value of maintaining all my relationships. I've learned it's easy to meet people if you consciously put yourself out there. Seek activities and arenas in which you have a genuine interest and passion and look to meet like-minded individuals from all walks of life—especially those five to ten years older than you. Then work hard to maintain those relationships. Never treat them as transactional or as a means to an end. Their value is in the perspective they give you and the opportunities and possibilities they help you see down the road.

Aman Ghose (linkedin.com/in/amanghose) is vice president for partnerships at Aquanow, Canada's largest digital assets and liquidity and infrastructure provider. He previously worked at Mastercard in product advancement and enterprise strategy and in new ventures at the Aditya Birla Group, a multinational Fortune

500 company, where he was a founding member of its Aerospace & Defense team. He graduated from Claremont McKenna College and received an MIB from The Fletcher School at Tufts University.

FROM MARSHALL
"LISTEN UP!"

Community lies at the heart of our fulfillment. What kind of life is earned if you live it alone? None of the people I have worked with believe they are self-made. They also appreciate that their choices and aspirations affect other people—that a community is not all one-way streets. Everything is reciprocal. But this reciprocity is not merely the two-dimensional kind between individuals. It's not the transactional I'll-scratch-your-back-if-you-scratch-mine reciprocity of aggressive networking. It happens when someone says, "I need help." And someone else, without making a "what's-in-it-for-me?" calculation, hears the plea and responds, "I can help."

Much of the good that you do for others without expectation of payback—comforting them, following up with them, connecting them to someone, or simply being present and hearing them—comes back to you whether you seek it or not, because this reciprocity is a defining feature of community. That is what Aman understands. And you'll never understand that, hear anyone's plea, or build that community if you fail to listen—really listen—to others.

Asheesh and I have said this many times in this book, and I'm going to say it again here: 80 percent of our success in learning from other people is based upon how well we listen.

If you can't listen to others, you'll soon find that your networks and relationships are often transactional and situational. That your community *is* mostly one-way streets.

You may *find* those friends five to ten years older than you on those streets, but you won't *make* them.

Listening and "people skills" become more important the older you get and the higher you go. Imagine a world where technical skills, educational pedigrees, even professional achievements no longer matter. Everyone is blessed with equal brains and talent. Everyone is highly skilled, well educated, and locked in a dead heat of accomplishment, posting the same "lifetime batting average."

Now, imagine that you lead an organization in this world. How would you hire people? How would you decide whom to promote and whom to cast aside?

Chances are you would start paying very close attention to how people behave—how they treat colleagues and clients, how they speak and listen in meetings, how well they extend minor courtesies to lubricate daily work and limit friction. Welcome to the real world at the higher levels of organizational life.

We apply these behavioral criteria to almost any accomplished person we work with, whether it's our boss or our plumber. But sometimes we forget to apply them to ourselves. And in turn, we forget that our behavior is key to our relationships.

Which is why I say, all other things being equal, your people skills become more essential the higher up you go. In fact, even when all other things are not equal, your people skills often make the difference in how high you go.

Imagine you're that leader again: Who would you rather

have as your CFO—a moderately good accountant who's great with people outside the firm and skilled at managing very smart people or a brilliant accountant who's inept with outsiders and alienates smart people? Not a tough choice, really. Candidates with superb people skills will win out every time, in large part because they will be able to hire people smarter than they are and lead them. There's no guarantee that the brilliant number cruncher can do that now or any time in the foreseeable future.

You, like everyone else, have certain attributes that helped or will help you land your first job. These are the kinds of credentials and skills that go on your resume. But as you become more successful, those attributes recede into the background and more subtle traits matter. Everyone around you is smart. You must be smart *and* something else.

What if you had to prepare a resume where you couldn't highlight where you graduated college, any academic recognition, or the big name of your current and previous employers? You can't boast about the profits you posted, the sagging division you turned around, or the product you launched and turned into a stand-alone brand. The only data you can put on your resume are your interpersonal skills (which, for the purposes of this exercise, must be documented and authentic). What would they be?

1. To be able to listen?
2. To give proper recognition?
3. To share information or credit for a success?

4. To stay calm when others panic?
5. To make midcourse corrections?
6. To embrace responsibility?
7. To admit a mistake?
8. To defer to others, even (especially) those of lesser rank?
9. To let someone else be right some of the time?
10. To resist playing favorites?
11. To say thank you?

Stripped of your technical skillset and your hall-of-fame-quality lifetime batting average, what are the interpersonal skills that will make you rise above the leadership pack? Pick one, any skill that you feel you're lacking. If you aren't sure, go ask your community.

29.

SHARE YOUR STORY TO INSPIRE OTHERS

A ya Youssef was born and still lives in a refugee camp in Lebanon with her parents, who were born in the same refugee camp. Her grandparents were brought to Lebanon as children by their parents when they fled Palestine back in 1948. None of that history has stopped Aya from writing her own achievement story. She is a JA alumna (from our chapter in Lebanon, INJAZ Lebanon), was one of fifty finalists (out of 3,500 applicants) for the first-ever Global Student Prizes (sponsored by the Varkey Foundation and Chegg.com), served as a student emcee of JA's global leadership conference, and graduated in 2023 with a degree in architecture from the American University of Beirut (AUB). What follows is part of her story as she told it to us.

AYA YOUSSEF

My passion for marine architecture started with a passion for the National Geographic *documentaries I watched on TV as a kid with my parents. You can imagine how excited I was then, when as a junior student at AUB, I had the chance to apply and was* selected for a two-month externship with the National Geographic Society and the Nature Conservancy. Throughout the externship, I became known as the girl who was passionate about water even though I have no idea how to swim. In fact, I am super afraid of water. But I love the sea. It gives me a wonderful feeling. I even fall asleep listening to water sounds.

During the externship, my concern with climate change and rising sea levels really started, which led to my pivoting in design and architectural focus and wanting to deal with rising sea levels from an architectural and materiality perspective. Studying architecture from that perspective is not that common. What was even less common was a girl like me even wanting to study architecture. I've never had access to any great cities, just what I could see on TV and online.

When I applied to the American University of Beirut, I wasn't even sure that would be my course of study, but that was more about what other people wanted for me. I thought about being a doctor to make my extended family proud of me. My dad did not go to university due to the war in Lebanon, and he and my mom kept asking me if I was sure I wanted to go into architecture. Being a doctor would give me opportunities. A female Palestinian refugee is not allowed to join the union of architects in Lebanon. "What are you going to do with the degree?" they kept asking. But their questions only made me more determined. I was so curious about architecture. I liked the practical side of building and creating. It was a totally new experience, beyond the books, and I wanted something new and challenging.

I also didn't see anyone approaching important architectural issues rooted in my experience and perspective. The biggest challenge facing young refugees is a lack of access to proper education and what that does to their mindset. But another major issue is the *architecture and infrastructure of camps, which lack open, green spaces. They also lack accessibility. I studied both those things, but for my undergraduate thesis, I returned to my love of water.*

I tried to find case studies about people trying to solve rising sea levels through architecture. Mostly what I found were floating cities or infrastructural resisting concrete. I thought, "This is how we solve the problem? We escape from it? We resist with worse methods?" So my undergraduate thesis discussed rising sea levels from an entrepreneurial and architectural perspective and designed some methodologies and solutions that would have social impact and work with our sea, rather than against it.

Because of my story, I knew I could combine my passion for entrepreneurship and architecture for social and global good, and my professors admired my passion and ability to approach the design process differently. I tried new technologies, software, concepts, and ideas to build my design proposals based on a merged version of everything I enjoy creating and accomplishing: my externship with National Geographic Society, my love of water, and my ultimate passion to make a change in any way possible on both a local and global scale.

That's why I say my story makes people realize what is possible. People picked me for the externship, admission to university, and other awards because I presented my story. But I share my story to show others what is possible and make changes to the things I care about. I started doing that in high school. In 2016, I started the first-ever coding club at my United Nations Relief and Work Agency school, sharing my self-taught knowledge and experience in coding with around twenty students who were willing and eager to learn something new. I wanted to reach students with a similar background to me—who had lived in or around a refugee settlement—because not many people knew how to learn how to code on their own or even what coding is. Yet that knowledge coming from someone like me opens up so many opportunities and, more importantly, revolutionizes a student's mindset by showing what's possible, what is there, and what they can be or do.

Through that club and my high school academics, I started noticing that the students also lacked access to resources about attending universities and earning scholarships in Lebanon. I had already been researching this information for myself and decided to start sharing what I found. I became part of an outreach team to spread the word about educational and scholarship opportunities at the best universities in Lebanon. I partnered a year later with two other changemakers with the same vision and mission, and we cofounded ToRead to increase the scale of our outreach and to bridge and fill in the gaps between high school students and universities/ scholarship foundations. The online platform allows those students to search, filter, and compare university and scholarship options they are eligible to apply to in Lebanon and abroad.

I am very proud that ToRead lives on without me, as I moved on in 2022 to cofound Step.propriate, which has designed a step that is placed at the bottom of a door to open it hands-free. In 2023, I was selected as one of the top six JA alumni to compete for $50,000 on David Meltzer's 2 Minute Drill on Apple TV. With Step.propriate, I am continuing to design for social impact, my community service, and my architecture work to make sure that every time I learn something that benefits me, I share it as part of my story. I love what I am doing, even if it is extremely experimentally experiential, and I know it will put me forward on that path to achieving my goals with my career. But I am not and don't want to be exceptional. My story is what makes me different, but there are a lot of me's out there. I know there are many people who have the same problems

I have, and I know my story can be powerful to them as much as it is for me. If I can show people like me that their story matters by sharing how my story matters, then I will have more people I can collaborate with, and we can make the changes we want to see in the world. (Find more about Aya at linkedin.com/in/ayayoussef1.)

I didn't include Aya's story in a separate comment because her story helped me articulate what I wanted to say in this final freestyle lesson. As I started writing this book, I kept coming back to a word that appears in the subtitle: timeless. *How do you make an idea timeless?* Many of the classic books I referenced in the Fixed section sold millions of copies in their authors' lifetimes and then millions more long after they passed away. How did they make these books timeless?

Aya's story made me realize that you can't *make* anything timeless any more than you can make someone love something. Love is a process that builds over time. You cannot force it; you feel it. What makes us feel the lessons in this or any book are not the words but the stories. *What good would the lessons in this book be without sharing a story that helped you feel them?* They would be empty words—maybe even platitudes—or far less memorable without stories to connect you to them and help you understand.

For me, this understanding of the power of shared stories to connect and inspire extends well beyond the mission of this book: I have made it a major part of my mission at JA Worldwide to invite young people to share their stories with us. This team effort culminated in 2022 with the launch of Youth Voices (YouthVoices.org)—a partnership between JA Worldwide, Cortico, MIT's Center for Constructive Communication, and Accenture—which captured firsthand stories from JA alumni from sixty-four countries. The site provided tools to highlight, analyze, and share these conversations, and the results sent a powerful message about JA's values and direction and the role JA programs have played in alumni's lives.

As we listened to our alumni stories and did our analysis, we learned quite a few things, too, which influenced our strategic planning when six key themes about JA emerged from the conversations:

- Self-efficacy
- Global citizen skills
- Learning experiences
- Thriving communities
- Youth empowerment
- Values

It's hard not to see how those themes have influenced not only my work at JA but my entire approach to this book and the process of modern achievement. I might never have seen that and been willing to open myself up to sharing my stories if those young people and everyone who became part of this book had not been so willing to share their stories with us.

Sharing your story requires a degree of vulnerability that helps you understand the process of your achievement, and that vulnerability is essential for becoming a leader. That may sound self-serving, but not if, like good leadership, the sharing is focused on serving others. That's how "sharing your story" differs from "presenting your story" (lesson six): the stories in this lesson and throughout this book are in the service of you.

That's how our stories stand the test of time: they help and empower you to achieve and see and become more through vivid examples of the possible. That's timeless.

SHARING YOUR STORY REQUIRES A DEGREE OF VULNERABILITY THAT HELPS YOU UNDERSTAND THE PROCESS OF YOUR ACHIEVEMENT, AND THAT VULNERABILITY IS ESSENTIAL IN BECOMING A LEADER.

"YOUR STORY HELPS PEOPLE REALIZE WHAT'S POSSIBLE"

As we did in the final lesson in the freestyle "self" section, Marshall and I thought it would be best to end this lesson with stories from Junior Achievement leaders sharing how their stories inspired others. The title for these comments comes from Aya. She is acutely aware, even early in her achievement journey, of how her story can, in her words, "magnify possibilities for others." But only if she continues to share her story and inspires others to share theirs. We hope these JA stories help you understand that our stories motivate us more than just the words in the title of this lesson and every lesson in this book do.

I grew up in Toledo, Ohio, in a loving, caring family, but education was not really a focus for my parents. My mother finished high school, but my father dropped out to join the Marines in World War II, where he rose to the rank of platoon sergeant. When he left the corps, he went to work in factories in Toledo—stamping plants, auto manufacturing, those sorts of things. The work was sporadic. We often ended up on food stamps and unemployment. That was the world I knew, and I didn't see any way education would help me make things happen differently for me. Not that I was a bad student, but I was very shy, and that didn't help.

Then the JA Company Program recruited at my school, and I signed up because this really attractive woman sitting in front of me signed up, and it was free. Lo and behold, it was a decision that changed my life. One of the JA volunteers who advised the student companies was a salesman and engineer who saw potential in me that no teacher or coach ever had. He made sure this shy kid with no love for education got elected vice president of sales of my JA company. So I learned how to sell and train other people on how to sell. In those days, that meant knocking on doors, and let me tell you, there's nothing more character-building than having a door slammed in your face. But when that first sale happened, a change came over me. It motivated me as a student and as a person for the first time in my life. I knew I could accomplish something—make something happen—and that people believed in me.

I stayed in JA the next two years of high school, becoming president the next year and then treasurer my final year. In fact, I became treasurer of the year in Toledo, Ohio, and went on to compete at the national level. I didn't win, by the way, but I did end up being the first person in my family to go to college with a JA scholarship. In fact, I never left JA. I worked for JA in college and after, working my way up from Toledo to the national organization, which merged with JA International in 2003 and opened my eyes to how we serve students in places like China, Russia, and the Middle East.

That merger motivated me even more to share my story directly and indirectly, like through Richard Teerlink, the former CEO of Harley-Davidson, who shares my story to motivate people to give to and volunteer with JA. I try to connect with young people like a high school student in California who was basically homeless and got involved in JA, and I had the opportunity to spend quite a bit of time with him. He ended up successfully graduating and now works for a film company.

I can't help everyone, but I am always looking for people who might benefit from hearing my not-so-rosy story and need some mentorship. I hope maybe I can have some of the motivating effect that JA volunteer in Toledo had on me.

I want people to know life is not something that just happens to you.

Jack Kosakowski

CEO, Junior Achievement USA

I initially wanted to become a diplomat and help change the world. But after gaining experience at the Italian Ministry of Foreign Affairs and working closely with Ambassador Uri Savir, the chief negotiator of the Oslo Peace Accords, I realized it would take me too many years to truly change the world as a diplomat. That's when I joined Uri's Glocal Forum.

Uri believed that one of the reasons peace accords do not succeed is that the decisions at the highest levels of government do not lead to tangible dividends for the population, especially for younger people. So he, together with Jan Stenbeck, created the Glocal Forum for city-to-city capacity building and youth empowerment. He had assembled a team of young people to think outside the box and come up with creative ideas. When a conference of mayors was organized in Rome in 2001, he asked us to come up with an entertainment program. What better idea than a concert in the Colosseum? From a seemingly crazy idea, we made history in the Colosseum: the first-ever concert at night with Ray Charles performing in front of three hundred mayors from around the world, including Abu Alaa from the Palestinian National Authority and Shimon Peres of Israel, who shook hands.

From that night, I learned about the power of music to cross borders and the power of youth to generate innovative ideas. These lessons continued to guide me as I managed teams and we organized engaging events. In 2004, the Glocal Forum, in collaboration with legendary producer Quincy Jones, launched the "We Are the Future" initiative, one of the largest fundraising events in Europe (and probably the world) to support children and youth in cities in conflict and post-conflict zones. The event was presented by Jones and Oprah Winfrey. Hundreds of artists—including Carlos Santana, Alicia Keys, Juanes, Cirque du Soleil, Andrea Bocelli, and Carmen Consoli—performed in front of hundreds of thousands of people in Rome's Circus Maximus and to a worldwide audience via MTV and Yahoo.

Before the concert, I also created partnerships with UN agencies and the World Bank. I shuttled between Washington, D.C., Los Angeles, New York, and Rome, meeting interesting people and organizations that supported the initiative. In fact, one day Uri was scheduled to present to Jim Wolfensohn, the president of the World Bank, in Paris, but during the meeting, turned to me and asked me to pitch it because I was young. I had to draw on all my skills to explain the "why" behind what we were doing. Jim bought into the initiative and asked me to work with the World Bank Institute to examine the World Bank's portfolio through a youth lens and see where we could connect the initiative with the Bank's existing portfolio.

I love to tell this story because it highlights how you don't have to "take the stage" yourself to make a difference. Working behind the scenes as a young person can put you in places that drive your career path. Today, I am more comfortable being in the spotlight—"taking the stage"—and am proud of the impact that I can make on the lives of young people in Europe.

Salvatore Nigro
CEO, JA Europe

I participated in the JA Company Program in Córdoba, Argentina, when I was seventeen and was asked to be an intern for the summer. That internship turned into a part-time assistant role when I was starting college. I sent three hundred faxes in just three days, trying to convince people to join a fundraiser event in our local office. That began a rapid ascent over the next decade-plus in JA, from working for JA Córdoba to being the head of JA Americas when I was thirty-three and eventually being selected as the Chief Development Officer of JA Worldwide, reporting to Asheesh directly as the first non-American to hold this important role.

One of the most transformational experiences that I ever had was in 1999, right after I joined JA Córdoba. The office was creating something called the International Forum for Entrepreneurs, which was something very disruptive for a city that is not Buenos Aires. Our intention was to bring delegations of young JA entrepreneurs from across the province and region to spend five intensive days in the mountains of Córdoba, participating in activities such as inspiring keynote presentations from famous role models, design-thinking workshops, and something we called "around the world in one breakfast," where each delegation would cook their typical breakfast. It was a mix of entrepreneurial empowerment and cultural exchange.

The second edition of the forum really changed the way I thought about how important it is to bring young people from all over the world to share stories and learn from each other. The way I saw it was these are maybe the future presidents of the different provinces and the next generation of business leaders. If we can have them connecting now and building understanding and empathy, then we are not just building entrepreneur networks but building a better tomorrow because of these relationships we are making now.

I carried this understanding of the power of this entrepreneurial spirit and the power of connection to my work at JA Americas. So when we were discussing having a global event, the JA Global Youth Forum, I told them what we had done in Córdoba for many years, and we started to plan something bigger. In July 2018, we succeeded in bringing young leaders from forty-seven different countries together in Mexico, with a focus on building their entrepreneurial spirit. Like during those first forums in Córdoba, some of these young people had never left their cities and towns. They came from rural areas in Latin America, urban areas in the Middle East, suburbs in North America, villages in South Asia, and everything in between. Young people always remember the experience of getting on a plane for the first time—as it was for many of these teenagers. Giving them a chance to see how big and different the world is transforms the way they see the world. They understand that the power of ideas lies in their diversity. They leave the event feeling like global citizens. The more I can help develop that in young people, the better it will be for the future of the business and the world.

Leo Martellotto
Chief Development Officer, JA Worldwide

30.

FREESTYLE YOUR CAREER

Freestyle lessons are about designing and innovating *you*, so how are you designing and innovating yourself in your career?

What is your modern achievement story?

What are your unique strengths? How did you discover them? How have you leveraged them as an aspiring leader or as you start your leadership journey?

After you reflect on these questions, ask yourself: *Based on your experience, what is your favorite achievement lesson you would share with others?*

Now share it!

Sharing your story can help inspire others. So when you're ready to share your lesson with others, allow us to help you. Go to **modernachievement.com**, click on "share," and if we choose your lesson, we will share it with our community of achievers!

CONCLUDING LESSON:

BE FIXED, FLEXIBLE, AND FREESTYLE

T his final lesson is best introduced by a Buddhist parable Marshall taught me.

On a blazing hot day, a young farmer covered with sweat paddled his boat upstream on a wide river to deliver his produce to the village. He was working hard to make his delivery and get home before dark. As he looked ahead, the farmer spied another boat heading rapidly downstream toward his. He rowed furiously to try to get out of the way, but it didn't seem to help. He started screaming, "Change direction, you idiot! You are going to hit me! Look out!" But it was to no avail. The boats collided with a sickening thud.

Enraged, the farmer cried out, "You moron! How could you manage to hit my boat in the middle of this wide river? What is wrong with you?"

Only then did the farmer realize that he was screaming at an empty boat that had broken free of its moorings and was floating downstream with the current.

The moral of this story is simple: there is never anyone in the other boat. We are always screaming at an empty vessel.

It's wonderful advice: accept that you are the source of your problems and reaction.

WHETHER YOU ARE
JUST STARTING YOUR
ACHIEVEMENT JOURNEY,
IN THE THICK OF IT,
HEADING INTO YOUR
FINAL THIRD, OR
REFLECTING ON THE
PATHS YOU HAVE TAKEN,
YOUR STORY IS ALWAYS
IN PROCESS, REGARDLESS
OF THE OUTCOME.
HOW YOU WRITE THAT
ACHIEVEMENT STORY IS
YOUR RESPONSIBILITY.

OK, maybe we are *often* screaming at an empty vessel. There are sometimes people in the other boat, just as there are things that happen to us that we have no control over. In any of those situations, we still have control over how *we* act, and that is where we should focus our attention and energy. Don't waste time with negativity. Adjust course and steer your boat forward.

This parable extends to modern achievement as a whole and what Marshall wrote in *The Earned Life: Lose Regret, Choose Fulfillment.* "We are living an earned life when the choice, risks, and effort we make in each moment align with an overarching purpose in our lives, regardless of the eventual outcome," he writes. "The reward of living an earned life is being engaged in the process of earning such a life."

There's that word again: *process.*

Whether you are just starting your achievement journey, in the thick of it, heading into your final third, or reflecting on the paths you have taken, your story is always in process, regardless of the outcome. How you write that achievement story is your responsibility. The choices, risks, and efforts you take and make are defined by your actions and reactions.

There is no one in the other boat.

There will, however, always be others in *your boat.* Sometimes we have no choice, like your family or teachers. Sometimes we choose whom to let aboard. No matter what, you need others with you on your journey. Relationships matter, for better or worse. Some will try to help you find your way. Others will tell you what to do—what to say, do, be, and become. How much you let those different people influence your choices on your achievement journey—to make it bigger or smaller—is also up to you. No matter your choice, you still steer yourself through the process of modern achievement.

As I said at the start of this book, modern achievement is a messy process and is only getting messier. Even if you choose one career path and pursue it from start to finish in your life, it will likely not be a linear progression to the "top." Being prepared for this process of modern achievement—for the inevitable stops and starts, zigs and zags, hurry ups and waits, obstacles and opportunities—requires balance.

Taken together, the lessons in this book are examples of how you can find that balance, choosing when to use which lessons and what parts of the framework as you achieve more and explore possibilities for your future—even as you are writing it! The Fixed-Flexible-Freestyle framework for organizing those lessons provides you with that balance—reminding you to learn, to collaborate with others, and to claim your individual power to grow, succeed, and lead.

Achieving that balance requires an open and creative mind. That's why the key to navigating the "waters" of modern achievement—and indeed life's journey itself—and all they throw at you is not to be fixed, flexible, *or* freestyle. It is to be fixed, flexible, *and* freestyle.

Fixed, flexible, and freestyle often seem to oppose or be separate from one another, but integrate them all in your life and you both increase your value and create opportunities to achieve more. The benefits of this go beyond your future success to include your mental health and wellness overall.

Balancing fixed, flexible, *and* freestyle reduces stress by allowing you to see achievement as a process and find success and fulfillment through your entire achievement journey, not just through the attainment of goals and objectives.

It helps you be more optimistic.

It forms the foundation for relationships that make for a good and happy life.

It reminds you that you have choices.

It reveals your values and what you value—and how that can change.

It compels you to learn by doing.

It attracts others who collaborate with you and push you to be your best.

It shows you how to have respect for others and their ideas, opening you up to new ideas and building communities.

It creates empathy.

It inspires and motivates others to be their best.

It embraces failure and mistakes as iterations to success—as part of the process of designing your life.

It empowers your creativity and curiosity.

It develops the skills you need to make an impact.

It makes you more grateful for what you have and what could be.

It builds the self-efficacy you need to stop worrying about the other boats coming toward you.

It moves you from *I can't* to *I can*.

ACKNOWLEDGMENTS

The original idea for this book was formulated over dinner in New York City just as the world was recovering from the COVID pandemic and people were returning to restaurants. Mark Thompson deserves our deep gratitude for hosting this pivotal dinner and for agreeing to be part of the book from the very start. Mark is our dear friend and colleague, serving as Marshall's collaborator for multiple projects and Asheesh's first executive coach.

Months later, we were connected to Jim Eber, an exceptional writer and thought partner, who helped us to refine the essential thesis of the book and connect it to lessons from our lives. Without Jim's adept touch, this book would be an academic tome without the relevance that comes from applying the Fixed-Flexible-Freestyle framework to the practical lessons in the book in a readable and enjoyable way. We are thankful to both Mark and Jim for their key roles in moving this project from idea to reality. If you are fortunate enough to work with Mark as an executive coach or Jim as a writer, count yourself privileged!

As the book came together, we interviewed several individuals who had helped shape our thinking by sharing their own lived experiences and lessons. These included some of the world's best leadership coaches, key leaders from Junior Achievement, and achievement-oriented young people from our experiences with teaching and working around the world. When we asked for their input for interviews and contributions, every one of them said yes, without hesitation.

A special thank you to the following individuals who not only said yes to be interviewed, but also agreed to include their own stories in this book: Amii Barnard-Bahn, Aman Ghose, Alex Osterwalder, Aya Youssef, Bill Carrier, Caroline Jenner, Clint Cadio, David Burkus, Harsh Shah, Howard (Yiq Zhenn) Leong, Jack Harris, Jack Kosakowski, Julie Carrier, Leo Martellotto, Lindsey Pollack, Maya Raichoora, Michael Bungay Stanier, Mikael Frølandshagen, Nelly Cetera, Salvatore Nigro, Sarah Rapp, Sanyin Siang, Simi Nwogugu, Whitney Johnson.

Our understanding of achievement in all of its forms has been richer because of the 100 Coaches network and colleagues from the JA network, past and present. Special thanks to those who have supported us on this journey of self-discovery in MG Connect groups and gatherings, YPO forum meetings, and JA gatherings and discussions, notably: Akef Aqrabawi, Alan Mulally, Alisa Cohn, Antonio Nieto-Rodriguez, Bonita Thompson, Brandie Conforti, Celia Deitz Valdespino, Carolyn Bassett, Carol Kauffman, Deepa Prahalad, Diane Ryan, Donnie Dhillon, Dorie Clark, Doug Winnie, Dune Thorne, Edy Greenblatt, Eddie Turner, Elliott Masie, Eric Schurenberg, Erica Dhawan, Fayzi Fatehi, Fernando Carrillo, Fiona Macaulay, Frank Wagner, Gabriela Teasdale, Gail Miller, Garry Ridge, Himanshu Saxena, Hortense le Gentil, Howard Morgan, Howard Prager, Hubert Joly, Jacquelyn Lane, Jeff Buckler, Jeff Slovin, Jen Goldman-Wetzler, Jeremy Isenberg, Jim Citrin, Jim Kim, Jim Sullivan, Joe Chase, Joe Tortora, Jonathan Benjamin, Josh Lutzger, Ken Blanchard, Laine Cohen, Maitali Chopra, Margie Wang, Mark Tercek, Martin Lindstrom, Michael McGovern, Michel Kripalani, Michael Kripalani, Mitali Chopra, Molly Tschang, Morag Barrett, Nankonde Kasonde-van den Broek, Noel Zemborain, Oleg Konovalov, Patricia Gorton, Pau Gasol, Peter Barkan, Peter Bregman, Pooneh Mohajer, Prakash Raman, Pranay Agrawal, Praveen Kopalle, Raj Shah, Richard Resnick, Rita McGrath, Rita Nathwani, Rob Nail, Robert Glazer,

Rodney Moses, Ruvi Kitov, Ruth Gotian, Safi Bahcall, Saloni Bowry Choudhry, Sally Helgesen, Sandy Ogg, Sanyin Siang, Sarah McArthur, Scott Osman, Sergey Sirotenko, Steve Rodgers, Subir Chowdhury, Taavo Godtfredsen, Tasha Eurich, Telisa Yancy, Telly Leung, Tom Moffitt, and Wendy Greeson.

One individual from the 100 Coaches network deserves special recognition: the designer and illustrator, Ayse Birsel. Ayse delivered the keynote address at JA's Global Leadership Conference in Bangkok and received a standing ovation. A few minutes after this speech, she agreed to be part of this project. Since then, she has provided the beautiful illustrations for the book, and donated her time and talent to advise us on all matters related to the book's layout and design. Thank you, Ayse!

Several friends and colleagues read early versions of the manuscript. Jacquelyn Lane, Jeff Hittner, Tere Stouffer, and Dave Mukherjee were particularly helpful with pointed feedback and constructive comments.

Special thanks to Brandon Coward, our editor from Amplify Publishing (home of 100 Coaches Publishing), for meticulous editing and valuable suggestions that have significantly enhanced the quality of the manuscript. The entire team at Amplify, led by Naren Aryal, has been a pleasure to work with.

Asheesh expresses profound gratitude to his wife and partner, Helen, for providing unwavering support through the ebbs and flows of his ambitious ideas and projects. Likewise, Marshall extends heartfelt thanks to his wife and partner, Lyda, whose support has been instrumental in the realization of his countless pursuits and endeavors. This book is dedicated to our children for their achievement journeys, but our spouses have lifted us, supported us, and protected us from ourselves in our own achievement journeys as recounted in many stories within these pages.

ABOUT THE AUTHORS AND ILLUSTRATOR

Asheesh Advani is the CEO of JA (Junior Achievement) Worldwide, one of the largest NGOs in the world dedicated to preparing youth for employment and entrepreneurship. During his leadership tenure, JA Worldwide has been selected annually as one of the top ten social good organizations in the world and been nominated for the Nobel Peace Prize. Advani is also an accomplished entrepreneur, having led two venture-backed businesses from start-up to acquisition. He is an in-demand speaker and regular contributor at major conferences, having served as a panelist or moderator at the World Economic Forum, the United Nations, the Young Presidents Organization, and Fortune 500 corporate gatherings.

Marshall Goldsmith is the founder of the Marshall Goldsmith Group and 100 Coaches. The inaugural winner of the Lifetime Achievement Award by the Institute of Coaching at Harvard Medical School and a Thinkers50 Management Hall of Fame inductee, he has advised more than two hundred major CEOs and their management teams. He is the author or editor of more than thirty-five books, including the classic *New York Times* bestseller *What Got You Here Won't Get You There*.

Ayse (pronounced *eye-shay*) Birsel is an award-winning industrial designer, speaker, author, and coach. In 2017, she was named one of *Fast Company*'s Most Creative People in Business, and *Interior Design* recognized her in 2020 with their Best of Year Product Designer award. Her work can be found in the permanent collection of the Museum of Modern Art. She is also the author of *Design the Life You Love* and *Design the LONG Life You Love*.

INDEX OF CONTRIBUTORS

Amii Barnard-Bahn	210–215
Ayse Birsel	274–278; 283–286
David Burkus	259–262
Clint Cadio	340–343
Bill Carrier	224–227
Julie Carrier	196–200
Nelly Cetera	328–329
Aman Ghose	369–374
Jack Harris	324–326
Caroline Jenner	323–324
Whitney Johnson	180–183
Jack Kosakowski	386–388
Howard (Yiq Zhenn) Leong	278–282
Leo Martellotto	390–392
Salvatore Nigro	388–390
Simi Nwogugu	326–328
Alex Osterwalder	235–239
Lindsey Pollak	154–157
Maya Raichoora	295–298
Sarah Rapp	355–360
Harsh Shah	308–311
Sanyin Siang	145–147
Michael Bungay Stanier	167–170
Mark C. Thompson	247–250
Aya Youssef	379–383